READING
WRITING
and
JUSTICE

SUNY series,
INTERRUPTIONS: Border Testimony(ies) and Critical Discourse/s

Henry A. Giroux, Editor

READING
WRITING
and
JUSTICE

School Reform as If Democracy Matters

James W. Fraser

STATE UNIVERSITY OF NEW YORK PRESS

Production by Ruth Fisher
Marketing by Hannah J. Hazen

Published by
State University of New York Press, Albany

For information, address the State University of New York Press,
State University Plaza, Albany, NY 12246

Library of Congress Cataloging-in-Publication Data

Fraser, James W., 1944–
    Reading, writing, and justice : school reform as if democracy
matters / James W. Fraser.
        p.   cm. — (SUNY series, Interruptions — Border
testimony(ies) and Critical Discourse/s)
    Includes bibliographical references (p.   ) and index.
    ISBN 0-7914-3405-2 (hc : alk. paper). — ISBN 0-7914-3406-0 (pb :
alk. paper)
        1. Education—Aims and objectives—United States.   2. Public
schools—United States.   3. Democracy—United States.   4. Education—
Social aspects—United States.   5. Multicultural education—United
States.   6. Critical pedagogy—United States.   I. Title.
II. Series.
LA217.2.F73   1997
371.01'0973—dc20   96-41493
                                                                         CIP

10 9 8 7 6 5 4 3 2 1

For Katherine

CONTENTS

ACKNOWLEDGMENTS

This book had its genesis in a series of conversations with Bruce Astrein and Adria Steinberg which led to our work on *Barriers to Excellence: Our Children at Risk* (Boston: National Coalition of Advocates for Students, 1985). At times we were fortunate to be joined in these conversations by others, especially Ann Bastian, Norm Fruchter, and the late Ken Haskins. While my thinking has evolved greatly in the ensuing years, those conversations are formative to what is here.

At different points in the development of this text Tanya McKinnon, Norma Rees, James Jennings, Marian Darlington-Hope, Leon J. Kamin, David Stratman, and Alan Cromer all provided invaluable comments. Elizabeth Wallace prepared the index and bibliography and also provided very important research help and editorial comment.

A part of chapter 2 appeared as the item on "Democracy" in *Philosophy of Education: An Encyclopedia* (New York: Garland Publishing, 1996). A much shorter version of my comments on the new right-wing historians appeared in *The History of Education Quarterly,* 36.2 (Summer 1996). An earlier version of chapter 6 appeared in *Teachers College Record,* 94.1 (Fall 1992). The material in chapter 1 is from *The Work of Nations* by Robert B. Reich. Copyright © 1991 by Robert B. Reich. Reprinted by permission of Alfred A. Knopf, Inc. I am grateful to all these publications for permission to reprint this material.

Chapter 5 was originally presented as a talk to the Computers and Education faculty of Lesley College, Cambridge, Massachusetts. I am especially grateful to George Blakeslee and Joan Thormann for their support in the development of this material. Chapter 3, and indeed all of this volume, is informed by and builds on the work in *Freedom's Plow: Teaching in the Multicultural Classroom* (New York: Routledge, 1994). I remain grateful to my co-editor in the earlier volume, Theresa Perry, for our work together.

Students and members of the faculty at Northeastern University, Lesley College, Wheelock College, and the University of Massachusetts at Boston will certainly recognize themselves in parts of this book. I am grateful for many classes and conversations. I am especially grateful to the staff, fellows, and faculty related to the Center for Innovation in Urban Education at Northeastern University for their support and encouragement.

At different times, Henry Giroux, Donaldo Macedo, and Paulo Freire have all encouraged me in this work and each has reminded me that being an academic administrator is no excuse for not continuing to write. I am grateful for their support and their prodding.

INTRODUCTION

I do not understand human existence, and the struggle needed to improve
it, apart from hope and dream. Hope is an ontological need. Hopelessness
is but hope that has lost its bearings, and becomes a distortion of that
ontological need. . . . I am hopeful, not out of mere stubbornness, but out
of an existential, concrete imperative.

Paulo Freire, *Pedagogy of Hope*

This book begins with a simple premise: The primary purpose of education in
a democratic society is democracy. This essential truth has been lost in much
of the contemporary educational debates. We have asked schools to do a better
job of preparing workers for a fast-changing economy. We have asked schools
to raise the academic standards so that students will achieve multiple literacies
at higher levels. These and other demands on schools are worthy and appropriate. But they also miss the most fundamental issue. Until we ask schools to
prepare our fellow citizens, until we view schooling for all of the nation's youth
as an essential element in the preparation of the next generation of active and
engaged participants in the common life of the nation, all debates about schooling will be trivialized and ultimately will miss the point.

A democratic society, indeed any society, will support schools for many
different reasons. But at the heart of the education in a democratic polity must
be a commitment to maintaining and expanding democracy itself. Any lesser
goal will ultimately fail to maintain public support for the enterprise of public
education or to foster a dynamic and self-critical democratic society. School
reform efforts which are not linked firmly to the constant expansion of democracy are doomed at best to a terrible smallness of purpose. In too many
cases efforts to improve schools which do not keep a democratic bias at their
core will unwittingly become antidemocratic in their long-term results.

The center which I direct at Northeastern University recently sponsored a panel on the future of public education. One of the panelists was a highly respected business leader who has developed a reputation for his support of efforts to improve the public schools. As we prepared for the panel he referred several times to his commitment to ensuring that his future employees received a better education than that available to those he was now hiring. I agreed with him but added, "I am also concerned about the education of your fellow citizens." When he looked puzzled, I added, "the people who are graduating from our public schools are not just your future employees or my future students in the university, they are also our fellow citizens, the people who will vote in our elections and ultimately the people who will shape the society and culture in which we live." While he did not disagree with me, it was clearly a new idea to him. I found myself wondering, Have we Americans become so divided that the very thought that graduates of urban public schools would be fellow citizens—peers in the shaping of our society—with prominent leaders in business and education be so surprising?

Reading, Writing, and Justice is written for those who want to be part of healing the divide in our society. It is written for all of those, students, teachers, parents, and advocates for public education who continue to believe that the struggle to create a truly inclusive and vibrant democratic society in our schools and in our nation is an essential effort. It is written, as one early reviewer said, to provide "argumentative ammunition" for defending schools and for placing school reform issues within the larger framework of an effort to keep and expand democracy. In 1932, George Counts published *Dare the School Build a New Social Order?*[1] In that brief book, Counts called on teachers to become agents for a more democratic society. Criticizing the highly individualistic nature of most 1930s progressive schools, Counts called on teachers to link education to social reform, including the transformation of the nation's then depression-ridden economy. In some ways, this volume is a similar book for the end of the century.

At the close of the twentieth century, debates about schooling in the United States are mired in a terribly limited vision of what is needed. In the name of practicality, too many important questions are being avoided. Whether it is the often heard request from teachers, "Just tell me what works," or the focus on using improved schools to strengthen the country's place in the international economic competition with Japan and Germany, school reforms are being judged on the wrong terms. While there is nothing wrong with asking for practical help in the means of instruction or with anyone wanting better economic prospects for themselves and their children, these and other

goals like them do not measure the full potential of schools. As Donaldo
Macedo has pointed out, the result of this focus on questions of only immediate relevance has been a tyranny of methodology and a "fetish of reform"
which never allows the larger question of purpose in the nation's classrooms,
in the programs to prepare future teachers, and in the national debates about
education.[2] While school budgets have been cut for the past two decades,
while more and more children are being born in poverty and without a "safety
net" of social services, while programs which were designed to support these
children are ravaged, most of the defenders of schools cannot bring themselves to ask the larger questions. Instead of focusing on whose interests are
served by the budget cuts, and the rapid decline in the status of too many of
the nation's citizens, much of education reform has been focused on the quick
fix, the new teaching method or school structure, which will "improve" the
situation. Instead of focusing on the development of the next generation of
active citizens, too much of today's education reform views students in terribly stunted ways, as potential workers with no lives beyond the job and no
need for skills beyond those involved in earning a living. We need to ask for
much more from our schools if the America society is going to be a safe,
dynamic, and thriving place in the twenty-first century.

Clearly this is an optimistic book. Indeed, I have been told many times
that the ideas contained here are naively optimistic, and that it would make
more sense to phrase them in the currently popular language of the nation's
economic competition. But, as I argue in chapter 1, that very language is part
of the problem. Even more seriously, our national aversion to a wide-ranging
discussion about democracy and democratic education is part of the problem.
I continue to hope that democracy—a radically inclusive democracy—can be
returned to the center of our educational debates. Ultimately I agree with
Paulo Freire, that without this hope we have lost our bearings. Perhaps this
is partly Scots stubbornness. It is also because I see optimism as essential for
the flourishing of a free society for all citizens. And I believe that schools
need to be one of the places where the conversation about the shape of that
society, and the models for the ways such a society can thrive, are developed.

While it is focused on what some see as a theoretical issue, democracy,
this is also a very personal book. In 1974 I was a monitor on the first day of
desegregation in the Boston Public Schools and I have been involved ever
since in efforts to make the schools of my city really serve all of the city's
children. Ten years ago I also found myself at the center of a campaign to
rewrite the regulations for teacher education in Massachusetts in an effort to
ensure that the next generation of teachers received a better preparation for

their work than their predecessors. At the same time, as an historian of education, I have watched with increased worry as the forces of reaction have gathered strength in this country. Nationally the last two decades have been a time of mean-spirited attacks on schools and all public institutions and ultimately on children and youth. In the midst of all of this I have become increasingly convinced that today's school reform efforts are really a struggle for the nation's soul. And in this situation the discussion of school improvement must not be allowed to focus on techniques and details but rather on the fundamental purpose of schools in a democratic society. In the face of growing inequalities among this nation's people and a lack of national will to remedy the situation, in the face of new levels of violence and racism, sexism, classism, and homophobia, I remain convinced that a different vision of school reform—one based on a focus on the best every student has to offer rather than the deficits which every human has—can be a means of rallying teachers, parents, and students in a campaign for a democratic school and an inclusive society. Without such a movement, in one form or another, the prospects for the twenty-first century are bleak indeed.

This volume draws on a long tradition of linking democracy and education. The thinking of John Dewey and W. E. B. Du Bois and Jane Addams, as well as the ideas of Thomas Jefferson, Paulo Freire, and Henry Giroux influence these pages every step of the way. It is important for us to remember that we are not the first generation to ask fundamental questions or to wrestle with the basic issues of the purposes of education. At the same time, we must not seek to canonize any of those on whose thought we draw. Manning Marable is absolutely right when he says, "Our generation's task is to build upon the protest traditions of the past, without becoming imprisoned by that history and the limitations of the vision of its leaders."[3] So the task of creating a dynamic democracy, an ever expanding vision of the liberating potential of education, is a never ending process in which the key to education is the journey itself.

Plan for the Book

The purpose of this book is to ask a simple question, what would it mean to take democracy seriously in today's debates about school reform? What would it mean, in the everyday practice of schools and teacher education programs, to keep the commitment to expanding democracy at the center of the enterprise? The chapters which follow offer no single answer, no one prescription. They are certainly not meant as a how-to manual on the ways to run a democratic school. They are, however, designed to consider the fundamental question "What would it mean to take democracy seriously?" in a number of specific instances which are important in today's educational debates: in the curriculum—questions of what is taught and how—in the use of technology, in school governance, and finally in the preparation of tomorrow's teachers. The result is not a definitive answer. Indeed, offering a definitive answer to the question would, in itself, run counter to the kind of democratic dialogue which is needed if real and meaningful educational reform is to take place. The text is intended, rather, to offer case studies, examples, provocative conversation starters for teachers, for administrators, for concerned citizens who still believe that democracy means more than capitalism, who long for a nation which truly embraces and builds on the wonderful contribution of each and every citizen, who are willing to take the risk of incorporating the diverse voices of all citizens in the educational debates, and ultimately who believe that schooling is about more than preparation for a job, but is rather a matter of building and rebuilding the great community, a society in which all citizens are free and equal. I plan to explore this theme of schooling for democracy in the chapters which follow.

Chapter 1, "Education Reform and Economic Renewal: Or, It Will Take More Than Robert Reich to Make Schools Work," explores the current emphasis on economic competition as the rationale for school reform and finds it wanting on both economic and educational grounds. The downward mobility of the majority of Americans requires political remedies and a long-term commitment to a different social order, not a quick fix in school reform. And the focus on preparing future workers for world markets deflects schools from the real role they should play in the economic crisis, preparing citizens who can envision a different economic and social order and who have the courage and will to bring their vision into existence.

Chapter 2, "Defining Democracy, Defining Democratic Education," seeks to place conflicting understandings of democracy and democratic education in both an historical and ideological perspective. There are many definitions of democracy which must properly be rejected. However, an understanding of democracy which includes the full and active participation of all citizens in both the benefits of society and in the very process of defining the social good is one which can compel wide allegiance and provide clear purpose for substantive school reform efforts.

Chapter 3, "The School and the Quest for a Multicultural Democracy," answers the question "What is the nature of the democratic society for which schools should prepare people?" with a clear affirmation of a multicultural democracy and a multicultural school curriculum. In this context, multiculturalism is not an add-on, but an essential way of viewing the curriculum and the task of the school. At the same time, the growing attack on multiculturalism, and the growing racism of our time, exemplified in the *Contract with America,* "P.C. debates," and works like *The Bell Curve* and *The Disuniting of America* needs to be viewed as a multipronged but coherent attempt to move the United States away from democracy to a new kind of fascism.

Chapter 4, "Toward a New Kind of Child-Centered Curriculum: The Individual Child and a Democratic Society" focuses on the individual student and the ongoing debates among progressive educators regarding the focus on the individual child versus the society. Educating the whole child, I argue, must mean attending to the many different needs of all children including physical and intellectual. But ultimately a democratic education requires a vision of each child not as a bundle of needs or a "human resource" for a competitive economy, but as a citizen with a critical role to play in the expansion of democracy in the future.

Chapter 5, "Technology, Democracy, and School Policy," examines the role of technology in a democratic educational system. The computer is but the latest of many tools which have been provided to improve instruction. These tools must always be tested in the larger democratic context. To the extent that they liberate and expand options, they should be embraced, while to the extent that they constrict and divide they must be rejected. Only with a clear overall goal for the schools can individual changes, such as the introduction of computers, be evaluated carefully.

Chapter 6, "Preparing Teachers for Democratic Schools," looks at the preparation of the next generation of teachers. Reforming teacher education has been a central goal of the reform decades of the 1980s and 1990s. Some important improvements of teacher education have been put forward while some reactionary changes have also been proposed under the same reform rubric. Only in the larger context of expanding democracy for all can the various changes in teacher education be carefully evaluated and implemented.

The basic goal in each of these chapters is the same—to explore the fundamental link between democracy and quality education, and to explore the results for educational practice if a true commitment to an ever expanding democracy were to be at the heart of all discussions about the changing institutional arrangements for delivering education in the United States. It is only when strengthening and expanding democracy is at the heart of any discussion of public education that the debate and the changes in curriculum and school structures will move forward in ways which liberate the students and build a larger society which is good for all.

CHAPTER ONE

Education Reform and Economic Renewal: Or, It Will Take More Than Robert Reich to Make Schools Work

In the life of a nation, few ideas are more dangerous than good solutions to the wrong problems.

Robert Reich, *The Work of Nations*

If there is a theme which has driven education reform in the United States in the last two decades of the twentieth century, it is the fear of America's economic decline and the need for urgent reform of the nation's schools in order to reverse the slide. The authors of *A Nation at Risk*, the 1983 Reagan administration document which did so much to start the current round of school reform, set the tone. They called for a major overhaul of the nation's schools because, "Our once unchallenged preeminence in commerce, industry, science, and technological innovation is being overtaken by competitors throughout the world." Since then the link between the fear that the United States is becoming a second-rate economic power and the need for school reform has been virtually indissoluble.[1] The same theme has continued to be echoed throughout the 1980s and 1990s. Both the decline in the standard of living for most Americans and the failures of schools to provide young Americans with a quality education are very serious problems. Indeed, both threaten the very fabric of a democratic society. But the link between the two is far more complex, and far less immediate, than is assumed in nearly all of the school reform literature.

The assumption of a link between economic and educational decline did not end with the reports of the early 1980s. In 1986, when the Carnegie

Corporation of New York wanted to launch a major effort to overhaul teacher education, the foundation created the Carnegie Forum on Education *and the Economy* (italics added). And the report which the forum produced, a report which included a number of significant recommendations for improving teacher education, was also framed with the warning, "Our ability to compete in world markets is eroding." The declining standard of living for many Americans seemed to be the starting point for all calls for education reform.[2] The fact that most thoughtful critics of contemporary teacher education programs were calling for radical surgery was, evidently, not sufficient for the leaders of the Carnegie Corporation. The report's authors felt that only by linking their plea for changes in teacher education to the nation's economic crisis could they get an audience for their generally quite wise prescriptions.

Most dramatically of all, the 1992 presidential campaign was fought around the same basic issues. Stanley Aronowitz and William DiFazio describe the incredibly effective use which Democratic candidate Bill Clinton made of the rhetoric which was begun in the report issued by Ronald Reagan's Department of Education:

> An important part of Clinton's approach to recovery was more money for education and a stepped up training and retraining, programs, the assumption of which is that development of "human capital" was a long ignored but important component of the growth of a technologically advanced economy. According to this argument, a poor educational system and inadequate apprenticeship and retraining programs would inevitably result in a competitive disadvantage for the United States in an increasingly competitive global economy.[3]

The rhetoric won the election, but hardly changed the national mood of worry. While the Clinton slogan "It's the economy, stupid" worked in 1992, two years later, Republicans promising their mean-spirited "Contract with America" took back control of the Congress for the first time in forty years. School reform took a back seat in Clinton's 1996 re-election campaign against Bob Dole, but came back into prominence in his second term. The re-elected president's 1997 state of the union message renewed the call for a national crusade for high education standards, a commitment that every child be able to read by the age of eight, support for the Carnegie initiated National Board for Professional Teaching Standards, as well as proposals for funding support for new school construction, charter schools, and a HOPE scholarship program. The relationship of education and the nation's well being seems likely to continue to be a subject of both high hopes and significant contention well into the next century.

In the realm of politics, a deep dissatisfaction, a "boiling point," as Kevin Phillips has described the majority of the electorate's response to the decline of middle-class prosperity can be expected to continue.[4] Economics, and a preoccupation with decline, have dominated national discourse, in politics and at the level of school-based reforms. In the realm of politics this focus is likely to lead to continued anger, continued radical shifts in power, and moves to "throw the bums out." In education the impact has been no less radical.

This theme of the need to reform the schools to stem the nation's economic decline has spawned the development of creative ideas and led to the provision of some badly needed energy and funds to schools. There is no question that schools are better off for the spotlight of attention which has focused on them, and on their failure to offer a quality education to a large percentage of students. As with the furor around the launch of Sputnik in 1957, when a plethora of new programs to expand science and mathematics education were spawned out of a fear that the Soviet Union was beating the United States into space and in the role of the world's leader in scientific literacy, the fears of the 1980s and 1990s have pushed school reform. In place of the fears of communism, the focus this time was the rapidly expanding economies of Japan and Western Europe, especially Germany. The students of those countries, so the argument has gone, are doing better in school and the industries of those nations are defeating the United States in world trade, resulting in a rapid decline of the standard of living for the average American.

As with Sputnik in the 1950s, the result has been change in schools. But far too often the result has also been misguided change which has terribly impoverished the educational discourse while misdiagnosing the problems in both the economy and the schools. In the 1950s and early 1960s, the result of Sputnik and the general fears of the cold war were the National Defense Education Act of 1958, significantly improved science and mathematics curricula—developed for the first time with financial support from the federal government—and a plethora of new research and reform projects focused on schooling. There was, at the same time, a significant increase in tracking—as policies focused on preparing the best and the brightest to overtake Soviet scientists and engineers—and a significant expansion of cold war paranoia in school politics. Attention to race, class, and gender discrimination or the terrible plight of many students with special needs was emphatically not part of the Sputnik era agenda. These things came to the fore a decade later as part of the agenda of the Civil Rights movement.[5] In the 1980s and 1990s, the results of the fears of economic enemies have also yielded both increased resources and a misunderstanding of the purposes of schooling in a democratic society, including in some places a new kind of tracking in the name of high standards. The time has come for anyone who is serious about meaningful school reform which will improve the opportunities for all of the nation's children—and not merely a select minority—to return to the fundamental questions which have been avoided through most of the discussion of reform in the last two decades: Just what is the link between schooling and the changing nature of the American economy?

What Really Is Happening to the American Economy?

In the early 1990s, two books appeared which are essential reading for anyone who seriously wants to understand the problems of the economy and of education. Robert Reich's *The Work of Nations* (1991) became something of a bible to the 1992 Clinton presidential campaign. It also provides an extraordinary analysis of the changing nature of the American economy and of the nature of work in the Unites States. *The Jobless Future* (1994), Stanley Aronowitz and William DiFazio's considerably more radical analysis of the changing nature of work at the end of the twentieth century, also places these changes in the context of both shifting economic and shifting philosophical and cultural movements regarding the nature of work, capital, and culture. Taken together, the two are fundamental texts for analyzing the relationship of economic change (and decline) and school reform. And taken together, both works lead to a quite simple conclusion: Problems with schools have not caused the current economic crisis and school reform alone won't fix it.

Both Reich and Aronowitz and DiFazio follow the lead of Bennett Harrison and Barry Bluestone in noting the rapidly increasing gap between rich and poor in the United States. What was still controversial and new when Harrison and Bluestone published *The Deindustrialization of America* and *The Great U-Turn* in the mid-1980s had become virtually common knowledge among economists and among American voters by the early 1990s.[6] The rich in the United States are becoming much richer and the rest—including the vast majority—significantly poorer. Reich provides one example which describes the growing separation quite clearly:

> In 1960, the chief executive of one of America's 100 largest nonfinancial corporations earned, on average, $190,000, or about 40 times the wage

of his average factory worker. After taxes, the chief executive earned only 12 times the factory worker's wages. By the end of the 1980s, however, the chief executive earned, on average, more than $2 million—93 times the wage of his (rarely her) average factory worker. After taxes, the chief executive's compensation was about 70 times that of the average factory worker.[7]

These are not modest differences. From 12 times to 70 times the average worker's after tax wages represents a very significant case of the rich getting much richer. At the same time, fewer Americans were able to even find work as "the average factory worker." The literature of the decade, and the experience of many citizens, confirmed that many factory workers were losing their jobs to find replacement work, if they found it at all, in much lower paid service industries. The combination of "labor-saving" technological innovation and the exportation of routine production work to countries with much lower wage scales has left the United States without the blue-collar jobs which were the backbone of the labor market for half a century.

At the same time, Reich's statistical example gives clear evidence of the impact of the changes in tax policy enacted during the early 1980s. While not all of the growing discrepancy is due to changed tax policies, the role of federal tax policy in equalizing the economic plight of Americans has virtually disappeared from economic calculations or the debates about the economy of the future.

In the same two decades in which education reform was called on to counter economic differences, the most well off Americans have become much more well off, while the majority of the country's citizens, and especially the poor, have become much poorer. At century's end, the much discussed "decline of the middle class" is a reality few will dispute. The question which remains, however, is the degree of causation between the educational crisis and the economic crisis.

Different economists focus on different reasons for the changes in the economy. Certainly a number of factors have contributed to the changes including poor planning on the part of American business leaders, the rapid replacement of many older jobs by machines and other computer-driven technology, the decline of organized labor, and the revolutionary changes in the tax code implemented during the Reagan years. Perhaps most significant is the fact that there is virtually no longer any such thing as an "American economy." To cite Reich again:

All Americans used to be in roughly the same economic boat. Most rose or fell together, as the corporations in which they were employed, the industries comprising such corporations, and the national economy as a whole became more productive—or languished. But national borders no longer define our economic fates. We are now in different boats, one sinking rapidly, one sinking more slowly, and the third rising steadily.[8]

Under such circumstances, Reich has cause to wonder at the ease with which the majority of Americans—approximately 80 percent—have "not vociferously contested the disengagement of the one-fifth whose economic future is becoming ever brighter."[9] While Reich provides some important answers to his own question, he also misses some of the key elements which must be part of the explanation of these changes.

The Globalization of the Economy

The place where Reich is most insightful, and most important for understanding the current education reform struggles is in his analysis of the changing nature of work in the United States and around the world. While some economists describe the shift from manufacturing to service-related jobs—with a consequent loss in wages for many—and while others describe the growth of the fortunes of the most well-off, Reich links these factors to a new categorization of work in the United States. He begins his argument with a simple assertion that the assumption of "the continued existence of an American economy in which jobs associated with a particular firm, industry, or sector are somehow connected within the borders of the nation, so that American workers face a common fate; and a common enemy as well,"[10] is simply no longer relevant. Given the complex web of international finance and the easy shipment of goods, ideas, and money across international borders, there is essentially no longer any such thing as an American economy (or any other national economy for that matter). On the contrary, there are citizens and workers in many different countries, competing with people who do similar work in their own and in different countries, across the world. The average income of Americans no longer represents anything except a numerical averaging of the money received by the sum of people who happen to live in a certain place at a certain time. It is not an interdependent set of variables related to a single national economy.

So when we speak of the "competitiveness" of Americans in general, we are talking only about how much the world is prepared to spend, on average, for services performed by Americans. Some Americans may command much higher rewards; others, far lower. No longer are Americans rising or falling together, as if in one large national boat. We are, increasingly, in different, smaller boats.[11]

As Reich goes on to note, the implications of these changes, for the notions of nationhood and community, for education, and for people's economic prospects have only begun to be explored.

The Nature of Jobs at the Beginning
of the Twenty-First Century

Having defined the extent of the globalization of the economy, Reich then differentiates the three "smaller boats" into which most working Americans are grouped as they face this world economy. These groupings significantly replace the older categories of workers in the United States and represent both types of work and types of international economic competition. They are:

Routine production services [which] "entail the kinds of repetitive tasks performed by the old foot soldiers of American capitalism in the high-volume enterprise." These manufacturing jobs have existed in both the older industries and in the newest emergent fields. Assembling the latest computer may be cleaner, but it is otherwise little different from assembling an automobile on the oldest of assembly lines, although the work is likely to be much lower paid in the former given the lack of unionization in the newer industries. In 1990 this kind of work included about one-quarter of the nation's workforce, a radical decline from mid-century.

In-person services represent the range of service work from retail sales to hospital and health care workers to food service workers and "among the fastest growing of all—security guards." These workers represent approximately 30 percent of the workforce and the percentage is growing rapidly. One of the significant differences between service and production work is that service work must usually be done "in person" and is thus not as easily exported as production. A second difference is that much service work has traditionally been stereotyped as nurturing work or women's work. And a third, not unrelated difference, is that most kinds of service work has traditionally been low paid.

Symbolic-analytic services are the work of problem-solvers and the creators of ideas and symbols including research scientists, most engineers, bankers, lawyers, writers, designers, and the growing numbers of consultants.

Like the first group, their jobs are easily internationalized. But unlike the first group, their numbers are growing, their pay is substantial, and the education required continues to make the elite of Americans very much eligible for this kind of work. Symbolic analysts represent approximately 20 percent of American workers.

The remaining workers, another 25 percent or so, are government workers—including teachers and other local government employees, federal employees such as the military, and physicians paid through Medicaid and Medicare—and a small number of farmers, miners, and other "extractors of natural resources" who together form 5 percent of the workforce.

These basic categories describe nearly all of the workers in the United States at the end of the twentieth century. Whatever the points at which one might take exception to Reich, and there are several, his analysis of the basic job categories into which America's workers fall at the end of the century are far more accurate than any other offered today. This analysis goes a long way toward explaining the job experiences of many of this country's citizens. As Reich has shown so convincingly, the links between workers in the different categories are significantly less important than their relationships to—and competition with—workers in the same category around the world.[12]

The Other Parts of the Story: What Reich Left Out

As important as *The Work of Nations* is to understanding both the nation's economic crisis and the future of schooling, there are a number of problems with the Reichian analysis.

Perhaps most important, Reich is significantly better on description than he is in asking questions of morality and the social good. In a critical review of *The Work of Nations,* Andrew Kopkind cites Samuel Bowles as seeing, "a critical flaw in the Reichian scheme . . . its indifference to promoting equality in economic relations." It is clearly true that the economy of the United States today is at a point where promoting equality is increasingly difficult, in part, as Bowles also says because, "You can't have a covenant with a labor force that's less than a fifth unionized. . . . There's no one to 'shake hands with'." From a purely economic perspective, there is good reason to question that "a skilled workforce will bring in multinational investors like miners to gold."[13] And even in Reich's own terms, there is serious reason to question how much good multinational investors who do come will do for the vast majority of the American workforce who will continue to be routine production and in-person service workers for the foreseeable future. Almost a century ago, John Dewey told his philosophy students, "the class divisions of industrial capitalism are incompatible with the ethics of democracy."[14] Reich gives little reason to hope that the class divisions of postindustrial world capitalism will offer any improvement in the class divisions in this society, but more seriously he fails to pay sufficient attention to the ethics of democracy.

A related problem with Reich's analysis is his weak examination of the other factors, besides the expansion of the global economy, which have exacerbated the class divisions and the economic stagnation for many in the United States. While he does provide convincing evidence of the way in which the changes in the Reagan tax code has aided the rich at the expense of virtually everyone else, while at the same time cutting off many of the countervailing social programs which were born out of both the New Deal and the Great Society, he does not explore, at any level of seriousness, the reasons why such politics prevailed.[15]

Race

Indeed, his virtually complete failure to deal with the power of racism is at the heart of Reich's weak political analysis. While he is careful to note the racial divisions within the workforce, he does not look at the power of racism in maintaining an unjust status quo. It makes no sense to discuss the fact that, "The four-fifths of the population whose economic future is growing more precarious has not vociferously contested the disengagement of the one-fifth whose economic future is becoming ever brighter,"[16] and not also discuss Willie Horton. At a point in the 1988 presidential campaign in which democratic candidate Michael Dukakis was making reasonable progress in challenging the impact of the national policies of the Reagan years in exacerbating the separation between the 20 percent who were prospering and the 80 percent who were in economic trouble (a ratio which should have guaranteed a Democratic landslide) the Republican campaign used furloughed Massachusetts prisoner Willie Horton's crime spree to make race—and specifically white fears of African Americans—and not economics, the key issue in the campaign. The Dukakis campaign never recovered. In a political world where such tactics are not unusual, and in which they are effective, any discussion of the divisions of Americans must begin with a thoughtful discussion of race.

Certainly any examination of the politics of the 1990s which does not include an analysis of race simply misses the point. Whether it is the "stop violent criminals" and "welfare reform" promises of the 1994 "Contract with America" or the way in which a campaign to repeal Affirmative Action dominated the 1996 presidential campaign, race and racism and "angry white males" seem to be dominant themes. And as long as the 80 percent who are losing ground economically are so divided, and as long as "angry white males" are given the rhetoric to turn their anger on people of color rather than the top 20 percent, class solidarity will be a chimera.

Gender

Race is also far from the only point of division. The American working class is also divided by issues of gender. And the conservative movement in this country has been brilliant in using "angry white males" as the backbone of their campaigns. In attacks on both abortion rights and welfare mothers, Republicans have used long simmering fears of sexuality and women's growing political strength to create a powerful backlash. While polls show a significant majority of the electorate favoring women's right to choose, conservative politicians have expanded the rhetoric of moral decline so that the issue of abortion rights, the successes which women have had in entering the workforce, and the perception of increasing family breakups have combined to fuel reaction.

The fact that American families are not collapsing and that Ozzie and Harriet have never been a reality makes little difference to the current campaigns to return to a past that never was. In an extraordinary study of the changing nature of American families, *The Way We Never Were: American Families and the Nostalgia Trap,* Stephanie Coontz effectively makes the case that the much revered nuclear family of the 1950s was a rare exception in the long stretch of American history and that even in the fifties, things were often not as they seemed. To give but one example from her careful study, the supposed mushrooming of teen pregnancy in the 1980s and 1990s does not fit with the facts of the 1950s. "In 1957, 97 out of every 1,000 girls aged fifteen to nineteen gave birth, compared to only 52 out of every 1,000 in 1983." But in the 1950s, teen pregnancy for white girls was often hid through adoption and a "fresh start," and across the races through marriage. "Young people were not taught how to 'say no'—they were simply handed wedding rings." How many of those who discuss the "problem" of teen pregnancy today note the almost 50 percent decline since the 1950s? But reality has seldom blocked the power of nostalgia in politics or public policy. And the "return to stable families" continues to be a pillar in the campaign to undo the gains which women have made in both economic location and in control of their own bodies which is the real shift of the last decades.[17]

Foreign Policy and the Domestic Economy

In a thoughtful essay written soon after the 1988 campaign, Stanley Aronowitz also noted a third pillar for the Republican ascendancy besides race and gender. This is the expansion of machismo into a hallmark of American foreign policy. When Richard Nixon ended the military draft, he took much of the force out of future antiwar movements, setting the stage for Ronald Reagan's brilliant ability to "displace a long list of domestic woes to patriotic fervor." The new patriotism has served conservatives well indeed.

> For at the very moment when international economic competition and the world-economic crisis were driving U.S. living standards down . . . the U.S. was beginning to flex its military muscle throughout the world. The new Cold War was more than a diversion; it reached down to the wounded (male) collective ego, providing it with renewed virility after the years of humiliation in Southeast Asia and equally taking its mind off the fact that middle- and working-class men were unable to support their families on a single income.[18]

No wonder that, six years later, the Republican take over of the House of Representatives was fueled by a *Contract with America* which included as a major plank a commitment to strong national defense and an end to "raiding the defense budget to fund social welfare programs and UN peacekeeping programs."[19] The fact that there is no powerful enemy or rational reason for such promises clearly has not detracted from their political effectiveness. The results are twofold: a frightening expansion of American militarism and economic colonialism and a complete inability of the American working class to vote or act in terms of unified economic interests.

The Decline of Organized Labor

While Reich does note the role of organized labor in bringing about the economic expansion of the 1950s and 1960s, he gives scant attention to the role of organized labor in bringing about the economic declines experienced by so many Americans in the 1980s and 1990s.[20] Of course, the industries which were at the heart of the labor organizations of the 1950s and 1960s have been among those hardest hit at century's end. While the leaders of the auto, steel, and other industrial unions may be faulted for not driving harder bargains, the globalization of the economy has been a guarantee of the deci-mation of their unions no matter what the unions and their leaders did. The way in which organized labor most significantly contributed to the economic dislocation is in what was not done. As Aronowitz and DiFazio argue:

> Ronald Reagan's dramatic and highly symbolic firing of 11,000 air traffic controllers in 1981 may be remembered as the definitive act that closed the book on the historic compromise between a relatively pow-erful, if conservative, labor movement and capital. As the American unions whimpered but offered little concrete resistance, employers' groups quickly perceived that it was possible to undertake a major frontal assault on labor's crucial practice, collective bargaining. The ensuing decade witnessed rapid deterioration in union power and there-fore a decline in real wages.[21]

While Reich might quarrel with Aronowitz and DiFazio on the relative im-portance of labor weakness in the decline in real wages, his failure to deal with the issue weakens his argument significantly.

The issue here is not primarily the impact of weak unions on the wages of traditionally unionized workers. Routine production workers who were unionized, and who did keep their jobs, were not among the worst to suffer in the recent past. Far more serious was the predicament of the many workers who did not keep their jobs. For these workers, the massive deindustrialization of the nation linked to the deskilling of the workforce meant a bleak future. As Reich notes so effectively, the jobs of many traditionally blue-collar work-ers were either mechanized or departed overseas in massive numbers. And traditional labor organizing could do little about these shifts.

But there is a point where organized labor has failed this country's work-ers quite spectacularly: in organizing in new fields. Replacement work for those who lost their jobs in the deindustrializing of America, when it could be found at all, was in very different fields and at much lower salaries. The laid-off steelworker who found employment on a computer assembly line could expect a 50–75 percent salary cut. These low-wage, nonunion jobs also offered fewer benefits and little prospect of advancement.

But the question must be asked—though surprisingly few economists have asked it—why hasn't there been a major unionizing effort in the newer industries, especially in in-person services?[22] If Reich is right that the in-person services are the jobs most resistant to exportation—by the very nature of the need for personal contact—be it from waitperson, health care worker, or cleaner—then these jobs ought to be prime cases for new labor organizing. The same case can also be made for the newer production jobs which have emerged. Aronowitz and DiFazio quote one long-time garment worker, "The only new work they create are the sweatshops in Chinatown, Greenpoint [Polish and Mexican immigrants], Brighton Beach [Russian, Jewish immigrants]. I don't know what they're going to do. These people work for peanuts."[23] But again, why isn't the union, which organized New York's garment workers so effectively for half a century, in the newer shops?

The answers are complex. The chilling impact of the Reagan years on any labor organizing cannot be overstated. The efforts to smash long-established unions from the air traffic controllers to meat packers in Minnesota have been exhausting. But the fact that so many of the newer workers are immigrants, people of color, and women must also be included in the equation. Until union movements in this country deal with diversity as opportunity rather than threat, they will be doomed to failure. Aronowitz and DiFazio are right: "With few exceptions, the U.S. working class movement is white, heterosexual, and male. The solidarity of the working-class is empty if it excludes workers on the basis of race and gender."[24] Organized labor in the United States has never conquered its white working-class male bias. And the result is a nation of citizens divided not only by the work they do but by race, ethnicity, and gender, in ways which make divide-and-conquer tactics easy and solidarity difficult.

It remains surprising, however, that so much of the economic analysis in the last two decades, often analysis done by people from a leftist perspective of one sort or another, has paid so little attention to the failure to organize among the unorganized. It is certainly true that many of the relatively well-paying industrial jobs of the 1950s and 1960s are disappearing from the United States and there is little organized labor can do about it. But those jobs were not always well organized. Indeed, a terrible price was paid by a generation of workers and labor organizers for the unionization of coal, steel, auto production, and all of the nation's major industries. Virtually any social or economic analysis of the United States which was done between the beginnings of the industrial revolution in the mid-nineteenth century and the 1930s would note the terrible salaries, benefits, and working conditions of the—mostly immigrant—workers in the nation's basic production industries. Only after a century of struggle did these jobs become the "good jobs with good wages" which are remembered with nostalgia now that they are gone.

Aronowitz quotes one important contemporary labor leader as saying, "This union can't be responsible for future generations or for the rest of the labor movement. We must be mainly concerned with our own."[25] This is the dominant tenor of organized labor in the United States in the 1990s. But imagine the reaction of a John L. Lewis or a Walter Reuther to such words! What happened to the vision of a better life for future generations and more and more of the nation's workers which animated the great organizing drives of the 1930s and 1940s? As David Bacon has asked, "Where is the social vision that will re-animate the labor movement, a vision of justice and equality to unite millions—union and nonunion, employed and unemployed—across all the lines of race and gender and ethnicity?"[26] Where indeed?

Surprisingly, even the most thoughtful of observers seem to fall into the nostalgia for the jobs and salaries of the two decades immediately after World War II. Even Aronowitz and DiFazio fall into this trap. They tell the story of DiFazio's father who began working as a New York longshoreman in 1937.

> He was working without a high school education and he made ten dollars a week more than his college-educated high school teacher. Since the late 1970s unionized jobs that require little more than the willingness to work hard and reward the worker with a decent wage no longer exist. In the 1990s there are almost no opportunities for workers with just high school degrees to make a decent wage and even fewer for those like Sebastian DiFazio without a high school degree but willing to work hard.[27]

Now a number of questions need to be asked about this rosy picture of mid-century opportunity. While Aronowitz and DiFazio certainly do make the point that these rules applied to white male workers much more than they did to people of color or women, others who tell the story leave that part out. (The teacher who made ten dollars a week less than the longshoreman was more than likely a woman.) And even Aronowitz and DiFazio seem to miss the point that Sebastian DiFazio's generation was virtually the only generation for whom his experience held true. By few standards would the New York longshoremen of the 1880s or the 1920s, laboring in the days before their union became strong, be seen as receiving the reward of decent wages. But even more important than accurate history is posing the right questions for the future. Certainly the vast majority of longshoremen have been replaced through the containerization and automation of the waterfront. But why can't the jobs which have replaced their work, in-person service jobs of the twenty-first century, jobs which Reich and others note are so unlikely to be exported to the lower-paying countries of the world, be the future of organized labor and the future of middle-class prosperity? Why not the equivalent of longshoreman or steel-worker wages in McDonalds, or for home health care aids? It is in the answer to that question that much of the nation's economic future rests.

The campaign for the presidency of the AFL-CIO in the fall of 1995 did provide new reason for hope for the emergence of a newly militant organized labor movement and a change in some of the directions of the past decades. When John J. Sweeney, president of the Service Employees International Union defeated AFL-CIO interim president, Thomas R. Donahue, in the first contested AFL-CIO presidential election in history on October 25, 1995, a new chapter in organized labor history may have begun. If Sweeney can deliver on his promises, then his election will have done more for the American economy, and especially for the majority of Americans who find themselves at the lower ends of the economy, than all of the school reform efforts of the last decade.

Sweeney promised increased spending on new organizing. His track record gives reason for hope. The Service Employees, which he has headed for fifteen years, spends 30 percent of its budget on new organizing while the AFL-CIO norm is closer to 5 percent. As a result, the Service Employees organized in new fields with some of the lowest paid workers such as the 20,000 home health aids added to the union's membership. These are exactly the kinds of low-paid, "in-person service workers" on whose future so much of the nation's economic prosperity—such as it is—rests. He also promised to bring more women and people of color into the union and the union's leadership and before the convention which elected him adjourned the executive council had been expanded from 17% to 27% women and minorities. As the *New York Times* reported the next day, the election marks "an emphatic shift back to the labor movement's militant roots." The *Times* also reported the new president of the United Automobile Workers as saying, "This is the first time in 20 years there's excitement. I heard someone say we have to defend the middle class. Well, that's right. But we've got to defend from the middle class on down." If these promises are fulfilled, then organized labor will be a significant player in determining the shape of the American economy in the twenty-first century; and the result will be a quite different and more democratic economy.[28] No wonder House Speaker Newt Gingrich criticized Sweeney's election as "a potential disaster" because it sends "a message of confrontation instead of cooperation."[29] Perhaps that is just what is needed.

The Cold War

There is yet another issue which needs significant attention if both the economic decline and the growing class separations of the United States are to be understood. For forty-five years the United States was locked in a Cold War with the Soviet Union. Throughout all of these years, the Cold War was the ultimate priority in the national budget. Education, job creation, health care, all lagged because their costs could not be covered after the heart of the budget was devoted to defense. During the years of greatest economic decline—the presidency of Ronald Reagan from 1981 to 1989—the defense budgets escalated significantly in a massive—and successful—campaign to outspend the Soviet Union on weapons and ultimately develop both massive weapons superiority and bankruptcy on the part of the old enemy. The problem, of course, is that in the process the United States came very close to bankrupting itself.

Economists have only recently begun to take stock of the massive dislocation of both the long years of the Cold War and the special spending of its last decade. In an underappreciated work of social analysis, Eric Alterman raises one of the fundamental questions which must be addressed if economic dislocation and educational decline are to be understood in meaningful terms rather than mere slogans. Long after the names of the major players have been forgotten, Alterman speculates, historians will ask some fundamental questions about these years:

> How was it, they will ask, that a nation so blessed with economic advantage, with such abundant natural resources, and with so sophisticated a guiding political class allowed itself to squander its national treasure and destroy the foundations of its prosperity and security in pursuit of enemies that had long ceased to threaten it? By what paradoxical rule of political science, they will wonder, did the United States embark on an orgy of military spending and colossal debt creation just as its enemy was collapsing and its own economy eroding?[30]

It is a question which everyone concerned with education needs to ponder seriously. This is much more than a matter of the slogan, "Won't it be a wonderful day when schools have all the money they need and the Navy has to have a bake sale to build a battleship." For more than half a century, military spending has claimed unquestioned supremacy, and the long-term disinvestment in education will take many years to counter, even if the start were made immediately. But there is more to the question than that. The largest question must be, Why was this allowed to happen? Why were two generations of Americans allowed to move through the schools and yet gain so limited a skill in critical thinking that very few voices ever rose to question the economic priorities or the economic devastation which was being wrought?

Of course, there were voices of dissent. Throughout the Cold War small numbers of pacifists and others challenged the basic focus of the priorities. And during the war in Vietnam, large numbers of Americans challenged both the killing and the economic priorities behind the war. The antiwar movement which toppled Lyndon Johnson and ultimately ended the war remains an underappreciated flowering of American democracy. A study is yet to be done of what was right in the education of young Americans in the 1950s which led so many of them to be willing to risk so much in ending the unjust war of the 1960s.

Even before the major buildup of the Vietnam War, Columbia Professor Seymour Melman wrote *Our Depleted Society* to warn Americans that the nation's self-image as the world's leader in basic industries and the production of consumer goods was disappearing. In 1965 he wrote:

Entire industries are falling into technical disrepair, and there is massive loss of productive employment because of inability to hold even domestic markets against foreign competition. Such depletion in economic life produces wide-ranging human deterioration at home. The wealthiest nation on earth has been unable to rally the resources necessary to raise one fifth of its own people from poverty.

And the reasons for the depletion were quite clear for Melman. "This deterioration is the result of an unprecedented concentration of America's technical talent and fresh capital on military production . . . . [M]ore than two thirds of America's technical researchers now work for the military."[31] And this was fifteen years before the United States government began the policies of deficit spending which in one administration moved it from a creditor to a debtor nation in the helter-skelter campaign for mutual bankruptcy with its erstwhile enemy.

The most famous American to worry about the military's cost to the nation's economic and cultural well-being made his case very early in the Cold War era. President Dwight Eisenhower not only coined the phrase "the military-industrial complex" in his farewell address, he spent most of his administration worrying about military expenditures. As David Halberstam has noted in his wonderful book *The Fifties,* Eisenhower "worried about the potential drain on the economy" of military spending and he "believed that the Joint Chiefs cared little or nothing about the dangers of inflation . . . . 'This country,' he once noted, 'can choke itself to death piling up expenditures just as surely as it can defeat itself by not spending enough for protection.' " And these worries marked all of the Eisenhower years. George Humphrey, his secretary of the treasury was one of his point people on the topic:

> Humphrey seemed to speak for Eisenhower's fiscal conservatism at an October 30, 1953, NSC meeting: "There would be no defense," he said, but only "disaster in a military program that scorned the resources and the problems of our economy—erecting majestic defenses and battlements for the protection of a country that was bankrupt."[32]

Where, we find ourselves asking, were the likes of George Humphrey and Ike himself as this country moved so close to bankruptcy, first at the time of the war in Vietnam and then more fully under the presidencies of Ronald Reagan and George Bush? Where were the public voices to challenge the massive transfer of public funds to the richest of the country's citizens who were part of the world of the defense contractors or the decimation of the Great Society programs? The sad reality is that beginning with the Kennedy campaign's emphasis on a "missile gap" in 1960, no subsequent American president has been willing to challenge "erecting majestic defenses" for bankruptcy. No wonder after thirty-five years, the nation is so close to the bankruptcy which Humphrey prophesied.

Toward a Different Analysis of Education and the Economy

At this point it is time to pause and ask a question about the shape of the chapter. Why so many pages of economic analysis in a book focused on the relationship of education and democracy? The answer is fairly straightforward. Far too much of the contemporary education reform movement is based on an attempt to solve the wrong problems with the contemporary economy. Many education reformers of the 1980s and 1990s have based the rationale for change in the schools on the needs of an American economy in crisis. The majority of economists from a range of political perspectives—while they agree that the economy is in crisis, that both capital and good jobs are fleeing the country and class divisions are growing to pre-1930s levels—focus their concerns quite differently. The globalization of the economy, the rapid advent of new technologies, the changing nature of work, the investment in arms over domestic spending, the failure to organize unions in the newly emergent industries, all of these far outrank any perceived failures in the schools as the causes of the current crisis.

If this is true, then something terribly strange is going on at the level of school reform. Justifying the need for a major restructuring of the schools on the economic crisis seems to be an extreme example of a good solution to the wrong problem. If the economic analysis contained in this chapter is accurate, most of the current school-reform ventures proposed today will do very little to improve the nation's economy. Deborah W. Meier is right that the problems with today's economy cannot be linked primarily to the schools, "as though it were illiteracy on the assembly line that undid Detroit!"[33] More seriously, by failing to diagnose the real problems in the schools accurately, too many of the proposed reforms are in danger of exacerbating rather than ameliorating the very real problems in the schools and in the education of the majority of this nation's youth.

So, the next question must be asked. If it does not make sense to call for school reform in the name of protecting the nation's competitive economic advantage, what kinds of economic questions do need to be raised in relationship to school reforms and what should the relationship of schooling and the economy be in a nation whose schools are dedicated to the ever greater expansion of democracy, including economic democracy? It is to the answer to these questions that the remainder of this chapter is dedicated.

If the starting point for all kinds of school reform is a commitment to democracy, then this commitment must be foremost in the analysis of the links between schools and the rest of the social structures, especially the economy. Democracy means many things, but among them are:

Equity—Education reform should, at a minimum, not contribute to further division of rich and poor. On the contrary, schools in a democratic society should foster a commitment to equity and be structured in ways which contribute to equity. Indeed, closing the growing gap between rich and poor, and the closely related divisions in this country by race, class, gender, and sexual orientation must be central to all reform policies.

Critical engagement—The economic challenges posed here and elsewhere are massive. Building a prosperous society for all of the nation's citizens, ultimately building a world of both peace and prosperity, will take the very best work of the minds of all citizens. Finding ways to avoid some of the economic foolishness of the past, the spending into bankruptcy for defense while the nation's infrastructure (including its schools) crumbles, for example will take the best that a generation of thoughtful, critical, and engaged citizens can contribute. And schools must be reformed so as to support the preparation of these kinds of citizens.

Democratic participation—In a haunting "Afterword," Robert Reich worries that the next generation of Americans could degenerate into a caricature of libertarianism. "There will be no sense of national community. Instead, Americans will secede into smaller enclaves of people with similar incomes, similar values and interests, similar ethnic identities. Pluribus without unum."[34] This decline in public spheres has been a worry of some of the most thoughtful of the nation's commentators for some time.[35] But a democratic schooling worthy of the name must be structured to counter these trends; must be a prime place in which a democratic society is both taught and modeled.

While the reforms proposed for a democratic education may be very similar to those proposed by reformers interested primarily in economic competition with Japan and Germany, the criteria for judging any individual reform will be quite different. It is one thing to say that we need to reorganize our schools so that a better trained workforce will graduate. It is quite a different thing, however, to say that we need change in schools to expand democracy, including economic democracy. If the latter is the goal, then democracy will be defined much more broadly and democracy must be the means as well as the end of the reform effort.

Throughout American history, school reformers have had difficulty coming to terms with exactly this division of purpose. Are schools primarily for the expansion of democracy and economic opportunity for all or are schools primarily for sorting and classifying citizens, separating the future winners from the future losers? As the historian James Anderson has written, "Both schooling for democratic citizenship and schooling for second-class citizenship have been basic traditions in American education."[36]

Certainly efforts throughout American history to link schooling to larger economic issues, and especially strategies with this end in mind which have been adopted during the reform decades of the 1980s and 1990s, have reflected both the democratic and the oppressive sides of the coin. If schooling for democratic citizenship for all, and not schooling for second class citizenship for any is primary, if equity, critical engagement, and democratic participation are the goals, there are a number of immediate reforms which are essential for the nation's schools. Ironically, some of these reforms are not too different from some currently being proposed and some well along in implementation. But the emphasis is different. The inclusion of people is very different. And the warnings and pitfalls which must be considered are sometimes virtually the opposite of those currently in the forefront of reform activities. It is to these examples that we must now turn.

The Standards Debate

As a new school year began, in September 1989, President George Bush and the nation's governors met at the historic University of Virginia campus at Charlottesville for an "Education Summit." The location was not accidental. If any president in American history had given voice to a powerful vision of the role of education in forging a democratic society it was the university's founder, Thomas Jefferson. And the 1989 summit's planners did their best to build on the historic associations.

President Bush and the governors, led by their co-chair Bill Clinton of Arkansas, began the process of creating a set of National Education Goals which could guide both federal and local education efforts. In his January 1990 State of the Union address, President Bush presented these goals to a joint session of Congress. Four years later, a new president, former Governor Clinton, presented the same goals as legislation to Congress resulting in the passage of the Goals 2000: Educate America Act, which expanded the role of the federal panel designated to implement the goals. Clearly the reform efforts begun in 1983 had come a long way.

With due deference to the American tradition of local autonomy in education, both the Republican and Democratic presidents insisted that not only implementation but the design of specific policies and curricula would remain at the local level. Goals 2000 did not mean a national curriculum for the United States. The role of the national movement was to build support, provide modest funds, and most of all outline the long-term goals themselves.

The goals were hardly likely to stir significant debate. Who could oppose the proposition that by the year 2000:

- All children in America will start school ready to learn.

- The high school graduation rate will increase to at least 90 percent.

- American students will . . . [have] demonstrated competency in challenging subject matter. . . so they may be prepared for re-

sponsible citizenship, further learning, and productive employment in our modern economy.

- American students will be the first in the world in science and
  mathematics achievement.

- Every adult American will be literate and will possess the knowledge and skills necessary to compete in a global economy and
  exercise the rights and responsibilities of citizenship.

- Every school in America will be free of drugs and violence and
  will offer a disciplined environment conducive to learning.

Who, indeed, could object?[37]

The national standards movement did not spring forth de novo at the
Charlottesville gathering. For over a decade, the National Council of Teachers of Mathematics (NCTM) had been working through a number of sub-
groups of its members to create the "Curriculum and Evaluation Standards
for School Mathematics," which was also published in 1989 and has served
as the granddaddy of a whole range of standards reports issued for the sciences, English, social studies, history, and other fields. With the creation of
the National Education Goals Panel as a joint federal and state effort, that
body took over the task of encouraging the development of national standards
in virtually every field of study. Ultimately the panel also took on an unex-
pected role of refereeing the fierce debates which some of the standards, most
notably those in history, generated between those who held radically different
interpretations of the history of the peoples of the United States.

At the same time, a number of foundations, led by the Carnegie Endowment, the Pew Charitable Trusts, the Lilly Endowment, and the Edna
McConnell Clark Foundation have been active in encouraging the development of "high standards, high expectations," in all schools. By supporting
intensive reform efforts in certain schools, these foundations seek to provide
models for the whole national campaign.

The opposition which has arisen to Goals 2000 and the standards movement has usually come from two perspectives. On the one hand, experienced
educators have rightly asked the tough question, Who is going to provide the
resources to meet these goals? What kinds of policies in terms of family
leave, Head Start, and expanded kindergarten programs will it really take to
ensure that "all children in America will start school ready to learn"? What
kinds of resources—for retraining teachers, for providing curriculum, in terms
of other incentives—will it really take to increase the high school graduation

rate to 90 percent? And what is the point of goals which have no meaningful resources behind them?

From another perspective, a new assault on Goals 2000 and the standards movement has been mounted. The conservatives who came to power in the 1994 election are of a different stripe than former President Bush and his first Secretary of Education, Lauro Cavazos. For the new generation of Republicans, any effort at national goals is a step towards a national curriculum and national control of education. The Gingrich Republicans have gone from a promise to "strengthen the rights of parents to protect their children against education programs that undermine the values taught in the home,"[38] to an all out assault on Goals 2000 as a national take-over of a parental and local responsibility.

Both the resource questions raised by sometimes jaded educators and the all-out assault on Goals 2000 by right-wing Republicans miss the point in the debate about higher standards for the nation's schools. The real issues have seldom been discussed. In an important exception to the general silence on the larger problems involved with the standards movement, Michael Apple has reminded us that in discussing standards one must also remember that, "In a society riven by social tensions and by increasingly larger inequalities, schools will not be immune from—and in fact may participate in recreating—these inequalities." And, "If this is true of education in general, it is equally true of attempts to reform it."[39] If one is serious about a democratic system of schooling, and using the reforms offered by the standards movement as a means to make schools more democratic, then two points should be obvious. First, there is no way that people seriously committed to the welfare of the next generation can oppose the broad outline of the national goals. At the same time, the question must be posed, what happens if a child does not live up to the goals? It seems like such an obvious question, but it has generally been avoided. And in the response to that great unasked question, the whole standards movement splits down the middle.

In fact, the split in the standards movement is very deep. On the one hand are those who argue that schools must be held accountable for high standards and for the success of every child in meeting the standards. On the other hand, there is a very different standards movement which argues that every child (and by extension their parents) must be held accountable for meeting the standards and if they don't it is their own fault and their own responsibility to correct the situation.

This split is virtually never discussed in the literature and the conferences which have marked the forward movement of the standards campaign. As one of the most respected and vocal of the standards supporters responded when this writer raised the question, "That is the issue we can't discuss. Our momentum comes from not looking at how much we disagree, but someday soon we are going to have to." As Apple has noted about many reform efforts similar to the call for standards, "they must have a penumbra of vagueness so that powerful groups or individuals who would otherwise disagree can fit under the umbrella."[40] Let us hope that the day of the discussion—and a recognition of the deep differences within the standards community—does indeed come soon for the differences are very important.

These two different approaches to standards yield radically different sorts of implementation policies. The former approach calls for a massive infusion of additional resources, both financial resources and training and motivation for educators and community leaders. It would be a significant shift for many of today's teachers to come to the point where they really believed that every child in their class could effectively meet all of the standards and that it was their responsibility to ensure such success. Anyone who has spent any time in the teachers room of almost any American school knows that a very different attitude prevails today. It is a significant shift for school boards and taxpayers to really believe that they must commit the resources to ensure that every school in the district and every child in each school really is provided an education that enables her or him to meet the highest standards. It will take, as noted above, major new investments to ensure that children enter school "ready to learn" or that they are in fact taught what they need in school.

On the other hand, the latter approach demands relatively little in the way of investment. Set the standards. Offer the tests to see if the students meet them. Separate the winners from the losers. It is a fairly simple and inexpensive process. Of course, another question needs to be asked about the latter approach: "Has anything actually been done to raise standards by this move?" As the old Highland Scots saying goes, "You don't fatten a sheep by weighing it." But weighing more than fattening seems to be a popular panacea today.

And the dangers for a democratic society of the "weighing the sheep" approach to standards have only begun to be explored. In Boston, in 1983, at the height of the first round of educational reform, the then superintendent proposed a new set of promotion requirements including grades, scores on citywide tests, and attendance. Many of us opposed those standards at the time. God knows, we wanted higher standards for the students in the Boston Public Schools as much as the superintendent did. What goes on in too many of the city's schools, in 1985 or 1995, is unacceptable. The schools, as they are, are not working, not educating many of today's youth. But the new standards, we argued, were also not the answer. Why not provide more individual support for students, provide more counselors, and, most important, provide different kinds of educational settings so that kids would stay in school, enjoy and be engaged in school, and learn in school, and then—and only then—look at the standards and begin to measure the results? But we lost.

A school committee which was anxious to respond to both national pressures for reform and a sense of crisis in the city schools adopted the standards as proposed. Remediation and support for achievement would come later; much later it turned out. Reform in Boston would begin with the standards. And the results were dramatic. The dropout rate increased significantly, to above 50 percent for those who entered high school in ninth grade. As a friend of mine who taught at one of the tougher high schools in the city said at the time, "By November, I have quite a few kids in my class who know that they have already failed to meet the standards, that no matter what they do from November to June, they will take my class again next year because they have failed the attendance standard. Now tell me how to motivate my class!" This is a recipe for failure, not for higher standards or increased student achievement.[41]

What is frightening is that this kind of individualized standards movement, in which the standards are used to divide students into successes and failures fits all too well with the kind of economic changes described by Reich and others. If it is true that there is a decline in the traditional middle of the economy and that workers are being separated more and more into high-paid, high-success symbolic analysts and the low-paid "sinking boats" of both the routine production workers and those who provide in-person services, should it really come as any surprise that the historic role of the school as the nation's great sorting mechanism should be expanded?

After all, what would schools look like if a cynical voice were to call for an education system designed to serve the new categories of work as they exist today?[42] While Reich admits it is implausible, he also notes that there is no reason why "in principle, all of America's routine production workers" should not receive an education to fit them for jobs as symbolic analysts. Nevertheless, he also notes that, "In practice, of course, the task of transforming a majority of the American workforce into symbolic analysts would be daunting."[43]

There is an alternative, though it is one few wish to discuss, especially the standards advocates. Again, Reich describes the current situation very well. "By the 1990s, the *average* American child was ill equipped to compete in the high-value global economy, but within that average was a wide variation . . . . [S]ome American children—no more than 15 to 20 percent—are being perfectly prepared for a lifetime of symbolic-analytic work."[44] What better way to keep the variation, and the sorting, intact, than a version of the call for high standards?

If one really wanted to ensure that 15–20 percent of the next generation were prepared for jobs as symbolic-analysts and the other 80–85 percent were prepared for routine production, in-person service, and/or long periods of unemployment, standards could serve well. If standards are raised, without any accompanying commitment to ensuring that all students meet the standards, then two things are accomplished, both of which are needed by the new emerging economy:

- Those who meet the standards continue to get a better and better kind of education, virtually the education which is required to be a systemic analyst. They receive the knowledge and the skills in critical thinking and team work which will yield success.

- Those who do not meet the standards do not stay in school, do not succeed, and they too are prepared—prepared to work at the cash register at McDonalds with the pictures of a Big Mac and a shake on it, or to mop the floor and change the bed pans in our hospitals, and receive low prestige and low wages. And if all goes smoothly, they will say, "I have only myself to blame, I didn't meet the standards."

In today's economy, the question must be asked, after all, what would happen if schools really succeeded? If schools really succeeded (by virtually any definition of success), if everyone stayed in and graduated from high school ready to take on the world and expecting a place in the world, it could be a social dynamite; the building of profound social discontent. If the American economy is not fundamentally reoriented, either so that full employment in meaningful work can be provided for all citizens, or so that alternatives to work of the sort proposed by Aronowitz and DiFazio become real and respectable, we must ask—Would George Bush or Bob Dole or Bill Clinton really want to preside over a nation in which over 90 percent of all youth graduated from high school ready for "responsible citizenship, further learning, and productive employment"? Are the leaders of either of today's political parties prepared to deal with that sort of social crisis?[45]

Sorting is an old pattern in education. If it is true that standards are being raised to improve the education of some, and to increase the pool of self-defined failures who will take the low-level jobs in the service sector, it would not be the first time that this has happened in American education.

There has long been a tradition within the field of education of saying that the real purpose of education is to serve the needs of industry. For decades school reformers have documented the tracking which goes on within schools, the tracking of some students—usually from upper social classes—to college and the professions and the tracking of other students—especially lower class students, women, people of color—to the working-class jobs in the factory and the service sector. The standards movement can be a vehicle for more of the same, much more of the same. It remains a serious problem that this possibility—in many places, this reality—has not been recognized more clearly by the progressives among the standards advocates.

There is a profound social discontent brewing in this nation and in this nation's economy. And whether by design or accident, many today are implementing reforms which will, in fact, produce a workforce and a population geared to the new two-tier economy which seems to be emerging with frightening speed.

There is also a clear alternative. Standards can be the standards for all. Schools can be provided with the resources but also the challenge of ensuring that they offer a range of structures, a range of learning options, and a range of resources so that every student succeeds and every student meets the standards. This is not an impossible dream.

Central Park East Secondary School is the most well-known example of a school built on the principles of the Coalition of Essential Schools, which includes a commitment to standards. "High standards are set for all students. Students must clearly exhibit mastery of their schoolwork." Yet at least at Central Park East, under the leadership of Deborah Meier and her colleagues, the high standards are linked to a sense of family in which students and teachers together—along with families and critical friends—are all invested in the ultimate success of every student. Everyone is ultimately expected to reach the same high standards. That is part of what it means for the school to be democratic. This is a very different way of doing business than in the vast majority of the nation's high schools. It is based on a democratic vision of both the way an individual school should operate and of the ways students should be prepared for participation in a larger democratic society. Only this kind of democratic dream is consistent with a democratic form of schooling for the citizens of the twenty-first century.[46] The recent publicity surrounding Meier's work is a useful reminder that this kind of school can be built even within the bureaucracy of a large urban school system. Democracy can be at the heart of the standards movement; indeed democracy itself can be the ultimate standard. The only remaining question then is one of will.

Of course, the call for high standards for all students, if it achieves any meaningful measure of success, is going to challenge all of the current assumptions about the link of education and the economy. Unless a Reichian nirvana is achieved in which everyone is a symbolic analyst, the real success of the standards movement would mean that many people would be "overeducated," that is, educated far beyond the needs of today's job market. That is a kind of social dynamite, but it could be a very healthy dynamite.

The emergence of a new generation of highly educated citizens, people ready to reexamine the fundamental assumptions about the nature of both democracy and the economy could be exactly the people needed to envision new ways of developing prosperity. These people could be the organizers of the next generation of labor unions, the Mother Joneses, John L. Lewises, and Walter Reuthers of the twenty-first century. They could also be the people who finally call the questions of U.S. militarism, and the racism, sexism, and homophobia which so divides today's working class. They could be the producers of a new kind of dynamic democracy in which the resources are truly used for the benefit of all. The production of democratic citizens who will not so much fit the economy as it is but rather challenge today's economic structures and dream of tomorrow's is not what most education reformers mean by school and work linkages. But it should be.

The emergence of a new generation of highly educated citizens in numbers far greater than the jobs available for them may finally force not only the issue of the link between education and preparation for work, but the central role of work itself in giving human life worth. *The Jobless Future* is not simply a work of economic analysis. It is also a book with a utopian vision. Aronowitz and DiFazio pose a fundamental set of questions which are virtually excluded from public debate today, though they are terribly relevant:

> If paid work is increasingly "unnecessary" in relation to technological possibilities, should it be encouraged? Assume in addition that in fact there are not enough jobs. Under these circumstances, what is the status of the traditional work ethic (which in actuality always means the compulsion to engage in paid work whatever the compensation)?[47]

If a new work ethic is to emerge; if a new understanding of the relationship of work to both individual and social well-being is to become clear, then skilled and self-confident people are going to have to attend to the issue. And a high-standards education for everyone could be just the vehicle to guarantee this sort of discourse.

But achieving a national commitment to high standards for all will not be easy. The campaign must begin with a clear focus on the issue. The standards movement cannot proceed as if the split down the middle of the movement did not exist. The differences between the call for high standards for all and high standards as a means of sorting is terribly fundamental. And if the question is not called, if the lines are not drawn, all of the dynamics of American education will push the standards movement in the direction of sorting and labeling the successes and the failures, those with a prosperous future and the rejects. Some of today's standards advocates will find themselves to have been agents of an illiberal educational agenda the results of which they do not like at all.

In any reform project, if one option is cheaper, easier to implement, and fits the needs of the economy as it is today better than the other, it is the side which will win the battle. This is especially likely in the political climate of the 1990s. As Apple warns, "the very real elements of democratic potential within the Standards can be washed away in a context of rightist reaction."[48] But that cannot be allowed to happen. And the work which must be done to ensure a different outcome is central to the battle for democratic schools and a democratic society.

The School-to-Work Movement

Perhaps nowhere has the struggle between schooling for democratic citizenship and schooling for second-class citizenship been stronger than in the school-to-work movement and its long predecessors in vocational education. In May 1994, President Clinton signed the School to Work Opportunities Act at a gala event on the White House lawn. The act was the culmination of years of work on the part of many people—and the merger of several streams of education reform in this country and worldwide. And like many such mergers, it left many of the underlying issues unresolved. For some of its supporters, the School to Work Opportunities Act was a means of using a new name to find additional funds for the traditional programs of vocational education. For others it was a fulfillment of the president's commitment to improving the training and education of all of the nation's citizens, especially those who were not college-bound. And for still others, it was a means of fulfilling a long-term vision held by many progressive educators in which the world of work—the "real world"—could become the laboratory in which all students learned. For the latter group, school-to-work was a tool to push the radical transformation of the education of all students—the college-bound and those planning on working directly out of high school—by breathing life into their studies through connections beyond the schoolhouse door.

Adria Steinberg, who has both written about and administered school-to-work programs, has described the splits in the movement very effectively:

> To the first group (which is the larger and more mainstream of the two), school to work programs are a way to serve the non-college bound. Although intending to create new opportunities for these students, this strand of the movement perpetuates the very social class tracking that created "the forgotten half" as this strata of students was aptly named in an important policy statement of the 1980s. Efforts to create programs for the non-college bound end up replicating the problems that have plagued vocational education for fifty years—low-level, watered down academics and job specific skills training.

In this version, school to work is a shiny new model of a very old and broken-down vehicle. And unfortunately, as Steinberg notes, this version does seem to be the dominant one. Fortunately, however, there are other options:

> The other strand of the school to work movement sees the possibilities quite differently. These policy makers and school practitioners also support school to work programs as an alternative, but with the emphasis on worksites as learning environments. This second group has its roots in the philosophy of John Dewey, who in the early years of the twentieth century propounded his views on "education through occupations." As he put it, occupations function as "magnet to attract and glue to hold" students interest.[49]

At a time of worrisome drop out rates; at a time when many students who remain in school have dropped out intellectually and are simply putting in time, a new kind of magnet or glue to hold student interest seems essential if meaningful change is to take place. And at a time when both the emerging world of work and critical citizenship for expanding democracy demand people who can respond quickly and thoughtfully to new situations, not merely follow instructions, learning from critical participation in the world of work offers wonderful new opportunities.

Fortunately there are educators like Steinberg and her colleagues at Cambridge Rindge and Latin School around the country who are building new programs for today's youth which engage the interests of a wide range of students through thoughtful engagement in real-world enterprises. Nevertheless, the majority of school-to-work programs, like their vocational education predecessors, define their students as "non-college-bound" and remain stuck in the tradition of low expectations, rote learning, and specific—and often irrelevant—skill training. Far too often they also remain stuck in a tradition of sex role stereotyping and expectations linked to the sex, race, and class of the student.

Many youth, and their parents, have long distrusted traditional vocational education programs. The tracking and the bleak futures are too well known to too many. Especially for people of color, people from working-class backgrounds, women, and their parents, the experience of Malcolm X was not atypical. As one of the top students in his eighth grade class in Mason, Michigan, the young Malcolm Little was taken under the wing of one of the schools most sympathetic teachers. One day Mr. Ostrowski raised the question of vocation: "Malcolm, you ought to be thinking about a career. Have you been giving it thought?" Almost off the top of his head Malcolm answered, "Well, yes, sir, I've been thinking I'd like to be a lawyer." Mr. Ostrowski's response remains a classic in American education:

> Malcolm, one of life's first needs is for us to be realistic. Don't misunderstand me now. We all here like you, you know that. But you've got to be realistic about being a nigger. A lawyer—that's no realistic goal for a nigger. You need to think about something you can be. You're good with your hands—making things. Everybody admires your carpentry shop work. Why don't you plan on carpentry? People like you as a person—you'd get all kinds of work.[50]

No wonder, "Why don't you plan on carpentry?" raises so many red flags for so many today.

Robert Reich has described in graphic detail what schooling might look like if it were truly geared to "serving the needs of industry" and to the divisions of work which he has developed. For most of the twentieth century, progressive educators have bemoaned the "factory system" which has predominated in the schools. From John Dewey to Samuel Bowles and Herbert Gintis they have noted the fact that in their organizational structure and in their curriculum the majority of the nation's schools virtually mirrored the factory system for which so many of the students were being prepared. In this sense, not just traditional "voc ed" programs, but the whole structure of schooling has been highly work oriented. And for most of the twentieth century, the majority of American jobs were in what Reich calls "routine production." And he also reminds us that the schools served this world of work quite well.

> Recall that America's educational system at mid-century fit nicely into the prevailing structure of high-volume production within which its young products were to be employed. American schools mirrored the national economy, with standard assembly-line curriculum divided neatly into subjects, taught in predictable units of time, arranged sequentially by grade, and controlled by standardized tests intended to weed out defective units and return them for reworking.[51]

It is a harsh, but surprisingly accurate picture of the kind of schooling which could be witnessed in far too many schools, at mid-century or century's end.

Reich also argues that this kind of schooling worked fairly well for much of the last century. It is only that the economy has left them behind. The current crisis in the link of schooling and the economy must then be seen in the fact that "most schools had not changed for the worse; they simply had not changed for the better."[52] And change for the better meant schools which could produce the workers most likely to succeed in the twenty-first century, symbolic analysts.

Many of today's school reformers will agree with Reich's analysis of both the success of the schools of mid-century and the needs for schooling as we enter the twenty-first century. But there is a problem here. Schools have never been training grounds for mere workers, for people are more than workers. In a critique of vocational education written in 1915, John Dewey asked the essential question of all school for work models.

> No one is just an artist and nothing else, and in so far as one approximates that condition, he is so much the less developed human being; he is a kind of monstrosity. He must, at some period of his life, be a member of a family; he must have friends and companions; he must either support himself or be supported by others, and thus he has a business career. He is a member of some organized political unit, and so on. We naturally name his vocation from that one of the callings which distinguishes him, rather than from those which he has in common with all others. But we should not allow ourselves to be so subject

to words as to ignore and virtually deny his other callings when it comes to a consideration of the vocational phases of education.[53]

In spite of the male only references of Dewey's 1915 words, he has set a broader standard for education in a democratic society than nearly any of the reformers at century's end. And by that standard much of American schooling at mid-century or century's end has been a significant failure. For Dewey, the student is preparing to be worker and citizen, preparing for ways to produce an income and for ways to live well. Would that more of the literature of the current reform era had such a broad conception of the purposes of schooling.

The point at which Dewey and Reich, and anyone else looking carefully at the majority of today's schools, would agree, however, is that too many schools in the 1990s still reflect the factory model. While the routine production jobs are disappearing, schools are still preparing students as if they were the norm. But not all schools. As Reich also reminds us, discussing either the economy or the schools of the United States as if the average were the norm is not useful. Just as the experiences of different kinds of workers are diverging more and more (with some in boats rising rapidly while most others sink at varying rates of speed), so too are the experiences of today's students diverging rapidly. Averages have no place in understanding today's economic or educational structures. On the contrary we must remember Reich's warning:

> By the 1990s, the *average* American child was ill equipped to compete in the high-value global economy, but within that average was a wide variation. . . . Fully 17 percent of American seventeen-year-olds are functionally illiterate. Some American children receive almost no education, and many more get a poor one. But some American children— no more than 15 to 20 percent—are being perfectly prepared for a lifetime of symbolic-analytic work.[54]

The rich are getting richer and the poor poorer not only in money but in the intellectual resources, the cultural capital, made available to them.

What has long been viewed as elite education takes on new meaning in the economy which Reich has described. As he notes:

> The formal education of the budding symbolic analyst follows a common pattern. Some of these young people attend elite private schools, followed by the most selective universities and prestigious graduate schools; a majority spend childhood within high quality suburban public schools

where they are tracked through advanced courses in the company of other similarly fortunate symbolic-analytic offspring, and thence to good four-year colleges. But their experiences are similar: Their parents are interested and involved in their education. Their teachers and professors are attentive to their academic needs. They have access to state-of-the-art science laboratories, interactive computers and video systems in the class-room, language laboratories, and high-tech school libraries. Their classes are relatively small; their peers are intellectually stimulating.[55]

For this fortunate minority, education works well. Indeed, "no other society prepares its most fortunate young people as well for lifetimes of creative problem-solving, -identifying, and brokering."[56]

But except for the high-tech elements, this kind of education is not new. Elite private schools have existed side by side with mass education throughout American history. Small numbers of students have been tracked to the top of public education, either in separate schools or separate programs for all of this century. The divisions between college prep and the vocational and general tracks are not new. Again, it was Dewey who recognized the inherently vocational aspect of all of the tracks when he wrote, "To a considerable extent, the education of the dominant classes was essentially vocational—it only happened that their pursuits of ruling and enjoying were not called professions."[57] Perhaps the current economic crisis has yielded a greater honesty at this point in the educational dialogue, if little else.

There is, however, a point at which the commitment to a democratic education and the school-to-work movement can converge. What would happen if the nation were to make a national priority of educating every citizen to be a symbolic analyst? Reich argues that it is theoretically possible. "[T]he global economy imposes no particular limit upon the number of Americans who can sell symbolic-analytic services worldwide. In principle, all of America's routine production workers could become symbolic analysts and let their old jobs drift overseas to developing nations." While one must question the morality of simply globalizing the split between rich and poor, the commitment to a better education for all Americans is certainly reasonable. Of course, commitment and reality may be two very different things. Providing all Americans with an education to be symbolic analysts would demand a great deal:

It would require early intervention to ensure the nutrition and health of small children and to enroll them in stimulating preschool programs.

And not even the most gifted of such children could aspire to such jobs unless the nation provided excellent public schools in every city and region and ample financial help to young people who wanted to attend college. Further, a large pool of symbolic analysts within the nation would require substantial additional investments in universities, research parks, airports, and other facilities conducive to symbolic-analytic work. Finally, to ensure that American symbolic analysts received sufficient on-the-job training, government would have to induce global enter- prises (of whatever putative nationality) to contract with Americans for complex problem-solving and -identifying.[58]

What if, indeed, this were to become America's educational goal? "As im- plausibly ambitious as these initiatives may seem, many other societies are pursing them: Japan, South Korea, Singapore, and several Western European nations have embarked upon vigorous programs of education, research, infra- structure, and on-the-job training, all designed to enlarge their pools of sym- bolic analysts."[59]

The goal of such a commitment could not be merely the production of more and more symbolic analysts. Reich and other economists can continue to debate the nation's and the world's capacity to absorb greater and greater numbers of such workers. But something more fundamental is at stake. View- ing education as simply vocational, whether vocational for routine produc- tion, in-service, or symbolic analytical work is, as Dewey argued, creating "a kind of monstrosity" who is nothing but a worker. But people are much more than the work they do. They are also lovers, members of families and com- munities, and citizens in a democracy. And for all of these roles, the educa- tion which will serve best is not far from that which is called for in the education of the symbolic analyst.

A democracy requires that all citizens be prepared for "pursuits of ruling and of enjoying," and not merely an elite. And so the education traditionally reserved for an elite must be made available to all. Only in this way will the education offered by society truly meet the test of offering schooling for democratic citizenship to all, schooling for second-class citizenship to none.

Ironically, the world of work offers one of the best opportunities for de- veloping this kind of democratic education for all. Adria Steinberg and Larry Rosenstock have described the ways in which the vocational education pro- grams in Cambridge, Massachusetts, have been completely overhauled so that the world of work has become the focus for study rather than the master of what is to be studied. Far from preparing for specific jobs, students in the

Cambridge program make the work of the city the unifying theme for their curriculum. "Cambridge is the 'text' as students investigate the neighborhoods, the systems, the people, and the needs that compose an urban community." In this process students use a project approach working with real clients. They are engaged in collaborative projects, and there are serious links between the students and faculty and community representatives. The air of reality, the links to solving real problems, and the requirement of collaboration all serve as Dewey prophesied as a kind of glue to maintain student interest and commitment.

Not surprisingly, this kind of education—which mirrors in many ways the education Reich describes for the symbolic analyst—has led more and more of the students in the program to decide to go on to college. At Cambridge Rindge and Latin School, the technical programs are no less college prep than those which formally carry the label. While still only a small minority among vocational education programs, schools like this can be found in many different parts of the country.[60] And they do represent an important alternative to the tracking which has been at the core of vocational education for the last century.

But the fundamental question of resources remains. If school budgets remain as they are now, only a fraction of citizens will receive the kind of education which they need and only a handful of schools will have the leadership of people who can bring about meaningful change. If, on the other hand, a major new national initiative is truly created, if education reform receives the emphasis in the next decades which the cold war has received in the past four decades, then amazing things are possible. It is thus to the question of money that we must turn.

School Funding

In the 1960s and 1970s, the issue of school financing was at the heart of many of the struggles to improve schools. Leaders of the Civil Rights movement and school advocates around the country pointed to the incredible differences in school funding between rich and poor school districts as both a symptom and a cause of the problems facing those committed to equal educational opportunity and quality education for all of the country's citizens.

For most of the twentieth century, school funding in nearly all states, has been based primarily on the local property tax. The result has been that rich communities had more money to support schools than poor communities—much more money. The percentage differences in per pupil spending between the richest and poorest school districts have usually been far greater than the percentage differences between the richest and the poorest states in the union.

It is not surprising that as the Civil Rights movement began to turn to school issues, challenges to this inequity began. And in the early 1960s, there was reason for optimism. In 1961 the California Supreme Court ruled that a system of school finance "which invidiously discriminates among students on the basis of wealth violates the equal protection guaranty of the state constitution."[61] Many hoped that the result of the *Serrano v. Priest* decision could be meaningful change in the distribution of school funds in California and a national movement in the same direction. Neither development took place, however.

In California, a combination of legislative inaction and legal challenges slowed the implementation of the Serrano decision to a crawl. And the optimism generated by Serrano came to a halt when the United States Supreme Court ruled 5-4 in a Texas case, *San Antonio School District v. Rodriguez,* that unequal school financing based on differences in the property tax could not be challenged, at least at the federal level. As happened so often during the succeeding decades, Justice Thurgood Marshall spoke for the Civil Rights agenda in dissent:

> The Court today decides, in effect, that a State may constitutionally vary the quality of education which it offers its children in accordance with the amount of taxable wealth located in the school districts within which they reside. The majority's decision represents an abrupt departure from the mainstream of recent state and federal court decisions concerning the unconstitutionality of state educational financing schemes dependent upon taxable local wealth. More unfortunately, though, the majority's holding can only be seen as a retreat from our historic commitment to equality of educational opportunity and as unsupportable acquiescence in a system which deprives children in their earliest years of the chance to reach their full potential as citizens.[62]

Little did Marshall know how long the retreat from equal educational opportunity would last.

After the San Antonio decision, progressive educational reformers tended to turn away from the issue of school financing. They did so in part out of a recognition that many issues besides money do influence the success of school reforms. They did so in part because of frustration, especially in large urban areas, with the capacity of school bureaucracies to eat up virtually limitless amounts of money and still not produce results. Finally, they did so out of a recognition that the political climate in the United States was not going to be conducive to further appeals.

California led in this retreat with the passage of Proposition 13, which severely limited a school district's ability to raise funds through the property tax. Quite a number of states followed California's lead. While it is true that the property tax burden had grown too steep for many, these votes also represented a turn away from concerns with the education of the next generation. This turn is dramatically exacerbated by the fact that close to three-quarters of today's voters do not have children in the public schools and in some urban areas such as Boston the figure is as high as 90 percent. This is not, primarily, a matter of the growth of private schools but rather the radical changes in the demographics of the United States. At a time when the population as a whole is getting older and when white middle-class families are having far fewer children, the split between voters and public school parents is growing. In many states the majority of children in the public schools are not white. However, the vast majority of voters are white. The growing reluctance of these voters to pay for the education of "other people's children" cannot be overlooked as a major hurdle to achieving equal educational opportunity.[63]

The result of the turn away from a national discourse about school finance is that the inequities in funds available to educate the nation's children remain glaring. Jonathan Kozol compares school spending differences in three of the major industrial states for the 1988–1989 school year. The differences are smallest in Illinois, where the City of Chicago spent on average $5,265 per pupil while Niles Township High School spent $9,371 and New Trier spent $8,823. In New Jersey and New York the differences are more stark with per pupil spending more than doubling between the largest urban districts and the richest suburbs. In New Jersey, Camden spent $3,538 while Summit spent $7,275 and Princeton $7,725. In New York, the city schools spend an average of $7,299 while Manhasset spent $15,084.[64] And even these differences do not tell the whole story, for per pupil costs traditionally underestimate the cost of an equal education between urban and suburban districts. The salaries negotiated by the urban teacher unions are usually higher than those in the surrounding suburbs. As a result of this one variable alone, the same "per pupil spending" purchases smaller classes and more individualized student attention in the suburbs than in the cities. In addition, the costs of far greater numbers of bilingual and special education students are also not reflected in per pupil averages. Thus, even if New York and Manhasset were at the same level of funding for their schools, it would be safe to assume that Manhasset would have significantly more money available for the education of the average—non bilingual, non-special-education—student. But the funds are not equal. Manhasset has more than twice the per pupil moneys as New York City!

If one looks at these numbers and then recalls Reich's description of the differences between the education available to the "average" American youth and to the 15–20 percent most likely destined for careers as symbolic analysts, a very stark picture begins to emerge. The accident of birth and residence in a select number of districts is a very powerful determinant of one's economic future. School spending remains one of the clearest points of division between the haves and the have-nots in the United States at the end of the century.

For all of the arguments that "money is not the primary issue," the kind of education which is received by future symbolic analysts costs a great deal more than the education received by the "average" American. And most calls to take up the challenge of providing a first-rate education, an education for both symbolic analytic work and active citizenship, is met with the stonewall of realism. "Of course, we can't talk about that level of money," we are told, "we have to be realistic." This is an odd state of affairs. For the first time in this nation's long pattern of rediscovering school reform, the majority of advocates for change seem to be arguing that no funds need to be spent to accomplish the change. In his July 1995 review of a number of the recent books on school reform, James Traub captures this majority sentiment:

> And where many liberals, including [Jonathan] Kozol, go wrong is in overestimating the importance of school spending. Of course, schools should have a decent physical plant, books that aren't falling apart, computers, and so on, but per-pupil spending, [James] Coleman noted, has virtually no correlation with school success.[65]

This is simply nonsense.

Traub's statement is wrong on several counts. It is easy to say that "Of course, schools should have a decent physical plant, books that aren't falling apart, computers, and so on," as if these were readily available in all of the nation's schools today. That is far from the case. Jonathan Kozol is but the most eloquent of a number of educators who have documented the appalling deficiencies in physical plant, text books, and computers in the schools which serve the nation's less well-off.

It is also interesting that Coleman's now thirty-year-old study continues to carry so much weight. Coleman was comparing the relative differences between socioeconomic background and school input in determining student success. And Coleman wrote before Ron Edmonds and others found more and more important exceptions to the general rules which he laid down.[66] That his work carries so much weight in the mid-1990s is a tribute to which people continue to hold onto research which confirms their self-interest, no matter what its accuracy.

The reality of school reform in the 1990s is that there is a high correlation between school success and the money spent. Many who might argue against this proposition are still likely to be willing to pay the tuition of elite private schools or high suburban property taxes to ensure that their own children receive the best of educational experiences. It would be hard to find any among those who so adamantly continue to cite Coleman who place their own children in the schools of the lowest spending districts, with the exception of the few elite examination schools which some cities use to continue the tracking among their own public school students. The best does cost a lot of money. The admissions officers at elite private schools and real estate agents in the more advantaged suburbs understand this reality quite clearly. It is time for education reform advocates to catch up.

Realism dictates that much more money is needed for public education in the United States. Indeed, the people of this nation face a fundamental choice. Are we, once and for all, going to admit that we have a two-track educational system, preparing some for active citizenship including both social, cultural, and political leadership and meaningful work while others are prepared for a second class kind of citizenship characterized by "deskilled labor" and passive enjoyment of a culture in which decisions are made elsewhere? Or is the United States, for the first time in its history, going to make a serious policy commitment to live up to the terms of democracy and provide all citizens with the fullest preparation for active participation in all aspects of the nation's life? That is the choice before us.

And the money can be found. Progressive school advocates have been far too timid in demanding their fair share of this nation's extraordinary resources. Most of those who do speak of a need for additional resources talk of ways to cut the costs in central bureaucracies or "frills" to fund basic reform. Certainly many school bureaucracies need to be trimmed, but that is only a very small start in addressing the needs of today's youth. Others talk of modest tax increases, often "sin taxes" which produce useful but very limited moneys around the margins of the economy. But virtually no one today is calling for a massive national campaign to meet the needs of today's youth. In times of war, in times of grave economic crisis, Americans have traditionally looked to the federal government. Why not now? Especially given the fact that there is a huge federal surplus waiting to be shifted—the continuing Pentagon budgets which have not been reduced in spite of the disappearance of the nation's primary purported enemy of the last forty-five years.

At the time of the savings and loan crisis, many commented on the speed with which the government found billions of dollars to live up to the commitment to insure the nation's banking system. At the time of the war in Vietnam and the time of Ronald Reagan's campaign to expand armaments until the Soviet Union was bankrupted, the nation found the funds. And, indeed, the funds which were spent on imperial campaigns abroad or arms build-ups at home are exactly the funds which should be transferred to today's schools. To put the matter most simply, to discuss reform in education and fail to make the case for a massive transfer of funds from the military to schools and related social service concerns is to admit that one is not serious about educational reform. All of the calls for high standards, all of the calls for effective school-to-work programs, all of the calls for a first-class education for all citizens simply ring hollow unless one is willing to talk about funding such a campaign. And the money is there, it is simply in the wrong part of the federal budget.

In the fall of 1991, just before the start of the presidential campaign which would catapult him into the position of secretary of labor, Reich wrote a somewhat wistful "Afterword" to *The Work of Nations*, "It is commonly assumed," he noted, "that, absent the Soviet threat, America can redirect its resources to the nation's domestic needs. . . . But this easy calculus presupposes a willingness on the part of Americans to redirect such resources rather than put the extra dollars back into their own pockets." Clearly, soon after the fall of the Soviet empire, Reich was detecting a reluctance on the part of many Americans to agree to the kinds of budget transfers which the nation so badly needs. Even though in the 1990s the United States clearly has the "capacity to rebuild the nation," it is less clear that we have either the national identity or the national will to do so. The consequences of not making the transfer are clear to Reich:

> Given these trends, without the external pressure of Soviet communism holding us together, America may simply explode into a microcosm of the entire world. It will contain some of the world's richest people and some of the world's poorest, speaking innumerable languages, owing many allegiances, celebrating different ideals.[67]

In America in the 1990s, one can move through almost any large metropolitan area and see this America in being. The distances from midtown Manhattan to

Harlem, from Chicago's Michigan Avenue to the South Side, from Boston's Newbury Street to Blue Hill Avenue are short indeed. And yet in the trip, the sight of the world's richest and world's poorest people can quickly be included.

Almost as if responding to Reich, the leaders of the Republican party in the House of Representatives committed themselves to running in the 1994 mid-term elections on a "Contract with America." Led by Newt Gingrich, 367 Republican candidates for the House of Representatives committed themselves to a common platform. The fact that they won the election and that Gingrich became the first Republican speaker of the House in forty years may have had more to do with President Clinton's failure to live up to the hopeful economic projections of the 1992 campaign than to the details of the "Contract," but the platform must nevertheless be taken seriously as a gauge to the national mood of America in the 1990s.

The Contract is quite clear in its "no" to the possibility of reducing defense spending to rebuild the nation, including its schools. "Our Contract with America includes a vote . . . to stop raiding the defense budget to finance social programs and UN peacekeeping; and to stop gutting Ronald Reagan's vision of protecting America against nuclear or chemical attack." Even absent the Soviet threat which justified Reagan's arms build up, the campaign must continue it seems. After all, the nation is in grave danger from "terrorist states such as North Korea, Iran, and Libya." And on the question of resources needed for improving the nation's schools, the only mention is a commitment to school choice. While the government is cutting federal spending on all social programs dramatically, in order to fund the Contract's commitment to a tax cut and a "firewall" between military and domestic spending," schools are promised that "Republicans believe parents know what's best for their children—not the government. Schools can accommodate the legitimate needs of students and their parents." In other words, vouchers, charter schools, an end to federal commitments to racial desegregation and gender equity and a federal blessing for separating the schooling available for those who can pay and those who can't. It is certainly a clear—and also a frightening answer— to the possibility of peacetime conversion of the nation's resources.[68]

Fortunately there have been some influential voices raised against this nonsense. A small but influential group of Democrats in the House have begun to challenge the Republican majority and the Clinton administration on exactly these issues. Los Angeles Representative Maxine Waters responded positively to the President's proposals in such areas as school construction but properly challenged him on where the funds would come from. Boston area Representative Barney Frank has been especially vocal in insisting that his colleagues—and the country—look at the promise of school reform (and other domestic spending) in its relationship to both military spending and commitment to a balanced budget by 2002. As Frank says:

> We're not in a zero-sum game, we're in a shrinking-sum game. And people are coming to understand that if you do not seriously reduce the military, then it's silly to talk about the government doing anything else . . . If you are not for cutting the military budget, then you are not for these social programs.[69]

Changing attitudes is going to take time, but honesty of this sort is the best hope the nation has that school reform in the twenty-first century is going to benefit all of the nation's youth and not merely a select and privileged few.

No issue of domestic policy has more far reaching implications for the nation's future. At issue are the most fundamental questions of democracy, whether the nation is going to value the contribution of all of its citizens or whether there will be a massive retreat into different enclaves, some reserved for the well educated and well to do and the rest offering the struggles of a marginal existence to the nation's majority. While the reasons for optimism may be scant at the present moment, the American people have risen to great challenges in the past. The issue today, for all who care about schooling, for all who care about living in a vibrant democratic society, is to state the issue with such clarity and such passion that the democratic option will prevail.

In this sense, the problem and the solution are the same. If the nation's schools can be energized to prepare a generation of deeply committed democrats, a generation enlivened by an ideal of the social good, then democracy will flourish and the good life will be within reach. If the schools, and the public will, cannot be mobilized, then the future is bleak indeed. The decision about whether the next generations of Americans are going to receive a quality education is a political decision which the people of the United States must make. And it is in the field of politics in the broadest sense of that term that the issue will be won or lost.

CHAPTER TWO

Defining Democracy, Defining
Democratic Education

> Democracy has failed because so many fear it. They believe that wealth
> and happiness are so limited that a world full of intelligent, healthy, and
> free people is impossible, if not undesirable . . . Such a world, with all its
> contradictions, can be saved, can yet be born again; but not out of capital,
> interest, property, and gold . . .
>
> W. E. B. DuBois, *Color and Democracy*

Defining a Democratic School Reform Movement

If democracy is to be at the forefront of education reform, if democracy itself
is to be one of the standards against which schools are judged, and if equity,
critical engagement, and democratic participation are to be among the purposes of reformed schools, then a clear definition of democracy is essential
before the reform enterprise can proceed. Citizens of the United States today
often find themselves wary of too much focus on the term democracy, especially in relationship to education. A century and a half ago, Horace Mann
noted that the link of schooling with democracy, "like most other very important truths, has become a very trite one."[1] And the triteness of linking
education and democracy has been exacerbated by the kind of simple minded,
and unquestioning patriotism which has been so associated with the term
democracy during the long decades of the Cold War.

But democracy can never be trite or unquestioning. Indeed democracy is
always a complex matter of questioning and constantly rebuilding and ex-

45

panding the understanding of society and the full participation of all citizens in the very definition and creation of the good society. When Malcolm X, shortly before his death, was asked to speak to a group of young civil rights activists from McComb, Mississippi, he told them, "If you form the habit of going by what others think about someone, instead of going and searching that thing out for yourself and seeing for yourself, you'll be walking west when you think you're going east, and you'll be walking east when you think you're going west. . . . The most important thing we can learn how to do today is think for ourselves."[2] In any generation, a genuinely democratic society requires citizens who take Malcolm's words very seriously, who think for themselves and who demand from the next generation the same kind of rigorous questioning and thinking. And the public school must be focused on this quest.

Yet if we look at the reality of public education in the United States we see much that is in need of being questioned and challenged. After more than a decade of talk about the need for reform in education, terrible things are happening in our schools and those things are not being challenged; they are often not even included in the debates about education. Jonathan Kozol has painted a haunting portrait of what is being done to too many children—poor children, children of color—in today's schools and yet, as he notes, "None of the national reports I saw made even passing references to inequality or segregation. Low reading scores, high dropout rates, poor motivation—symptomatic matters—seemed to dominate discussion."[3] After reporting in gripping detail on the horror too many children experience growing up and attending school in contemporary America, Kozol concludes, "Surely there is enough for everyone within this country. It is a tragedy that these good things are not more widely shared."[4] But in spite of the valiant pleas of Kozol and others, that need for a wider and more democratic sharing of the good things of this land has not been included in much of the discussion of educational reform of late.

At the same time, those of us who have been arguing that the curriculum of the schools must truly reflect and empower the wonderfully diverse multicultural/ multiracial heritage of today's students find ourselves increasingly under attack from voices as prestigious as historian Arthur M. Schlesinger Jr., who in a surprisingly mean spirited attack on multicultural education argues:

> Whatever the particular crimes of Europe, that continent is also the
> source—the unique source—of those liberating ideas of individual lib-
> erty, political democracy, the rule of law, human rights, and cultural

freedom that constitute our most precious legacy and to which most of the world today aspires. These are European ideas, not Asian, nor African, nor Middle Eastern ideas, except by adoption. . . . There is surely no reason for Western civilization to have guilt trips laid on it by champions of cultures based on despotism, superstition, tribalism, and fanaticism.[5]

What an odd interpretation of history. Schlesinger is too sophisticated an historian to believe this, but he has caught a part of the spirit of the times.

This view of a Eurocentric nation is a long way from the inclusive democratic ideal which was expressed at the beginning of the century by Jane Addams:

We have learned to say that the good must be extended to all of society before it can be held secure by any one person or any one class; but we have not yet learned to add to that statement, that unless all men [and women] and all classes contribute to a good, we cannot even be sure that it is worth having.[6]

A truly democratic system of education then begins with a commitment to extending the best society has to offer to every citizen and at the same time ensuring that every citizen has voice and power in defining the nature of the social good itself not merely receiving as "best" the social good of one of the nation's many ethnic groups.

In the arguments about multicultural education, "political correctness," and the kind of history to be taught in schools, the much older arguments about the nature of democracy are reflected yet again. While few today openly argue that democracy should be the preserve of a limited number of male citizens, there are great debates about the kind of democratic culture which should be taught in the schools. On the one hand are those who see democracy and culture as emerging in Western Europe and flourishing in North America and who thus teach a conception of culture which is Eurocentric in its core while adding the stories of other peoples and cultures around the margins. On the other hand are those who argue that the only culture worthy of a democracy is one which fully and equally embraces all of the people, female and male, from all races and classes, and thus teaches a multicultural view of history in which the contributions of the many—as well as the repeated attempts by various elites to control power and culture—make up the heart of the history and the school's curriculum.

Schools today, in far too many cases, are not reflecting a democratic ideal and are not structured in democratic ways. Schools in which there are terrible inequalities in the experiences of different children, schools in which far too many are tracked and sorted into a dead-end future, schools in which the cultures of many students are excluded or ridiculed are not worthy of a democratic society. But they are the norm in too many places in this country.

Democracy—and a democratic system of public education—is a matter of much more than elections and democratic governance. It is also more than ensuring the basic liberties and meeting the basic needs of all. It is even more than ensuring a healthy economy. It is, as Jane Addams insisted, a vision of the good society in which the good is both shared and defined by all.

If we then propose that the purpose of public education in a democratic society must always be to build more democracy, we must include a democracy which operates at many levels:

- In the conception of the larger society as an inclusive (and therefore multicultural) society which builds on the strengths and contributions of all citizens.

- In the conception of the individual citizen as a person with basic rights, including the right to full participation in defining and benefiting from the social good, but also with a voice and power which must be honored in the democratic dialogue.

- In the conception of the school classroom as a place where democracy can be both created and modeled in the kind of social interaction, mutual respect, and the voice given to all players, especially students, but also teachers and parents.

This notion of democracy is built on an understanding of the democratic citizen as both a participant in a just society and as a unique, empowered individual. Both of these elements are essential to education for democracy.

If the purpose of schools is really to help foster this kind of multilayered democracy, then schools designed to foster this democracy will have some very easily recognizable characteristics. They will be:

- Schools in which all students, whatever their race, class, gender, are treated as individuals who can learn successfully; where tracking and other structures which limit the expectations of some students are eliminated.

- Schools in which critical thinking and engaged conversations are part of the process of learning; where teachers do not pour information into their students, but where mutual inquiry marks the approach to all parts of the curriculum, including reading, writing, and arithmetic.

- Schools in which a sense of community is fostered, in which parents and community people are welcome, in which teachers are treated with respect, in which children and adults learn together.

- Schools in which the contribution of students from many diverse cultures are valued as contributing equally essential parts of a common American history and the making of a new American community; in which girls and boys, and students of all races and classes are valued for the contribution they bring, not as problems to be dealt with.

- Schools in which the financial resources are present to buy textbooks, keep the buildings in repair, and pay the teachers; schools which in their material resources reflect the commitment of a larger society deeply devoted to its young and its future.

Other items can be added to the list. All of the items can be viewed as utopian dreams by "realists" bent on balancing the budget without a tax increase or maintaining a status quo. But unless our schools have the resources, financial and moral, to begin to build a new and better society for all of our citizens, the society in which every one of us lives is going to be increasingly impoverished and frightening.

Either public education will be part of the solution to this fundamental crisis in our nation's life, or our schools will continue to perpetuate the inequality and separation which has been too much a part of our land. Meaningful school reform—and the development of a strong public commitment to the institution of schooling—must have at the heart of its agenda a commitment to building an American democracy in which the contribution of all citizens is valued and in which the potential of all citizens is developed if democracy itself is to survive and flourish.

Ironically, the last two decades which have seen a dramatic upsurge in concern with schools has seen the least discussion of the link between democracy and schooling of any time in the last 150 years. While much of the previous link between school and the larger society was a romantic and very limited understanding of democracy, the ideal was there. What is remarkable in the current round of school reform is the gradual disappearance of any discussion of the link of education and democracy.

During a time of unprecedented "reform" in the nation's schools a commitment to democracy has received, at best, a cursory and polite nod. And this failure to attend to fundamental questions of the structure of national life and individual citizenship can be seen in almost all perspectives within the educational debate. Education, Americans are being told today, should be supported in terms of the economy and the need to maintain the nation's competitive edge in world markets. Yet there are so many other pressing national issues to which a more democratized school can make a significant contribution.

At the end of the twentieth century, the United States is a nation in trouble. While the public dialogue seems to focus on a diagnosis of the problems primarily in terms of the loss of the nation's economic hegemony in the world and the long running economic recession, other basic problems exist—the infrastructure is crumbling, the intractable issues of poverty, racism, sexism, and fear remain for far too many citizens, a sense of optimism that things can get better or that a more inclusive community can exist is sadly lacking. The end of the Cold War has brought into heightened relief the inability of most of the nation's leaders to envision a positive meaning to democracy.

Manning Marable has named the failure of vision in this nation and has done much to prescribe the kind of changes which are needed while noting, "the most important missing element in American politics today is vision." He goes on to ask:

> When did the last politician you heard say something like, "What would it really take for this society to abolish unemployment, poverty or homelessness? What would it really take to attack the drug traffic in our central cities, to construct a system of mass transit, to reduce pollution, and to uproot racism and sexism?" A political vision of emancipation is more than a set of ambitious goals, it's the courage to state what's wrong with our society, and to call upon people to resolve collectively these problems.[7]

This lack of vision comes, Marable and many others note, not from a lack of information but from a lack of political courage or a fundamental fear of the impact of real democracy on the power and comfort of today's elite.

The last decades have not been kind to those who would propose alternative visions. The Civil Rights movement of the earlier parts of the century represented a very different vision of this nation as the "beloved community." But that vision was undermined significantly in the late 1960s and 1970s and attacked directly in the 1980s. Thus Marable notes, "For black Americans, the central political characteristic of the 1980s was the conservative reaction to the legacy of the Civil Rights Movement, and the apparent capitulation of both political parties to a more conservative and repressive social order."[8] For all Americans, this conservative reaction changed—and dramatically limited—the terms of the debate. In an extraordinary study of the changes in American politics during the 1980s, Eric Alterman has written of the 1988 elections:

> Thus it was wholly irrelevant to the 1988 campaign that vast majorities of the American people had ceased to view the Soviet military as an important threat to their well-being. Nor did it turn out to matter much that economic power and influence had come to play a far more important role on the world state in determining the nation's well being than the size of its military, and that more than two thirds of Americans surveyed at the time felt that way. . . . Those candidates who refused to place this contest [the cold war] at the very center of their political agendas—and who refused, therefore, to subordinate all other national problems to its achievement—were to be dismissed as foolish, naive, and "McGovernite." Their funding and hence recognition levels diminished accordingly. . . . The environment, our education system, our economic infrastructure, the health of our cities, our ability to compete on par with Germans and Japanese—these were issues that, when push came to shove, were not even peripheral when compared with the long twilight struggle of the never-ending Cold War.[9]

Alterman is simply describing the latest version of what Antonio Gramsci named earlier in this century when he talked of the hegemony of the ideas of a politically dominant culture driving all other world views out of public discourse, but he is doing so in graphic detail.[10] And it is certainly the interrogation of ideas, the constant checking to be sure that many different ideas, even some which might be "dismissed as foolish, naive," are heard, which must be at the heart of both a quality educational process and a democratic discourse worthy of its name.

A democratic discourse is much wider than the limited sphere of electoral politics. Yet even in the more limited arena of campaigns and elections, our democracy is failing us. Many today comment on the abysmally low voter turn-out and the vacuous nature of political discourse in the United States in the 1990s. Eric Alterman has noted an obvious, but too easily overlooked reality when he writes, "If ideas have consequences for society, then so, too does their absence. . . . But our lack of coherent political discourse is really quite a serious problem."[11] Why aren't educators voicing this concern and committing the schools to raising the level of the discourse? Why isn't the current state of political campaign debate, as well as the nation's economic problems, and the even more fundamental issues of creating a political system which gives true voice, and true power to all citizens in shaping the future . . . why aren't these things at the heart of the debate about schooling?

In the midst of this situation, public education has been the subject of much discussion and many prescriptions. But there has been very little vision of the role of a strong system of public education in building a truly democratic society; that is in challenging the hegemony of any given set of ideas in society. Given the lack of vision about democracy itself, this situation is not surprising, but it undermines all efforts to build a clear consensus about the role of education in strengthening American democracy as we enter the twenty-first century. Ironically we are, at the same time, asking too much and too little of our schools. While asking them to restore the nation's competitive edge, we are not asking them to prepare citizens who will grapple at the deepest level with the nation's problems, including its economic problems, and with the crying need to create a truly democratic society and culture for the first time in the nation's history.

In 1927, John Dewey posed the question:

> What are the conditions under which it is possible for the Great Society to approach more closely and vitally the status of a Great Community, and thus take form in genuinely democratic societies and state? What are the conditions under which we may reasonably picture the Public emerging from its eclipse?[12]

And what, we must ask, would it mean for schooling in the United States to be fundamentally organized around seeking answers to these questions—to creating in its classrooms and in the minds of its students new visions and new mechanisms for creating the "great community" a more genuinely democratic society in the nation and the world?

Defining Success for Democratic Schools

Clearly there are major problems in public education. Some will ask how schools can be expected to take on the development of a larger democratic discourse when they cannot teach many students to read and write? Many believe that our schools are failing across the board. Some are ready to dismantle the whole system of public education. Thus we have the private enterprise notion of school vouchers. A Christopher Whittle can talk of creating a West Berlin [his schools] so that the East Berlin of public education will fall.[13] And his for-profit idea seems to him—and to respected educational leaders like Benno Schmidt—as just the way to go. At the same time, political leaders in many of the states and in Washington propose reform measures that offer far too little money and far too much testing and sorting. How, we must ask, is a new testing program going to help those students who do not do well on the tests? How is the teacher-punishing idea of abolishing tenure supposed to improve the morale of those who struggle daily to educate students in spite of too few resources and too many problems? Most of all, how are any of the current proposals for funding public education going to provide the basic textbooks, school buildings and numbers of teachers needed to make schools work? The reluctance to provide sufficient financing for public schools and the Whittle attack on the whole enterprise of public education are part of a national consensus that has been gelling since we were told, a decade ago, that our nation is at risk; that our schools have fallen into such desperate shape that, if another country had done this to us, we would have seen it as an act of war. Clearly this is a level of negativism to which we must attend!

With so many voices giving public schools a failing grade, why have so few asked, "What is success?" Perhaps the answer seems obvious. But, if the definition of success is so obvious, why is it spelled out in such little detail? All of us have a right to ask, by what standard will we measure our schools? I propose three standards which must be included in any definition of success for this nation's schools:

- *Schools must ensure critical literacy for all students.* We want our schools to prepare our children in reading/writing/arithmetic. We want all citizens to know the basics of how to read, communicate, and understand the power of numbers in our society. Graduates need skills and the confidence which true literacy gives them in their own lives and as active participants in the larger society; they must have the ability to debate the fundamental issues facing society with a skill lacking among today's leaders. Schooling must also lead to a knowledge of a wide range of literatures and cultural traditions, and to an ability to critique and ultimately create their own art. And we must be confident that our schools provide these skills to all, not merely to an elite in the top tracks of public or private schools.

- *Schools must prepare all students for meaningful work and for an understanding of the economy in which they live.* Part of the purpose of schooling must be to prepare citizens for meaningful work. School policies which fail to help students understand and prepare for economic realities are misdirected at best. Democratic citizens do not thrive without satisfying jobs and democracy itself does not last for long in continuing economic depression. We want graduates prepared for jobs but also for understanding the economy and culture in which their skills will be used. Changes in federal vocational education policy which mandate that students must have exposure to "all aspects of the industry," point the way toward a curriculum which will prepare active players in a democratic nation not passive cogs in an economic machine.

- *Schools must—perhaps most significantly—prepare citizens for a democratic society.* From the earliest days of public education in North America, the purpose of public education has been to foster democracy. People could learn to read and write at home. People could be prepared for work through apprenticeship. But the school was the place where a diverse group of young citizens came together to model the larger society we hoped to create. Schools often fail in this task. (We can all give examples of the kinds of failure which we have seen in our schools in terms of building a democratic community within them or calling youth to commit themselves to one in the larger society.) But we have come to a sad state of affairs when the definition of school success includes a cursory—and sometimes embarrassed—nod in the direction of democracy before we move on to the "real" business of preparing for a competitive economy. Meaningful school reform must begin with a commitment to building an American democracy in which the contribution of all citizens is developed and valued; where racism, sexism, and other forms of divisiveness are challenged and ultimately eliminated; where the society is structured for the benefit of all citizens and not a small elite.

The Bias for Democracy

This is a book with a deep bias about the purpose of public schooling. Following in the tradition of John Dewey, I believe that the fundamental purpose of education in a democratic society is supporting democracy. And like Dewey, when I say democracy, I am not talking merely about voting and teaching people the rules of the system. I am, rather, talking about the fundamental nature of democracy: the commitment to equality for all people, the commitment to individual liberty and the right of every citizen to give voice to her/his ideas, and, most significant, the commitment to the building up of a better community for all people—beginning in the classroom and extending to the larger society in which the school is located and in which its graduates will live.

A commitment to democracy has been part of the discussions of schooling in this country since at least the time of Thomas Jefferson, who reminded us that the best safeguard against tyranny is "to illuminate, as far as practicable, the minds of the people at large."[14] Throughout the decades after Jefferson, Americans continued to argue, as did Horace Mann, that public schools were essential to democracy because, "a republican form of government, without intelligence in the people, must be, on a vast scale, what a madhouse, without superintendent or keepers, would be on a small one."[15] This link of education to the success of democracy has continued to be echoed well into the twentieth century.

Of course, Jefferson and most of his successors failed miserably in living up to their own ideals. Schools in this country have never been fully agents of democracy. But if hypocrisy is the tribute that vice pays to virtue, I remain concerned that at least some portion of virtue remain a part of the public dialogue about education in the United States. And I worry that is changing. As Barbara Finkelstein has warned us,

> Americans, for the first time in a one hundred and fifty-year history, seem ready to do ideological surgery on their public schools—cutting them away from the fate of social justice and political democracy completely and grafting them onto elite corporate, industrial, military, and cultural interests.[16]

Until we change that reality, all discussions about defending public education, about what is success in school threatens to degenerate into a discussion about technical jargon or a romantic quest to return to a simpler past.

I realize that in the 1990s I risk being called a romantic for this focus on democracy. There are those who argue that we must "be practical," and being practical means focusing education on beating the Japanese in the struggle for world markets and ensuring the nation's continued economic dominance in the "new world order." There are also those who have given up on the term, and there is reason for sympathy for that position, for there has been a debasement of all of the terms of discussion today. But I still find myself hanging on to that older vision; I still find myself saying with Langston Hughes:

> LIBERTY!
> FREEDOM!
> DEMOCRACY!
> True anyhow no matter how many
> Liars use those words.[17]

It is a vision which has sustained generations in a struggle for a better society and it must not be abandoned lightly.

In his extraordinary study of African American education in the South after the Civil War, James D. Anderson catches this deep tension between vision and reality.

> The history of American education abounds with themes that represent the inextricable ties between citizenship in a democratic society and popular education. It is crucial for an understanding of American educational history, however, to recognize that within American democracy there have been classes of oppressed people and that there have been essential relationships between popular education and the politics of oppression. Both schooling for democratic citizenship and schooling for second-class citizenship have been basic traditions in American education.[18]

As Anderson thoroughly documents, the hypocrisy of many education advocates, from the slave-owning Jefferson on, did not dim the commitment to education for democracy within the slave and newly free communities of African Americans. "There developed in the slave community," he concludes, "a fundamental belief in learning and self-improvement and a shared belief in universal education as a necessary basis for freedom and citizenship."[19] It is that fundamental belief, nurtured throughout the history of this nation and often strongest among some of those who received the least from the democracy, that I want to argue must be returned to the center of debates about education.

The events surrounding the Rodney King beating, the acquittal of the police officers, and the subsequent uprising in Los Angeles in the spring of 1992 are but one of many reminders of how deeply racism and discrimination mar the fabric of democracy.[20] The words of the 1967 Kerner Commission, for all of their nostalgia about the past, are more true with each passing year: "Our nation is moving toward two societies, one black, one white—separate and unequal."[21] Either we will use our schools to create a new open, diverse, and equitable democracy, or we will continue "separate and unequal" and increasingly violent and repressive in maintaining that separation. It is this choice which must be the fundamental test of all proposals concerning the future of education in this nation. The situation today is not good. We see the signs of new levels of hate, and new levels of division all around. But we had better return to the basic task of building a "great society," a true community soon, or we will not do it at all. In order to attend thoughtfully to building a new sense of community and a new link between a democratic ideal and improved futures for our children, it is also essential to look carefully at the long and sometimes tortured history of the links between schooling and democracy.

Defining Democracy

Of course, democracy means many different things to many different people. For some, democracy is but another code word for the "American way of life," and especially for corporate capitalism which is now being exported— in its most virulent form—to the nations of the former communist world.

For others, however, democracy is something quite different, and much more humanistic. Democracy has been defined many different ways by different people in different historical contexts. At one level, democracy refers to a government based on the consent of the governed as opposed to dictatorship or oligarchy based on birth, wealth, or simple power. There are, however, a number of variables which appear along the spectrum of the differing definitions of democracy. The consent of the governed can be a fairly passive acceptance of the rule of a leadership class. On the other hand, it can mean active involvement in the business of government by citizens at every level, not merely through voting but through the development of communities of active and equal citizens.

When James A. Beane and Michael W. Apple seek to make the "case for democratic schools," they naturally include issues like the democratic structure of social institutions, the "open flow of ideas, regardless of their popularity," and "concern for the welfare of others." But perhaps most important, they also include "Faith in the individual and collective capacity of people to create possibilities for resolving problems." It is in this last item that the real test of a democratic society or school must be made. It is not sufficient to provide freedom to individuals and services to all, important as these are. A real democracy is more than this. A really democratic society is a school or a larger society structured around the belief that the solutions-and not just the problems-reside with the people and that all of the people, if fully empowered, will be wiser than any small minority or vanguard.[22]

Living up to this level of trust in people is rare. In most governments which have called themselves democratic, the ranks of citizens whose consent was required has also been significantly smaller than the people as a whole. Women, slaves, people without property or birth rights have more often than not been excluded from the government of states referred to as democratic. And the contests over inclusion and over the rights and responsibilities of citizenship continue to be at the heart of current debates about democracy.

The link between democracy and education has also been a matter of debate since at least the time of Aristotle. And since the time of Aristotle, the definitions of both democracy and education have also been fluid. Since the Aristotelian state was based on the wisdom and virtue of the rulers, a democracy demanded a widespread education which would ensure both the wisdom and the virtue of the next generation of citizens, both those called to specific office and those doing the calling.

At the same time, however, the great contradiction of Aristotle's definition of democracy was the limited base of citizenship. Citizens were free men. Women, slaves, and foreigners were excluded from his definition. And the exclusion by gender and by caste was as central to Aristotle's definition of democracy as the inclusion of the free citizen. Both the inclusive and the exclusive elements of Greek democracy influenced the education needed for citizenship. The free male needed a preparation in the exercise of freedom and leadership, while women and slaves needed preparation in the virtues of submission to their respective roles. Thus Aristotle argued that the definition of virtue—and education for the virtuous life—depends on one's position in the society. Democratic education was a very different thing for a free citizen and for a dependent noncitizen.[23]

In what became the United States, both the inclusive and the exclusive definitions of democracy also continued to influence democratic education. Among the nation's founders, Thomas Jefferson provided perhaps the best definition of democracy as a form of government in which all authorities derive, "their just powers from the consent of the governed." Jefferson was equally clear that the kind of democracy he articulated needed a new kind of education to prepare citizens fit for the new free and democratic nation. Throughout Jefferson's long career the themes of expanding democracy, and of education as central to democracy, appear again and again. The best way to protect against tyranny, Jefferson always insisted, was to educate all of the citizens and especially the leaders while also ensuring that "those who form and administer" the laws and the government, "are wise and honest." And, as with Aristotle, the contradictions of exclusion—of women, of slaves, of indigenous peoples—also remained in place in Jefferson's world.[24]

Unlike many of his contemporaries, Jefferson understood the contradiction between his call for liberty and democracy while allowing the second-class status of women and the slave status of African Americans. More fundamentally, of course, those who were excluded understood all too well the limits of the democracy espoused by the revolution of 1776. Whether it was Abigail Adams reminding her husband to, "Remember the Ladies . . . [and] Remember all Men would be tyrants if they could" or Langston Hughes in, *Freedom's Plow* giving voice to the slaves who also believed Jefferson's words, "And silently took for granted; That what he said was meant for them," the struggle to expand democracy paralleled the development of the new government.[25]

In 1779 Jefferson proposed, unsuccessfully, that Virginia revise its educational system to fit the needs of the democracy for which its soldiers were fighting. There were two elements in Jefferson's "Bill for the More General Diffusion of Knowledge," both of which fit his own Aristotelian worldview. As a means of safeguarding against a return to tyranny, Jefferson proposed a system of schooling throughout the Commonwealth which would ensure that every free male child would receive at least three years of basic instruction and thus be able to read, write, and participate in the democratic political process. At the same time, Jefferson also proposed a restructuring of the College of William and Mary to ensure that citizens of all ranks would be able to attend, thus perpetuating a leadership class of virtue and wisdom, regardless of the wealth of their families of origin.[26]

Perhaps the most dramatic expansion of education, in the name of democracy, in the United States came at the time of emancipation. With the end of the Civil War, the great contradiction in Aristotelian and Jeffersonian democracy began to take different shape. The dual themes running through democratic education—education for full and active citizenship and education for second-class citizenship and obedience—were challenged in fresh ways. For newly freed slaves, going to school, learning to read and write, were essential steps in the process of freedom. Seldom had the language of democracy been so central to the development of literacy and schools. As W. E. B. DuBois asserted, "Public education for all at public expense was, in the South, a Negro idea." The system of public education in the South—in spite of Jefferson's earlier attempts—was a creation of newly freed African Americans seeking to embrace a democratic ideal.[27]

In the first decade after the Civil War, when newly freed slaves were able to control their own schools, and in many cases the legislatures of the states of the old confederacy, the creation of a democratic system of education which ensured not only literacy and technical mastery, but full-scale citizenship, was the goal. With the end of reconstruction after 1876, these themes went underground throughout most of the South as reactionary forces gained power, but they would emerge again a century later in the educational agenda of the Civil Rights movement.[28]

At the beginning of the twentieth century John Dewey emerged as one of the leaders in linking and also expanding the notions of democracy and democratic education. For Dewey, the commitment of democracy to education was only superficially explained in the belief that popular suffrage required well-educated electors. At a much more fundamental level, Dewey insisted, democracy is more than a form of government, it is a way of building up the common good and the common community. If democracy is more than a system of government, but rather a whole way of understanding and living in the great community, then the implications for education are significant. In 1899, Dewey wrote:

> When the school introduces and trains each child of society into membership within such a little community, saturating him [or her] with the spirit of service, and providing him [or her] with the instruments of effective self-direction, we shall have the deepest and best guarantee of a larger society which is worthy, lovely, and harmonious.[29]

The progressive education movement, as defined by Dewey, was a means of preparing self-confident, active citizens ready to engage in the continuing process of social evolution and community building. For Dewey active learning, self-directed study, participation in school governance, were not merely new and more effective means of instruction, they were ways of creating in the school the small scale model of the larger democratic society, a society which is not only well-governed, but "worthy, lovely, and harmonious." In a sense, Dewey was the first American philosopher of education to take seriously Alexis de Tocqueville's observation in his 1835 *Democracy in America* that the American democracy always threatened to degenerate into anarchic individualism unless the forces of community were as central to democracy as those of individual liberty.[30]

Though often called the father of progressive education, Dewey actually found himself highly critical of much of the movement that went by that name. Dewey continually warned of the danger of progressivism declining into mere techniques of instruction and concerns for the successful development of individual children—often the children of those wealthy enough to send their offspring to expensive private progressive schools. He also engaged in political battles with those who, also in the name of progressivism, sought to centralize educational authority in increasingly elite superintendent's offices and school boards. For Dewey, democracy required the full participation of all citizens, children in the life of their classrooms, teachers and other citizens in the development of curriculum and school policies.

William Edward Burghardt DuBois spent a long and illustrious career expanding the borders of both democracy and education. Known best for his militant rejection of gradualism and his commitment to immediate and full emancipation of African Americans, DuBois regularly returned to the issues of democracy and education. Most significantly, DuBois rejected the exclusion which had been part of the definition of democracy from the time of Aristotle. For DuBois democracy worked for all or it worked for none, embraced all or embraced none. Writing while the Ku Klux Klan was an open and powerful force in national politics and even the best of white progressives, including Dewey, often wrote as if African Americans were invisible, DuBois gave intellectual voice to the yearnings of the nation's excluded. In that voice the stage was set for both the Civil Rights movement and for many of the struggles which have been waged about education in the twentieth century.

For DuBois, a democratic education contained the double elements of skill-building and the development of character and wisdom. From the days of his famous debates with Booker T. Washington, DuBois rejected manual education for African Americans as a sure means of continuing second-class citizenship. Writing during the Second World War, DuBois noted that the technical skills, the manual skills, were in higher order than ever before, and yet the world was in chaos. "It has been organized twice in the last quarter of a century for murder and destruction on a tremendous scale." He called for an education which would teach both how and why, both mastery of technique and the character to use techniques for human good. DuBois understood the need for both. "Technique without character is chaos and war. Character without technique is labor and want." The combination of both was required if democracy was to flourish.

Still, for Du Bois, character and the building of the good society was at the heart of the matter in education. He reminded those in the 1940s or 1990s who focus too much on skills or standards that these are not enough:

> But when you have human beings who know the world and can grasp it; who have their feelings guided by ideals; then using technique at

their hands they can get rid of the four great evils of human life. These four evils are ignorance, poverty, disease and crime. They flourish today in the midst of miraculous technique and in spite of our manifest ability to rid the world of them. They flourish because with all our technical training we do not have in sufficient quantity and for a long enough time the education of the human soul.[31]

Would that the "education of the human soul" were more seriously at the forefront of education reform for the century ahead.

In the United States in the 1950s, 1960s, and 1970s, the Civil Rights movement became the chief arena in which democracy continued to be defined and the links of democracy and education fought out. From the 1954 United States Supreme Court decision in *Brown v. Board of Education of Topeka, Kansas,* through the struggles to integrate school systems throughout the country, to the passage of the first Civil Rights act since reconstruction, and expanding provisions to meet the needs of bilingual and special education students, and the campaigns for equal resources to educate all citizens, the Civil Rights agenda has been at the forefront of school politics in the second half of the twentieth century. Also beginning in the 1960s, but expanding rapidly in the 1980s and 1990s, the struggle around the school curriculum, the struggle for the culture to be taught and passed on in school, has expanded the debates about the nature of a democratic education.

Of course, linking democracy and education has not been confined to the United States. The most widely read exponent of a link between democracy and education in the second half of the twentieth century has been the Brazilian educator Paulo Freire. Beginning with his work in adult literacy in Brazil, Freire developed a conceptualization of education in which the struggle for democracy, for the illiterate student to become a free subject participating in the transformation of society, is the key to both democracy and literacy. Expanding on Dewey's notion of the link between democratic education and community building, Freire has insisted that the process of liberation becomes both the reason for literacy and the means to literacy.

When democracy is linked to education, it then demands that the central purpose of education be the nurture and development of a powerful sense of agency and voice among all students in all schools. It is not enough for democratic schools to successfully transmit a static culture to all students, or to give all students the skills needed for successful future employment. A democratic educational enterprise in Freire's vision must always be in the business of preparing a new generation to reshape the culture, economy, and polity of the society in ways which build on the best which every citizen has to offer and which constantly expand the very notion of democracy itself. It is this kind of democratic education of which he speaks when Freire insisted on a pedagogy of the oppressed:

> a pedagogy which must be forged with, not for, the oppressed (whether individuals or peoples) in the incessant struggle to regain their humanity. This pedagogy makes oppression and its causes objects of reflection by the oppressed, and from that reflection will come their necessary engagement in the struggle for their liberation. And in this struggle this pedagogy will be made and remade.[32]

When education is placed at the service of liberation, and a continual remaking of the understanding of liberation for all peoples, then it is truly a democratic education as that term is defined in this book.

After a courageous and distinguished career in recasting educational theory, Freire in his sixties took on the job of Secretary of Education (superintendent of schools) for the city of San Paulo, Brazil. At the meeting of the American Educational Research Association in Chicago in April 1991, he reflected on his two and one half years as a superintendent. He said, "we have only two problems in achieving the fulfillment of our dreams, "our patience and our impatience."[33] Freire went on to say that we who want to build a democratic, progressive educational vision usually fail either because we are so patient that we wait forever for the right moment to act, or we become so impatient that we give up on the whole enterprise of education. We cannot allow ourselves either luxury.

On the brink of the twenty-first century, debates about democracy and education are not a luxury. They are essential if the American society of the new century is to be worth living in for the majority of American citizens. The dangers and the opportunities are both real. Manning Marable is right:

> Finally, we must infuse our definition of politics with a common sense of ethics and spirituality which challenges the structures of oppression, power and privilege within the dominant social order. Can we dare to struggle, dare to build a new democracy, without poverty and homelessness; can we dare to uproot racism, sexism, homophobia, and all forms of social oppression? Can we dare to assert ourselves as an emerging multicultural democratic majority for peace, social justice, for real democracy?[34]

Those are the real questions facing today's schools and today's educators. Answering those questions positively is a challenge worthy of the best which today's educational reformers and today's students have to offer. And making the schools one of the prime vehicles for answering these questions positively will mean an education reform movement worthy of being called democratic.

CHAPTER THREE

The School and the Quest for a Multicultural Democracy

> We have learned to say that the good must be extended to all of society
> before it can be held secure by any one person or any one class; but we
> have not yet learned to add to that statement, that unless all men [and
> women] and all classes contribute to a good, we cannot even be sure that
> it is worth having.
>
> Jane Addams

Democratic Education and Multicultural Education

To talk of democracy in the United States at the end of the twentieth century
is to talk of multiculturalism. To talk of using schools to foster democracy
means that multicultural education must move to the very heart of the educational enterprise. Unless all groups are included, democracy loses its meaning. There cannot be democracy for those who are descendants of Western
European immigrants, and not for those who have come from other lands.
There cannot be democracy for men and not for women. There cannot be
democracy for those whose families have been here for generations, but not
for those who have arrived in the last decade—from Central and South
America, from Southeast Asia, from Ireland, from many corners of the globe.
There cannot be democracy for whose who came to these shores willingly,
but not for those who came here in chains or were here to be conquered by
Columbus and his descendants. And there cannot be democracy when some
groups are seen as creators of the dominant culture while others are only its

65

recipients, at best its beneficiaries. Jane Addams was right, unless all people contribute to the social and cultural good, we cannot even be sure that it is good.

As Theresa Perry and I have previously argued, multiculturalism is not a passing fad. It is fundamentally a matter of how we view teaching and the future. "If there is to be democracy in the twenty-first century, it must be a multiracial/ multiethnic democracy. Unless all groups are included, democracy loses its meaning."[1]

If the discussion of multicultural education is placed at the heart of redefining democratic education, then it becomes much more than a matter of adding some additional stories to the school curriculum. It involves revisioning the curriculum, and ultimately the nation's culture, as one in which all groups, whites who are descendants of European immigrants, and the wide range of people of color in this country, all tell their story and all see their stories included as equal components in the development of a new national culture.

Some of the potential for the school to be the location for the building of this new culture was recognized by John Dewey when he wrote, "The intermingling in the school of youth of different races, differing religions, and unlike customs creates for all a new and broader environment."[2] But multicultural education must move further. The goal is not just intermingling, it is ultimately a mutual project to build a new and quite different culture for all.

In the process of building a new multiethnic/multiracial culture for this nation all people and all cultures must contribute. But, at the same time, it must be recognized that not all people and all cultures begin the process on an equal footing. The dominant culture in this country has been white, European, and male for more than 200 years. People of color, people whose family origins are non-European, including indigenous Americans, and women have not been recognized as full participants in defining the culture of this nation. Indeed, only a small percentage of the white males of European origin have been recognized as full participants. The issue of changing the power dynamics—of giving not only voice but the power of full participation—must be at the heart of the multicultural agenda. When issues of power and oppression are not recognized, multiculturalism can quickly degenerate into a sentimental exchange of exotic information. When the issues of power and oppression are at the center of the debate, however, the potential for truly engaging in the development of a multicultural democracy in the United States—a democracy very different than anything which has been known up to this time—becomes real.

The decision to engage in this process of building a new common culture has significant risks for all involved. All of the participants will see their own cultural heritage reshaped in the interaction with others. But it is fundamental to the meaning of democracy that all participate not only as recipients of services but in the very business of shaping the culture. It is only when a multicultural education curriculum involves opportunities for all participants in this increasingly diverse society to make their own contribution to the definition of the social good that we have the basis for a democratic system of education.

A commitment to a multicultural education and a multicultural nation makes special demands on those who teach in any field, but especially in history, literature, and related fields which carry the nation's cultural story. I have been asked, "How can we add more stories and more traditions, we haven't got time to cover the curriculum as it is?" But, in fact, the issue is much more fundamental. A multicultural approach is not just adding stories at the margins of the curriculum. It involves a complete rethinking and retelling of the nation's cultural narrative. It involves a different way of looking at the history and culture of the United States so that the stories of the traditionally voiceless have as much weight as the stories which have long been told. This is a significant task. It involves hard work and new research for teachers, putting some of their expertise at risk. In schools which are fortunate enough to have a diverse student body it means allowing a range of students to bring their expertise to the teaching and learning process. But without a commitment to that effort, any talk of building a multicultural democracy in schools will be a matter of tinkering at the margins.

The lands which now make up the United States have always contained diverse ethnic groups. In the 1860s, at the time of emancipation, many parts of the South had African American majorities and in spite of the massive immigration to the North which began around World War I, many southern counties still have African American majorities. Northern cities have seen their ethnic makeup change many times, with the Irish immigration of the 1830s and 1840s and the Italian and Eastern European immigrations which began in the 1890s through the twentieth-century immigrations of African Americans from the South, Puerto Ricans from the island, and more recently a range of Latin Americans and Southeast Asians. Many parts of the southwest have always had Latino majorities, no matter which flag flew overhead. And little over a century ago several of the present states of the union still had Native American majorities. Those who have only recently discovered diversity have not been paying attention.

It is important to remember in this context that the issue of bilingualism is also not new. James Crawford has noted that in 1664 when the British took control of Manhattan Island from the Dutch, "at least eighteen tongues were spoken on Manhattan Island, not counting Indian languages." Before the end of the seventeenth century, Philadelphia had thriving German-language schools which would last into the twentieth century.[3] The nation's urban centers have had more diversity for more time than is generally recognized. At the same time, throughout the nation, many different ethnic groups conducted schools of their own, either bilingually or only in their own tongue. Thus as Diego Castellanos says:

> For much of the 19th century, certainly before the 1880s, the structure of American public education allowed immigrant groups to incorporate linguistic and cultural traditions into the schools. . . .Wherever immigrant groups possessed sufficient political power—be they Italian, Polish, Czech, French, Dutch, German—foreign languages were introduced into elementary and secondary schools, either as separate subjects or as languages of instruction.[4]

And in much of the southwest, Spanish was the dominant language when vast areas were annexed to the United States, and Spanish remained the language of instruction in many educational institutions well into the twentieth century.[5] It was only as a result of the anti-immigrant, "Americanization" movement of the turn of the twentieth century and the virulent anti-German feelings aroused by World War I that the nation's first bilingual schools were terminated.[6]

Nevertheless, while America has been both multicultural and bilingual much longer than it has been a nation, for most of our history various cultures and peoples stayed quite apart from each other or, in the case of slavery, annexation in the southwest, and the European conquest of Native Americans, met on terms which completely denigrated one culture involved in the meeting. The people of the United States have been thrown together in this last generation as never before. The people of different races and different colors in this country have been thrown together by changing social patterns, by the immigration of new peoples from Central and South America and Southeast Asia, by the struggle of all people for a share in the American dream. The time has come in this nation's life when we must, as Martin Luther King, Jr. reminded us, "either live together as brothers and sisters, or perish separately as fools." Yet at this same time there has been significant movement to turn back the vision of the Civil Rights movement in American politics.[7]

But the reality of the nation's demographic changes is such that King's words, though powerful, do not go far enough. It will not work to say that we must accept diversity or perish. If democracy is to flourish in the United States of the twenty-first century, if the nation is to avoid a new kind of apartheid, then this nation must embrace diversity as a great gift, as a means of living in a new, and much better, and more diverse world. The good old days were not so good for any of us. And for far too many of us, the old days were not good at all. The future can be quite different. We can build a world in which the diversity of peoples makes the society richer for us all. And school classrooms which effectively build on the multicultural diversity of the nation's people can be one of the prime locations for beginning to build this new society.

Nearly every one of the national education reports which were issued in the 1980s contained some variation on the theme of the nation's growing diversity. As one report said, "The broad outlines of the problem can be seen in the numbers. First, Blacks, Hispanics, and Asians account for a rising proportion of the school population . . . By around the year 2000, one out of three Americans will be a member of a racial minority."[8] Given the age disparity between whites and people of color, it must be expected that the majority of students in many of the nation's schools will be non-white in the years ahead. But the question must be asked, why is this diversity so often viewed as a problem to be solved? Well meaning as it is, some of the calls to deal with diversity in the classroom sound too much like the Public Health Officer warning us that a measles epidemic is coming. As we enter a new century we are going to have to embrace—not merely tolerate—a multicultural world if we are going to give any meaning to the word democracy. Indeed, in our day, any talk of democracy which is not fully inclusive is simply meaningless.

The dialogue about the kind of society which we want—the kind of society which schools should help to foster—is in itself a part of the democratic process which we must nurture. It is only through dialogue, through the sharing of hopes, fears, frustrations, and ideals that we will begin to build the new social order of which we want our educational system to be a part. As Maxine Greene has noted, we must nurture our own vision of the good society—the democratic society—because "it is only through the projection of a better social order that we can perceive the gaps in what exists and try to transform and repair." Greene continues hopefully, "I would like to think that this can happen in classrooms, in corridors, in schoolyards, in the streets around."[9]

This is a very clear goal for educators. We must look clearly at our whole society and the diversity of peoples who are here, and then rather than accept things as they are and call on the schools to prepare students to live in this world as it is with all of its inequities and unhappiness, to instead project a better social order and try to live up to it.

To do the latter, to try to talk about a new vision of the good society, a vision which truly embraces the rich, multicultural diversity of our people, is to talk about the true nature of democracy. Democracy is, after all, much more than a method of holding elections and selecting leaders. Democracy is primarily a matter of how we live together, how we build community together, or as John Dewey said seventy-five years ago, "A democracy is more than a form of government; it is primarily a mode of associated living, of communal experience."[10]

In many ways, the Civil Rights movement is the paradigm for this kind of democratic education, and it is no accident that the battle for equality and integration in schools has been one of the primary battles of late-twentieth-century educational politics. At its core, the Civil Rights movement's focus in education is a matter of building a new vision of the good society. . . .or, in the words of Martin Luther King Jr., "the beloved community." It is a matter of building what Beverly Harrison has called a utopian vision "in that it envisages a society, a world, a cosmos, in which . . . there are 'no excluded ones.' "[11]

Education for a world where "there are no excluded ones," is one of the great opportunities available in today's urban schools. For all the difficulties with the process, one of the legacies of the forty-year-long struggle to desegregate public education, especially in the urban North, is that today's classrooms, in some cases, represent the best available microcosm of the nation of the future. It is possible to imagine a school classroom in one of the nation's cities, in which there is:

- One child whose parents are middle-class professionals who came from some other part of the nation to take good jobs in the city's hospitals or universities

- One child, a third- or fourth-generation resident of the city, born to teenage parents who live in public housing

- One child who was born in war-torn Cambodia, whose parents remember the horrors of Pol Pot, and who escaped first to a refugee camp in Thailand and only recently came to this city

- One child who is the product of artificial insemination, whose loving parents are a lesbian couple

- One child, another third- or fourth-generation resident, whose Irish-Catholic or Italian-Catholic forebears have been part of the city's political establishment for decades

- One child who is a great-grandchild of slaves from Africa.

And so on and so on, altogether an amazing collection of all sorts and conditions of God's people. And the question is, how do we view this class?

- The conservatives will say: "We need to get tough, we must make sure that they all meet high standards, and if some of them don't it will be their own fault."

- The liberals will likely say: "This class includes many students with social problems, many of these children have a cultural deficit, and we need to provide remediation to many of them so that they can fit in to the culture of the schools and of the larger society."

- But why can't we ask a different question: Why don't we view this class as a wonderful opportunity—an opportunity to begin a new American culture, an opportunity to view these children, and their parents and their teachers, as a wonderful microcosm of the new social order which we desperately need but cannot really envision.

It is important to recognize that in too many cases, this classroom still does not exist. For all the struggle to desegregate the nation's schools, Jonathan Kozol's observations will ring true for anyone who has spent time in city schools during the last decade. Speaking of his visits to schools around the nation between 1988 and 1990, Kozol writes, "Most of the urban schools I visited were 95 to 99 percent nonwhite. In no school that I saw anywhere in the United States were nonwhite children in large numbers truly intermingled with white children."[12] Kozol's observation fits the reality more often than the classroom envisioned above. And yet, the struggle for a different kind of school and classroom continues. It is important to recognize the democratic potential in this sort of struggle especially at a time when the national mood seems less and less interested in the justice of the *Brown v. Board of Education* decision.

We need new ways for this nation's diverse peoples to come together and mutually envision a new culture and the nation's classrooms are an ideal place to begin. As Norma Rees, once said:

We white liberals have tended to view education reform as our opening the doors of our society and our culture . . . and inviting people of color, the diversity of people in our society, to come in and join us. [And if we are good liberals, we have even crafted affirmative action programs to bring many into our world.] But I hear people saying now, "we don't want to come in to your culture, we want to sit down together and build a new culture."[13]

That is something quite different, and much more exciting. But the process of building a new culture can only take place in the interaction of people who bring different cultural traditions to the table. This has long been the case in popular culture. American music, literature, and religion has long reflected a wide range of cultural influences. And the school classroom has the potential to be an ideal meeting place in this quest for a new culture of diversity.

Not everyone today is interested in building a new common culture. It is not only the Arthur Schlesingers and other advocates of maintaining Eurocentric dominance while other cultures are admitted at the margins who oppose the idea. There are times when advocates of an Afrocentric curriculum, advocates of separate bilingual programs, and others also seek to maintain a distinct culture above building a new one. In the short term, such actions are often essential. Until children and communities have a strong sense of the confidence which comes from pride in one's identity, they enter the larger dialogue at a distinct disadvantage. Until people know their own heritage well, it is impossible for them to make their unique contribution to the building of a new culture. But when short-term strategy becomes long-term goal, something very important is lost. We need to remember Robert Reich's haunting warning of a twenty-first century America in which "Americans will secede into smaller enclaves of people with similar incomes, similar values and interests, similar ethnic identities."[14] If that is the future, it may be a future in which many different and distinct cultures survive, but it will not be a future of equality or opportunity for the heirs of many of those cultures.

Two very influential books, Allan Bloom's, *The Closing of the American Mind*, and E. D. Hirsch's *Cultural Literacy*, both published in 1987, bemoaned the lack of a set of common cultural assumptions in the United States today, and then Hirsch went so far as to publish his list of the 5,000 things, names, proverbs, quotes, and so on that every literate American should know. While Hirsch drew his list from an embarrassingly white/male/ Western set of concepts, he was an equal opportunity cultural imperialist; he wanted everyone, people from all backgrounds, to learn his list. This is not what I am talking about in a discussion of building a new culture.

It is, indeed, quite a different matter to recognize that what is needed in the United States is a commitment to build a new, and as yet unrecognized, culture in which all citizens—Native Americans and immigrants from Africa, Asia, Europe, Latin America, and the Pacific Islands—make their own contribution and play their part in the design of new cultural assumptions, in which the current mainstream culture is but one of the many represented. This kind of commitment to cultural diversity is serious business. It does not mean that we are satisfied to learn each other's Thanksgiving customs and honor Black History month and St. Patrick's Day. It means learning enough to seriously engage together in building something quite new and as yet unanticipated. And the dialogue necessary to build this culture cannot happen unless there is a wide diversity of races and cultures represented among the students, parents, and teachers of the schools where it is being created.

The philosopher Maxine Greene describes what it will take to build this new culture when she insists:

> We need spaces . . . for expression, for freedom . . . a public space . . . where living persons can come together in speech and action, each one free to articulate a distinctive perspective, all of them granted equal worth. It must be a space of dialogue, a space where a web of relationships can be woven, and where a common world can be brought into being and continually renewed."[15]

This is, I believe, a worthy goal for education, this building of a common world which can be brought into being and continually renewed.

Political Correctness

Any discussion of the centrality of multiculturalism in democratic education leads, unfortunately, directly to the recent debates about the issue of political correctness. Does advocating the importance of a multicultural perspective in the curriculum mean saying that there should be a politically correct line from which there can be no deviation? Certainly some of those who have raised the specter of a politically correct line engulfing campuses and textbooks would say so. But the reality is exactly the opposite. In arguing for diversity, for inclusion, for the widest possible spectrum of ideas, perspectives, and information in the curriculum of the school, the advocates of a multicultural democracy are moving in exactly the opposite direction.

The call for a multicultural perspective is not, and cannot ever be, a call for narrowing the curriculum, for cutting off debate or for defining one set of information as "correct" and the rest as excludable. Any multiculturalism is, by definition, a discussion of multiple perspectives.

- If anyone, in the name of multiculturalism, demands a narrowing of the curriculum, of academic discourse, to the "politically correct," they are not being true to the purposes of multiculturalism.

- If, on the other hand, anyone attempts—as many other of today's conservative academics are doing and as their predecessors have done for generations—to limit the debate to their definition of a "politically correct" Western canon which reigned in academia a generation ago, they too must be called to account.

Multiculturalism and academic freedom must go hand in hand.

But there is something very strange going on here. A whole group of authors have suddenly burst on the scene accusing some generally unnamed opponents—but focusing especially on those of us who call for multicultural perspectives within the curriculum—as people who demand political correctness.[16] In reading these books, one wonders where the universities are which are being painted as being taken over by the "tenured radicals." The whole political correctness debate seems to be a matter of setting up "straw men" and then attacking them. Campus debates have throughout history often been heated and pointed. There is no question that there have been times when leftist academics have inappropriately favored their allies, as have academics of every other perspective. This must always be resisted. But there is little serious evidence that there is suddenly a new political line—some amalgamation of leftist political thinking and multiculturalism—which has taken over academia. Indeed, there is far more evidence on the side of those who argue that higher education, like must of the rest of the country, has been engulfed in a rising tide of apathy and conservatism in the aftermath of the Reagan-Bush administrations.

There are two other issues which must be considered in this debate:

1. First, we must look honestly at the issues of power. The canon of Western European authors has held sway in academia for a long time. The call by authors like Allan Bloom and E. D. Hirsch for a clear canon of what must be taught in our colleges is merely a call for what has been business as usual for most of this century.[17] It is those of us who are arguing for the inclusion of non-Western materials, those of us who argue that while we must read Jefferson, we must also read Langston Hughes's commentary on Jefferson, and while we must read Shakespeare, we must equally read Marquez and Malcolm and Toni Morrison and Alice Walker and Amy Tan, who have the uphill fight. And to brand those who call for inclusion, who call for a broader curriculum and who must often fight hard battles for that kind of inclusion, to call that narrowness is both dishonest and a means of shifting the power back into a more narrow set of hands.

2. It is also important to note the timing of this assault. Beginning in the fall of 1990, books, articles, and television programs suddenly discovered a

crisis on college campuses and elsewhere in which, "In the name of 'sensitivity' to others and under pain of being denounced as a sexist or racist, the postmodern radicals require everyone around them to adhere to their own codes of speech and behavior."[18] The issue has made the cover of major news magazines and the evening news. Why now? Who is at risk and who gains by the debate? Again, the answers seem to be obvious. At the very moment when, mostly because of the pressure coming from an increasingly diverse student body in higher education, there is finally beginning to be a new openness and a new expansion of the curriculum, suddenly those who call for openness are called narrow. It is as if the right in this country, looking out and seeing new changes on the horizon, has assumed that those who call for change would use the tactics of McCarthyism perfected by the right, and so they recoil in fear. And in their fear they have coined a new phrase which places virtue on the side of tradition and vice on the side of change. It is a neat trick. But it is a dirty trick, and we must resist it.

Academic Racism and the Attack on Multiculturalism

It is part of the reactionary times in which we live that more and more "academic" attacks on multiculturalism and directly on people of color are appearing. While Arthur Schlesinger may have been among the earliest and most prominent voices, a long line of right-wing scholars have joined the parade including people like Roger Kimball and Dinesh D'Souza.[19] Indeed dressing up racism and the fear of difference in an academic cap and gown seems to be one of the growth industries of the 1990s. And the attacks have become meaner and stronger, embarrassing even the Schlesingers and their early allies.

The apotheoses of this trend appeared in 1994 with the publication of *The Bell Curve: Intelligence and Class Structure in American Life* by Richard J. Herrnstein and Charles Murray. Herrnstein and Murray build on the pseudo-scholarly tradition of Arthur Jensen using a distorted scientific evidence to "prove" that higher intelligence is found among whites than people of color and that there is little that can be done to change this.[20] As one group of thoughtful reviewers noted, "*The Bell Curve* gives a sophisticated voice to a repressed and illiberal sentiment: a belief that ruinous divisions in society are sanctioned by nature itself."[21] Clearly this is the academic version of sentiments which are all too common in other parts of American society, be they political discussion, office talk, or the informal conversation in many living rooms.

Perhaps most frightening, however, is the fact that *The Bell Curve* is not a lone exception in contemporary scholarship. More and more books are appearing with equal virulence. One recent publication, *Molding the Good Citizen* by Robert Lerner, Althea K. Nagai, and Stanley Rothman, purports to be a new look at the history of textbooks in this country. In fact, it is an excursion into curriculum history which adds another volume to the new genre. An analysis of this volume is useful as a sample of the new conservative scholarship.

Molding the Good Citizen[22] is *The Bell Curve* of curriculum history. Like Herrnstein and Murray's text, it hides its reactionary political agenda behind a facade of concerned inquiry and the pseudo-science of a coding scheme for analyzing the content of high school history texts. But this book is not science or history. Russell Jacoby and Naomi Glauberman have said of *The Bell Curve* that it has struck a chord, a frightening chord, in the American psyche. "For many readers the graphs and charts of *The Bell Curve* confirm a dark suspicion: the ills of welfare, poverty, and an underclass are less matters of justice than biology." And Herrnstein and Murray "pose as feckless seekers of truth who are bucking liberal conformism."[23] Only a short time later, it seems, the same approach has come to the history of education.

The text of *Molding the Good Citizen* begins with a thoughtful—and accurate—assertion:

> If American history and civics textbooks have become a battleground, it is because they now serve as the prayer-books of the United States's civil religion. . . .Yet problems emerge because we do not all agree on what is best for the nation or what our civic culture is all about.[24]

Many other historians have noted the same reality. In the secular culture of the United States, the school becomes the carrier of the culture. If they had stayed with that theme, if they had analyzed the way in which texts are a battle ground for contending forces in the country's civil religion, these authors might have made an important contribution.

In the next several chapters, however, the authors of this text paint a conspiracy theory of the movement which began with John Dewey and other progressive educators at the turn of the twentieth century, but gathered steam rapidly in the 1960s and following.[25] If Lerner, Nagai, and Rothman's work has a thesis, it is a reprise of the kind of conservative education history popular in the 1950s which viewed the history of twentieth century American schooling as a disaster originated in the mind of John Dewey. *Molding the*

Good Citizen brings the conspiracy theory up to date, including participants in the civil rights, feminist, and antiwar movements as well as those struggling for equal rights on the part of gay and lesbian citizens (a cause of special worry to them) in the litany of those who are corrupting American history as it is taught to our children. It is as if Dewey and *The Social Frontier* progressives of the 1930s and 1940s have been joined by the WEEA [Women's Educational Equity Act] Program and the publishers of multicultural curricula in a century-long crusade to enlist the schools for what is variously described as democratic socialism or "collectivism."

Up to this point, *Molding the Good Citizen* can be considered as a new and provocative addition to the literature of curriculum history. Many would disagree sharply with its conclusions, but differing interpretations are part of the process of building greater understanding. But is this really what is going on here? Is this book really a conservative addition to the scholarly dialogue aimed at ever more sophisticated notions of historical truth. I think not.

In fact, the book is filled with dishonesty parading as historical research. The analogy with *The Bell Curve* fits at several points. At no point is the link clearer than the use which Lerner, Nagai, and Rothman make of their supposedly quantitative research to create a "scientific" basis for their conclusions. The use of a novel "coding scheme" for rating the changes in U.S. history texts over the last half century seems to "prove" their case that the nation's texts have been taken over by radical feminists, multiculturalists, and their allies. But one needs to read this text very carefully. If that happens, a very different kind of research technique emerges.

Example: On pages 30–32 the authors describe the rapid domination of progressive education in the nation's school in the 1930s and 1940s through a kind of "group think" methodology in which teachers were forced to participate in study groups with the predetermined outcome of a schoolwide commitment to a collectivist and socialist –as opposed to an individualistic and capitalistic—ideology. They go on to assert, "Ravitch pointed out that teachers who 'impeded' that process were fired."[26]

Historians of education are left wondering at such an assertion. Few other careful studies of American schools in the 1930s and 1940s report the massive dismissal of public school teachers for failing to embrace socialist collectivism. While many teachers were fired for ideological reasons in the nation's schools during the 1930s and 1940s, nearly all such cases were for the opposite reasons. Teachers were fired for being "communists," for lacking sufficient patriotism, and in the case of some for their membership in the NAACP. If there were teachers who were fired for insufficient devotion to socialism, the cases were either very few and far between or have gone unreported in nearly all serious histories of the era.[27]

Lerner, Nagai, and Rothman, however, do provide a reference for their assertion, Diane Ravitch's *The Troubled Crusade: American Education, 1945–1980*.[28] And Ravitch does, indeed, make the claim, asserting: "Teachers who impeded the 'democratic' group process were fired; in one school the principal fired half the faculty and replaced them with teachers who had trained in progressive methods." And Ravitch too has a citation for her assertion.

Ravitch's footnote indicates two sources: N. C. Turpen, "Cooperative Curricular Improvement: To Formulate a Plan for Securing Community Understanding, Cooperation, and Support in Making Basic Program Changes in the High Schools of Alabama" (Diss., Teachers College, Columbia University, 1941), pp. 129–30; Caswell, Curriculum Improvement [Hollis Caswell, *Curriculum Improvement in Public School Systems* (New York: Bureau of Publications, Teachers College, 1950)], pp. 293–94. Caswell's more widely available work has no mention of teacher terminations. Turpen's 1941 Teachers College dissertation does indeed tell a story of a principal who, in the fall of 1940, was given permission by his superintendent and school board to terminate ten teachers who were not cooperating in his efforts to implement the new State of Alabama core curriculum. The core curriculum, as also described by Turpen, "replaces the time which was previously given to the required subjects of English and social studies. Subject matter lines have been erased in the core which consists of a study of life problems drawing material from all organized bodies of subject matter."[29] It takes quite a series of leaps from one example of the termination of a group of teachers for failure to support a state mandated progressive, integrated core curriculum to the kind of widespread reign of terror for failure to support socialist collectivism which these authors imply. And to imply that such happenings were commonplace or the normal reasons for teacher termination in this-or any— era of American history simply flies in the face of reality.

Example: Lerner, Nagai, and Rothman pride themselves on the fact that their study of the history of texts, unlike previous studies, is quantitative as well as qualitative.[30] They base their boast on the coding scheme which they have developed for reporting the total number of women and men, whites, African Americans, Native-Americans, Latinos, Asians, and others who are given a specific mention in a total of fifteen high school history textbooks published from the 1940s to the 1980s. Having coded a total of 4,285 people who are given sufficient mention in these texts over five decades, the authors are able, so they claim, to trace the growing representation of women and people of color [they use the term minorities] over the years. Not surprisingly, given the unstated ideological base of the book, the authors find that:

> Using both the quantitative summaries of change over time and the case studies of individual characters we find that American history textbook authors transformed the texts from scarcely mentioning blacks in the 1940s to containing a substantial multicultural (and feminist) component in the 1980s.[31]

They are clear that this "elaborate evaluational and pictorial overrepresentation of women and minorities" represents a clear distortion of the goals of teaching American history. Indeed, they coin the term "filler feminism" for the growing representation of women in these texts. They also complain that both women and African Americans are portrayed favorably more often than white men.[32]

What is the reality behind their statistics? If one reads closely, the sea change they describe consists of a growth of the total percentage of women represented in the texts from 5% in the 1940s to 13% in the 1980s.[33] For African Americans, the percentage growth is from 0.1% up to a whopping 8% in the 1980s.[34] To do further statistical analysis on these numbers, such as the complaint that 10–15% of men are given negative or mixed ratings while almost no women are (that is none of the 13% of the people in these texts who are women) or that 94% of blacks are rated positively which is a higher figure than for whites (94% of the African Americans who made it in, who are 8% of the total people)[35] is to distort the meaning of statistical research and to create a pretense of scientific objectivity which has nothing to do with reality. In one chart which "proves" the unfairly positive ratings given to African Americans and women in more recent texts, the authors describe the portraits of 123 black men compared to 1,665 white men and 23 black women compared to 183 white women.[36] Such comparisons are meaningless, unless they are meant to prove that both people of color and women continue to be significantly underrepresented in even the most recent high school history texts.

There is a further issue here for historians. In their complaints about "filler feminism" and the so-called over representation of people of color and women, the authors are continuing a "great man" view of history. Indeed, they are quite explicit about this approach. "Most of American history is male-dominated," they explain, "in part because women in most states were not allowed to vote in federal elections or hold office until the twentieth century." And again, "Reading about the 'contributions' of women and minorities to any particular field does not show how most historically salient characters, who were neither women nor minorities, conceived of their civic duty and acted so as to measurably shape historical events." From their perspective, voting, holding office, and reflecting on civic duties seem to be the only keys to shaping history.[37]

Have these authors never heard of E. P. Thompson or Herbert G. Gutman?[38] Hasn't the field of American history, including hopefully American history texts, been shaped by Thompson's insistence that history focus on, "the agency of working people, the degree to which they contributed, by conscious efforts, to the making of history."[39] And among working people, as opposed to the presidents, leading capitalists, and best-selling authors whom Lerner, Nagai, and Rothman seem to favor, are many more women and people of color. To find representative examples from these groups, to use specific examples to give voice to the historically voiceless, is not a distortion of history but the very best effort to tell history accurately and carefully. The authors of *Molding the Good Citizen*, of course, disagree. One of their final pleas is that, "The teaching of history with due attention to the impact of great men has the benefit of reducing the sense of fatalism and hopelessness, which is the characteristic vice of democratic historians, history textbooks, and egalitarian society."[40] Apparently the participants in the civil rights, women's, and pro-democracy movements of this century should still be characterized by fatalism and hopelessness until they are caught up in the dream of individual achievement as great [white] men.

Example: Perhaps nowhere are the conclusions of *Molding the Good Citizen* more offensive than in their description of the changes between the 1940s and the 1980s in the ways the story of European and Native American encounters are told. In this case the authors bemoan what they see as a decline in historical accuracy leading to the fact that:

> The authors of the 1980s texts go to some trouble to indicate the numerous shortcomings of whites in understanding and appreciating the Indian way of life. The books, however, fail to point out the numerous shortcomings of the Indian way of life, including the widespread practice of torturing captives to death.[41]

They want a return to history of the encounter as it was taught in the 1940s. Indeed, Indian torture appears on nearly every page of this chapter, while the genocidal practices of the European are simply not mentioned. It is amazing that a book which claims to call for a return to "objectivity" can first mention the word genocide in its last pages and then in a dismissive note that "Christopher Columbus, on the other hand, once viewed as a courageous explorer, has descended to the level of a genocidal criminal."[42]

In this case, the model which these authors embrace is David Saville Muzzey whose 1943 and 1952 texts were among the most used in the decades immediately after World War II.[43] As they view him, "Muzzey (1943) does not have a pro-European bias, but a civilizational bias . . . he is a 'cultural hierarchicalist' "[44] This they see as good. The authors devote a full chapter to what they see as an increasingly romanticized portrait in the more recent texts of the cultures of the peoples who were "discovered" in the Americas, while they critique as unfair the growing criticism of the Europeans who brought more "advanced" technology and civilization to the continents.

In their whole discussion there is no interrogation of the notion of advanced "Western civilization" as it was experienced by Native Americans. Lerner, Nagai, and Rothman's references to barbarism simply does not fit what is becoming known about the increasingly sophisticated nature of many of the native cultures. But more important, what is really barbarism? These authors critique the most conservative of the 1980s texts for its statement regarding the arrival of Europeans, "For some [Indian tribes] it meant the end of their native American civilization. For some it meant slavery. For nearly all of them Europeans brought shock, disease, and change."[45] This analysis, they seem to say, is unfair to the Europeans. Indeed for the majority of natives, the encounter with Europeans meant quick death. Shock, disease, and change were for the lucky ones! What is the political agenda behind the call to return to Muzzey?

Example: In their closing chapter, the authors return to their basic complaint. Progressive educators, followed by their feminist and multiculturalist successors, "sanctioned a massive injection of the educators' own values into curricular developments and classroom teaching wherever this proved politically feasible."[46] The result of this new politicization, they argue, is a rapid decline in historical knowledge on the part of most Americans, a growing cynicism about the nation and the development of an "adversary culture of intellectuals"[47] who are not fostering a sense of national unity.

Each of these conclusions deserves consideration. While it is certainly true that progressives, feminists, and advocates for multicultural education have contended for a voice in the interpretation of American history in the schools, they have been far from the only ones—or the most successful ones—doing so, as *Molding the Good Citizen* implies. One comes away from reading this book with the assumption that prior to the Progressive Era the teaching of American history was fully objective. Have these authors never read the texts of William Holmes McGuffey or Charles A. Goodrich and their successors, who set the patriotic, Protestant, and Eurocentric tone of nineteenth-century American history texts?[48] Have they never heard of the campaigns by the National Association of Manufacturers and the American Legion for control of history texts in the 1940s or the Heritage Foundation in the 1980s? Certainly they do not bother to tell their readers this part of the story.[49]

It is in the discussion of the supposed educational decline which has taken place as a result of the changes during the last fifty years that these authors most clearly show their real political agenda. "What are the consequences of textbook changes?" they ask. "[W]e believe that changes in their content have played a role in the overall decline in educational achievement that many have criticized."[50] And who are the many who have studied the decline? In addition to the ever present Ravitch, now linked with Chester E. Finn, a new source appears, an article from *Public Interest*, "What's Really Behind the SAT-Score Decline?" by none other than Charles Murray and R. J. Herrnstein.[51]

If one pursues their argument, one discovers that, in fact, the decline they describe assumes some unspecified golden age in which all Americans knew their nation's history well and were able to draw on that knowledge as a basis for thoughtful reflection and civic responsibility. Such a situation is indeed a goal—though the definitions of both reflection and civic responsibility differ significantly—but it is hardly a portrait of any moment in this nation's past.

In such "research," *Molding the Good Citizen* follows quite closely the research methodology of *The Bell Curve*. My colleague Leon Kamin has provided one of the most careful analyses available of *The Bell Curve*'s "scientific" methodology. He has found case after case of references to studies which do not say what Herrnstein and Murray assert they say or studies which are naked prejudice parading as science. Reviewing the work of two scholars who provide much of the research foundation for *The Bell Curve*, and their use by Herrnstein and Murray, Kamin concludes:

> To admit Lynn and Rushton into the scientific mainstream—I'll say it bluntly—is a betrayal of science. . . . Herrnstein and Murray's defense of Rushton's racist claptrap—"we expect that time will tell whether it is right or wrong in fact"—is couched in the tones of moderation and reason. In my view both the work and its defense are contemptible."[52]

Unfortunately the same must be said of *Molding the Good Citizen*.

Historians of education, like most others in the academy, have had a long history of heated debates. But while the disagreements have been heated and sharp, they have seldom been marked by the fundamental dishonesty which the new right is parading as scholarship in the United States in the 1990s. Many progressive scholars have provided a careful critique of *The Bell Curve*. It is important for other scholars to take on other similar volumes, such as *Molding the Good Citizen*, so that the pattern, as well as the problems with Herrnstein and Murray's volume, are made clear.

There must be a means to make a distinction between difference—including radical and sharp differences—and plain historical dishonesty posing as a perspective within a debate. Writing in *Rethinking Schools* about *The Bell Curve*'s Charles Murray, Adolph Reed Jr. says: "Liberals have never frankly denounced Murray as the right-wing hack that he is. They appear on panels with him and treat him as a serious, albeit conservative, fellow worker in the vineyard of truth."[53] With a few important exceptions which have emerged since he wrote, Reed is right in his charge. Unless a clear distinction is made between disagreement and plain dishonesty and unless progressive educators are able to effectively challenge both the mean-spiritedness and the dishonesty of the current reactionary assault, the future of scholarship, like the larger society, is going to be bleak.[54]

The School and the Struggle for Cultural Diversity

There is more to be done than challenging the assertions of the right, however. A new scholarship of diversity and difference needs to emerge. One of the nation's leading scholars to focus on the issue of difference, Henry Giroux, sees an important opening for progressive educators in the larger debate surrounding "political correctness." Giroux, in a chapter co-authored with David Trend, reviews the debates of the 1980s:

> Within the last decade, conservatives such as Allan Bloom, E. D. Hirsch, Diane Ravitch, Pat Buchanan, and Senator Jesse Helms have been able to beat progressives at their own game. They have placed the issue of culture and difference at the center of the debate about education and democracy. They have asserted the primacy of the political in invoking the language of culture and in doing so have let it be known that culture is a terrain of political and ideological struggle. The general ideological parameters of this struggle are partly revealed in the words of syndicated

columnist Pat Buchanan, who has urged his fellow conservatives "to wage a cultural revolution in the 1990s as sweeping as the political revolution in the 1980s."[55]

Giroux recognizes that what "is being valorized in the dominant language of the culture industry is an elitist view of self and social development based on a celebration of cultural homogeneity, an undemocratic approach to social authority, and a politically regressive move to reconstruct American life within the script of Eurocentrism, racism, and patriarchy." Nevertheless, as Giroux sees it, the right's shift of the battle about democracy from the strictly political to the cultural field, opens important opportunities for progressives. In *Border Crossings* he analyzes, "the implications that this struggle over culture has for redefining a language of critique and possibility that is capable of challenging the authoritarianism and cultural amnesia that is the hallmark of a new cultural conservatism."[56]

In expanding the terrain of the contest from simply matters of governance to the whole of the nation's culture, and in demanding that culture itself be democratized, Giroux is following in the steps of John Dewey who always insisted that "democracy as a social idea," is much more than mere "political democracy as a system of government," and that the "idea of democracy is a wider and fuller idea than can be exemplified in the state even at its best."[57] But the battle today is to move far beyond Dewey in building a notion of "democracy as a social idea," which truly expands the boundaries which have traditionally limited all of those who by virtue of race, class, gender, or other kinds of difference were not included in the dominant culture. Thus Giroux criticizes Diane Ravitch, among others, for a failure to include "a notion of difference and citizenship tied to a project of substantive critical democracy that extends the principles of justice, liberty, and equality to the widest possible set of economic and social relations."[58]

Giroux also calls on teachers, and other "cultural workers" to serve as public intellectuals who pose a far different notion of democratic culture from the celebration of a European hegemony which is far too dominant in today's discourse. In this struggle, cultural workers need to reclaim the diverse histories of this nation's peoples from a single dominant "monologue of totalizing narratives," they need to rewrite political and pedagogical practice, and they need to develop a new kind of "Prophetic Criticism," which involves "the deliberate notion of unveiling, negating, and problematizing." But most important, teachers and other cultural workers need to develop a new "language of imagination."

This is a language of democratic possibilities that rejects the enactment of cultural difference structured in hierarchy and dominance; it is a language that rejects cultural, social, and spatial borders as shorelines of violence and terrorism. In opposition to this view, the concepts of democracy, border borderlands, and difference must be rewritten so that diverse identities and cultures can intersect as sites of creative cultural production, multiple resources, and experimentation for expanding those human capacities and social forms necessary for a radical democracy to emerge in this country.[59]

At precisely the moment when far too much of the nation's cultural elite seem to be constricting the notion of democratic culture to a matter of simply passing on the western heritage unchallenged, Giroux is speaking the language of an expanding and newly varied democracy. It is only this brave and imaginative understanding of democracy which will result in an educational system and a nation worthy of the term democracy in the decades ahead.

Reflections of a White Male

It is not possible to write about democracy and multiculturalism and not at the same time reflect on my own location in this conversation. I must also look at my own place as a white male whose current status as a college professor and administrator is certainly middle class. So many of my contemporaries seem to be fleeing from the dialogue. I find myself wondering about their fear, and my own. From my own, quite different perspective, I find myself seeing with bell hooks a situation in which "all of a sudden, professors who had taken issues of multiculturalism and cultural diversity seriously were backtracking, expressing doubts, casting votes in directions that would restore biased traditions or prohibit changes in faculty and curricula that were to bring diversity of representation and perspective."[60] What about my votes, my decisions as an administrator? Keeping a vision of a multicultural democracy alive requires both a long-term commitment and a very specific day-to-day examination of specific actions.

In the shadow of the *Contract with America*, fear seems to be taking many forms. In the neighborhood where I live, many are voicing the language of "angry white males." Suddenly it has become popular for white males, some working-class and some quite well off, to assume the position of victim and to blame people of color and women for their plight in an economy in which

they can no longer see upward mobility as a reasonable expectation. I sup-
pose the anger can provide a kind of cultural norm to fill the emptiness of
consumerist society. And I must sympathize with many who are experiencing
the downward mobility of a constricting national economy and are not sure
what to do with it. The economic situation in the United States is increasingly
oppressive for many, including many white males. Angry white maleness
may play well in an era of rapid change and confusion. But in the long run—
and not very long at that—it is a recipe for fascism, an excuse for developing
fear and hate into a political program which marginalizes everyone else and
calls on still marginalized white males to serve as the shock troops of the
"new world order." While the elite of this new world will still dispense with
most of their followers once they are no longer needed, participation in the
culture of anger can, in the short run, give a sense of power by differentiating
them from "the other" who is seen as the enemy. This is much like the
security which the old racism gave the poor and working class whites of the
old South. There must be a better way. Fascism is a means of death for
everyone.

At the same time, the fear and hate are not limited to self acknowledged
"angry white males." As already noted, academics as distinguished as Arthur
Schlesinger Jr. seem to be infected with the disease. How else to account for
his diatribe, "It may be too bad that dead white European males have played
so large a role in shaping our culture. But that's the way it is. One cannot
erase history."[61] One wonders—by what definition of our culture?—"that's
the way it is" in whose version of history? But the frightening thing is that
Schlesinger is not alone. Indeed, the angry white male syndrome seems especially alive among liberal academics.

Neil Postman, whose writings have influenced my own views of education for some time, is suddenly among those saying frightening things.
Describing multiculturalism as a "reversion to undiluted tribalism," Postman joins Schlesinger in the attack. Like Schlesinger, Postman sets up
Leonard Jeffries as the spokesperson for multiculturalism and then proceeds
to attack Jeffries as if he spoke for all advocates of multiculturalism. Following from this line of thinking, Postman asks, "Why should the public,
which is largely of European origin, support a school program that takes as
its theme their own evil?"[62] By what analysis does a call for teaching
American history which describes the contribution of the many diverse
cultures represented in the American people or a call for analyzing the
differing power relationships among Americans, including attention to the
issues slavery and genocide, of oppression by race, class, and gender, sud-

denly become this kind of demonization of all whites? Only in the mind of a very fearful or guilty observer.

But Postman does more than that. He sets up a clear hierarchy of values in which the historical norms of upper class, white, European-American society represents the cultural apex and all others descend from that. Thus he argues, "the level of sensibility required to appreciate the music of Robert Waters is both different and lower than what is required to appreciate, let us say, a Chopin étude."[63] Why? One does not have to be a fan of Waters to ask, by what definition of musical sensibility is one form higher and another lower? Such ranking of culture can only proceed from fear, and fear is a very dangerous basis for building an inclusive society or even a thoughtful approach to culture.

But "angry white male" rhetoric—whether in its street corner or its academic variety—is not the only danger undermining the establishment of a serious multicultural society today. Paulo Freire, speaking as a Brazilian, an outsider, has caught another aspect of the conversation among the races in contemporary America.

> In the relations between blacks and whites, if I am not completely mistaken, there seems to be, on the part of many whites who do not regard themselves as racists, something that encumbers them in their dealings with blacks, and prevents them from mounting an authentic battle against racism. Here is what I mean. It seems—at least to me— that whites have strong guilt feelings with regard to blacks. And if there is anything that annoys those who suffer discrimination, it is to have someone dealing with them in a guilty tone.[64]

How right Freire is. How annoying to be in a multiracial conversation and see other whites adopt a tone of seeming deference, which is really another way of withdrawing from the conversation, hiding one's sense of superiority behind a mask of pseudo-respect which effectively marginalizes the other person.

And Freire is also right, the only solution to the problem is for whites— people like me who are white and male and—in my adult incarnation middle-class—to engage as actively and contend as vigorously as anyone else in the conversation. Unless I join in the conversation with respect but also as a person who is proud of my ideas and proud of what I can bring to the encounter, I am not engaging in building a real multicultural conversation or a multicultural society. I agree with Freire. In my relationships with people of color, with women, with all of those who represent the diversity of this society, I have to take the risk of saying clearly and completely what I believe and who I am. "What I ought to be doing is discussing and debating things with them, disagreeing with them, as new comrades, or at least as possible comrades-to-be, comrades in the battle, companions along the way."[65] How much more open and satisfying a way to live and be.

In asking the question of the role of whites, I am also helped by the long-term vision of the Civil Rights movement. It is a vision spoken in many forms. At the end of World War II a young Adam Clayton Powell published a book called *Marching Blacks* in which he looked at the emerging post-World War II world. And in that he cited a white whom he saw as an ally of the new Civil Rights movement, Edwin Embree who wrote:

> The white man [I suspect that Embree was just being sexist when he said "white man" but for our purposes that is exactly the word I want—for I want to discuss both gender and race] of the western world is offered his last chance for equal status in world society. If he accepts equality, he can hold a self-respecting place . . . And he may continue to contribute much. . . .But if the western white man persists in trying to run the show, in exploiting the whole earth, in treating the hundreds of millions of his neighbors as inferiors, then the fresh might of the billion and a half nonwhite, non-western people may in a surging rebellion smash him to nonentity.[66]

That was written in 1945, but it is still terribly relevant at the end of the century.

In the conversation which Freire describes, in the vision of Edwin Embree, there is no talk of whites as evil or of giving up ones right to contend for what one brings to the culture or what one believes about the culture. Actually viewing oneself as evil, or as a representative of evil, is disempowering. It makes one, to say the least, a useless ally. Ultimately it is a distortion of what it means to be human.

There is, however, something very significant which must be given up—the belief that one is at the center of the culture. What a white male must give up to join the multicultural world is a Copernican view of culture—with the white males of Europe at the center—and replace it with a modern world in which many cultures, many galaxies, spinning together, sometimes crashing against each other, represent the whole of a much larger and more dynamic society and culture. It is, apparently, a frightening change for many. Just as significant authorities threatened Galileo and others for proposing to view the sun and stars differently, for proposing a complex view of a much larger solar system—so many of today's authorities threaten those who propose new and more diverse ways of viewing culture. But in both cases, with or without the threats, the changes will come. And the opportunity to be a full and active participant in the new culture is all that anyone or any group—whatever their background—can ask.

Building a Vision of a Democratic Education:
A Difficult Task

The commitment to building a truly diverse multicultural educational system is not an easy one. All of us who are teachers must commit ourselves to new learning for ourselves as well as our students. All of us must agree that there will be times of friction. To try to build a school which represents many perspectives means inevitably that there will be clashes and misunderstandings. There is a long, hard struggle involved in beginning to build a new world, and there will be opposition in many forms.

It is important not to romanticize the reality of the multicultural struggle. Advocates of multiculturalism have undermined our cause because we have sometimes failed to recognize the mistakes that inevitably will be made in the development of a new culture. bell hooks is right:

> Some folks think that everyone who supports cultural diversity wants to replace one dictatorship of knowing with another, changing one set way of thinking for another. This is perhaps the gravest misperception of cultural diversity. Even though there are those overly zealous among us who hope to replace one set of absolutes with another, simply changing content, this perspective does not accurately represent progressive visions of the way commitment to cultural diversity can constructively transform the academy. In all cultural revolutions there are periods of chaos and confusion, times when grave mistakes are made. If we fear mistakes, doing things wrongly, constantly evaluating ourselves, we will never make the academy a culturally diverse place where scholars and the curricula address every dimension of that difference.[67]

This reminder is essential if we are to continue to struggle even when things are most difficult.

Diversity can and will lead to clashes. When we bring people from different cultures together in the school it is inevitable that there will be misunderstanding, fear, and tense moments. That is part of the process of learning about each other and from each other. Giroux is right, "democratic societies are noisy."[68] A homogeneous school may be quieter and simpler, but it will not help us in the process of building a better tomorrow.

Even more difficult, however, valuing diversity can also lead to clashes with the larger society. The youth we educate, if we take even small steps toward this sort of diverse democratic education will ask all sorts of questions. And questioning children and youth make people nervous.

Thirty-five years ago, James Baldwin, in a talk to teachers, said:

> The purpose of education, finally, is to create in a person the ability to look at the world for him or herself, to make his or her own decisions, to say this is black or this is white, to decide whether there is a God in heaven or not. To ask questions of the universe, and then to learn to live with those questions, is the way a person achieves identity. But no society is really anxious to have that kind of person around. What societies really, ideally want is a citizenry which will simply obey the rules of society.[69]

If educators begin to truly embrace the multicultural future, and use that embrace to build a new multicultural, democratic present, we are going to have all sorts of students asking all sorts of embarrassing, uncomfortable questions of the society, and of ourselves. And while we may welcome these questions, even when they get uncomfortable, the society we live in today does not welcome these questions.

All societies are uncomfortable with dissent. America in the last decade has grown even more uncomfortable. As the novelist E. L. Doctorow said in a commencement address at Brandeis University in the spring of 1989:

> Something poisonous has been set loose in the last several years as we have enjoyed life under the power and principles of political conservatism. I don't know what to call it—a gangsterdom of the spirit, perhaps. In fact part of this poisonous thing that I'm trying to describe is its characteristic way of dealing with criticism: It used to be enough to brand a critic as a radical or a leftist to make people turn away. Now we need only to call him a liberal. Soon "moderate" will be the M word, "conservative" will be the C word and only fascists will be in the mainstream. And that degradation of discourse, that too, is part of this something that is really rotten in America right now.[70]

Doctorow spoke in 1989. In the following decade, the "degradation of discourse" has expanded on many fronts.

The challenge today is to find ways of talking about an education which leads our students, our graduates, and ourselves as educators, to reject mindlessness in any form, to demand—for ourselves and our students—the alert, critical, engaged consciousness which can only come from thinking minds in dialogue with—and ultimately in community with—people who bring different stories, and tell different tales, so that something truly new can emerge.

The process will not be easy. There will be hard times and anger, and it will be worth it, for we will be living in a society, at least in our schools, and perhaps in our larger community, which has begun, if only in small ways, to resemble the community we want.

Building a vision of an open and inclusive multicultural democracy in the United States is utopianism at its best, but it is also very practical. Educational dialogue needs to be practical. But it is also true that the desire to be immediately practical, to be immediately relevant, has impoverished our dialogue and kept us from larger goals and larger visions. There has been too much hiding of larger questions and values, too much reluctance to discuss the meaning and purpose of education in the fear of being impractical. And as a result the general public has turned away from many of the debates within the education community, viewing them as both boring and self-serving. It is time for that larger discussion.

And in that discussion, it is important to come down on the side of efforts which lead to a larger American society which is quite different from the one we have now, one which is not greedy and mean spirited, but rather one which is built on the energies and wonderful diversity of this nation's people. If that happens, then the essential purpose of education in a democratic society will have been established as never before.

CHAPTER FOUR

Toward a New Kind of Child-Centered Curriculum: The Individual Child and a Democratic Society

We cannot, by talk about the interests of children and the sacredness of personality, evade the responsibility of bringing to the younger generation a vision which will call forth their active loyalties and challenge them to creative and arduous labors.

George S. Counts, *Dare the School Build a New Social Order?*[1]

Progressive educators in the United States have long been split between those who focus primarily on the need to use the schools as a vehicle for building a more just and democratic society and those who focus on the needs of the individual child; the so called child-centered educators. While generations of reformers have called for a reconciliation between the two wings of the movement, the split remains.[1] And throughout the twentieth century, this split has undermined efforts to use schools as a vehicle for building a more democratic society.

It was in response to his concern with exactly this split that in 1900 John Dewey wrote:

We are apt to look at the school from an individualistic standpoint, as something between teacher and pupil, or between teacher and parent. That which interests us most is naturally the progress made by the individual child of our acquaintance . . . Yet the range of the outlook needs to be enlarged. What the best and wisest parent wants for his

93

[and her] own child, that must the community want for all of its children. Any other ideal for our schools is narrow and unlovely; acted upon, it destroys our democracy. . . . Here individualism and socialism are at one. Only by being true to the full growth of all the individuals who make it up, can society by any chance be true to itself.[2]

It remains true today, only by being true to "the full growth of all the individuals," all the diverse range of individuals who populate its schools, "can society by any chance be true to itself." Dewey may, at times, have been naive about the incredible range of children and youth who will attend school, and the many different educational strategies and curricula which are needed to serve them. In addition, we need to attend carefully to Amy Gutmann's concern that different groups of citizens in a democracy might arrive at quite different interpretations of what represents "the best." In the name of preserving a range of democratic choices Gutmann says we need to remember that wise parents disagree: "A democratic society must not be constrained to legislate what the wisest parents want for their child, yet it must be constrained *not* to legislate policies that render democracy repressive or discriminatory."[3]

Perhaps Dewey and other turn of the century progressives were overly optimistic about society's potential to come to consensus without the imposition of a repressive conformity. Democracy must involve freedom—including the freedom to differ significantly—as well as an emphasis on community. But freedom cannot include either the freedom to oppress others or the freedom to ignore the needs and contributions of one's fellow citizens. Gutmann provides an important reminder that much repression can happen in the name of doing good. But her conclusion asks too little. Of course, democracy must include freedom from coercion. But it must involve more than that. It must also include a commitment to giving and receiving the best from every citizen, especially every young citizen. So the basic point remains, the needs of every individual and the needs of society must always be linked, however often American educators have tried to separate them. We cannot settle for an education for "other people's children" which is anything less than excellent.

Child-centered educators have made very important progress in designing more effective and liberating ways of teaching children. But the child-centered movement, by itself, always remains an instrument to maintain the status quo. Often the children who receive the best child-centered education are students in elite public or private schools, while the majority of the nation's youth continue to receive an education still too close to the factory model of the nineteenth century. Thus Samuel Bowled and Herbert Gintis have a considerable base on which to make their charge that "A co-opted free-school movement, shorn of its radical rhetoric, could play an important role in providing employers with young workers with a 'built-in' supervisor."[4] As noted in chapter 1, this danger becomes all the greater as the economy splits increasingly between the 20 percent of citizens who provide "symbolic-analytic services," and who need a highly individualized education and the vast majority who are experiencing downward economic mobility and seem to be receiving an education to match.[5]

On the other hand, there cannot be a democratic education which does not focus on the needs of the individual child—every individual child—as an object of concern. Liberty and liberation for all is an essential element of democracy. The twentieth century has seen too many tragic examples of what happens when the rights and needs of individual citizens, including very young citizens, are forgotten, forgotten often in the name of a larger social good. Democratic schools must meet the needs of every child and youth in them, and ultimately democratic schools must view each student as a democratic citizen who will play his or her own role in expanding the nature of democracy itself.

Progressive educators, democratic educators, must therefore always hold to the commitment to use schools as a vehicle of a more just society and as a means of liberating every individual student in the institution. This statement seems obvious, but the reality is sadly lacking whenever one views education in the United States today. Indeed, the schools of the nation and too many of the national policies have taken on an increasingly anti-child tone. The nation's children are too often viewed as a "human resource" in the struggle for economic markets or ignored completely in the discussion of national priorities.

America as an Anti-Child Society

America today is an anti-child society. There is, of course, a soft sentimentalism about children which is displayed in parts of the media from the greeting card industry to television advertising. The hard reality is quite different, however. We see the evidence in far too many places that this nation does not care about children.

Children and Poverty

More and more of this nation's children are living in poverty. The legacy of the years of the Reagan and Bush administrations is a situation which Jacqueline Jones reports that 26 percent of children in the South fall below the poverty line and the figures are only somewhat better for other parts of the nation, "the poverty rate among black Americans was 28 percent, compared to 8.8 percent among whites," and government reports speak of the nation's 150 "worst hunger counties."[6] Something is wrong with a land as rich as the United States which has statistics and realities like these and a federal government which moves even more funding away from programs which address the needs of children and youth.

And on the streets of our cities, children are murdering children and few are expressing outrage at the horror. Except for a very few visionary leaders and grieving families no one is saying, business as usual must stop, we must deal with this murder immediately. There is something very wrong when discussion of reform of the schools is focused on test scores or skills needed in international competition, yet homicide is by far the leading cause of death among African American youth and AIDS is killing more and more young people of every race.[7] Marian Wright Edelman is addressing something very deep in the fabric of American society when she says:

> I don't think I've ever seen more people who are aware that something fundamental has come loose in this country. What in the world has happened to us, that we've become so numb, so spiritually dead? Our children are dying like flies. A child dies from guns every ninety-eight minutes in this country, and from poverty every fifty-three minutes, and from child abuse every seven hours. Is there one shred of evidence that punishing children will change the behavior of parents? I am sick and tired of begging people not to hurt children.[8]

It will, of course, take more than begging to change this reality. We need to understand and then change a social reality in which children, especially "other people's children," are not valued.

In his extraordinary book, *Amazing Grace*, Jonathan Kozol paints a portrait of the lives of children in one part of New York City, the South Bronx, and adjacent streets in Harlem. One of the youth interviewed by Kozol understands this nation's view of many of its children and youth better than most sociologists.

> It's not like being in a jail. . . . It's more like being "hidden." It's as if you have been put in a garage where, if they don't have room for something but aren't sure if they should throw it out, they put it there where they don't need to think of it again.

Another of Kozol's informants asks, "If the people in New York woke up one day and learned that we were gone, that we had simply died or left for somewhere else, how would they feel?" and she proceeds to answer her own question, "I think they'd be relieved. I think it would lift a burden from their minds. . . . I think they look at us as obstacles to moving forward."[9] Obstacles, a burden, something hidden—this is America's view of far too many children and youth as reported by some of the more eloquent among them.

It is important to note that poverty is not confined to large cities. Indeed, as Jones also reminds us

> In the late twentieth century, in absolute terms, the locus of poverty in the United States was not black, Northern, or urban . . . the faces of poverty were many, and scattered throughout the nation. Some of the poorest regions, such as the Lower Mississippi Valley; the old Cotton Belt in the South; the Appalachian Mountains; and Native American reservations in Oklahoma, New Mexico, and Arizona . . . [and] the rural poor of New England stayed "hidden by the trees," though their standard of living approximated the lowest in the nation. Four out of every five people in Washington County, Maine, lived below the poverty line.[10]

This extraordinary range of poverty in the United States means that there is a potentially powerful constituency to challenge the status quo, yet the reality of the divisions in the nation, especially the great divide of racism and the pervasive nature of sexism which still excludes women from many economic calculations, and the simple fact that so many of the poor are too young to vote, means that unity on the issue is very difficult to achieve.[11]

Poverty for children in the United States is a result of a lack of will on the part of too many of the nation's citizens to fight for the kinds of changes which are needed. Barbara Ehrenreich is right, "No viable human society condemns its children to death. Yet, through public policy and private indifference, we have guaranteed that our poor, inner-city children will lead lives stunted by heartbreak, violence, and disease."[12] Poverty of this sort is not an accident or an inevitable part of the human condition, it is a social policy choice in America, and—given the current national mood—it is going to expand rapidly.

The evidence of what could be done, if there was the will to do it, is quite clear. Beginning with Social Security in the 1930s, American social policy has virtually eliminated any higher rate of poverty among old people, when compared to the population in general. It is quite different when programs for children are involved. Thus Jones notes,

Aid to Families with Dependent Children payments, which in 1988 went to less than 5 percent of the American population (10.8 million individuals, almost all of them women and children), were stigmatized as "welfare," while Social Security was not. The federal funds committed to AFDC represented less than 2 percent of the national budget; over a seventeen year period (1970–87), real benefits fell by 37 percent. . . . A plethora of scholarly research demonstrating (in the late 1980s, for example) the positive effects of even relatively modest programs, such as prenatal education for pregnant women and early childhood programs for their offspring, had little effect on the priorities of national policy makers.[13]

The matter then is clearly one of national priorities and commitment rather than economic necessity. Jones wrote this well before President Clinton and Congressional conservatives united to "end welfare as we know it" and to push the nation's economic priorities even further away from the needs of children or any citizen in poverty.

In response to these statistics and the reality of national policy, Manning Marable is right when he argues:

The moral poverty in contemporary American society is founded, in part, in the vast chasm which separates the conditions of material well-being, affluence, power and privilege of a small elite from the masses of others. The evil in our world is politically and socially engineered, and its products of poverty, homelessness, illiteracy, political subservience, race and gender domination. The old saying from the sixties—we are part of the solution or part of the problem—is simultaneously moral, cultural, economic and political. We cannot be disinterested observers as the physical and spiritual beings of millions of people of color and the poor are collectively crushed.[14]

It is only when this moral poverty is challenged with a vision of a new multicultural democracy that the needs of this nation's children and adults will be met in a meaningful way.

Lack of Support for Schools

When it comes to support for education, to the funds needed so that our schools can succeed and prosper, so that our schools can serve the children who are sometimes refugees from mean streets, abusive situations, or plain hunger, the same mean-spiritedness of these times is clearly evident. It is important not to understate the case; an examination of the impact of many of the public policy decisions being made clearly points to the reality that the needs of children are a very low priority and the resources needed by those who work with children are in very short supply. Almost every day the media reports another failed challenge to some tax limitation scheme or another politician voicing fear that an opponent has a secret plan to raise taxes. We read of recent upturns in the economy and improvements in the tax base, but still the "no new taxes" pledge remains, at incredible cost to children and schools. It is time for educators to be more blunt. The "no new taxes" commitment—shared across the board by far too many Democrats as well as Republicans at both the state and federal level—represents a direct assault on the children of this society. It is a frightening break with what Horace Mann long ago called the "sacred obligation" to secure the needs of the generation which will come after us.[15]

While the issue of school financing—and underfunding—is explored in more detail in chapter 1, it cannot be divorced from a discussion of the nation's attitude toward its youth. No unbiased analysis of the funds available for the education of many of the students in this nation could lead to a conclusion that children and youth are valued in this society. Again Jonathan Kozol's interviews tell the story more effectively than many statistics:

> "Do you think America likes children?" Mrs. Washington asks me. . . . "I don't think so," she replies, and hands me a clipping she has saved. The story, which is from *Newsday*, is about an abandoned steel plant that is going to be used this fall as a school building. The factory, which is next to a cemetery and beside a pipeline that carries "combustible fuel," is in an area, according to a Board of Education engineer, that "appears to be a dumping ground" for "tires, rugs, and parts of bodies." Because of unexpected overcrowding some 500 children will be forced to go to school there.[16]

Thurgood Marshall's eloquent dissent in the Supreme Court's 1973 school funding decision is becoming a tragic understatement at the end of the century. The current system of financing in education in the United States represents an, "unsupportable acquiescence in a system which deprives children in their earliest years of the chance to reach their full potential as citizens."[17] The political climate of the 1990s gives little reason for optimism that the retreat will not continue.

Why This Anti-Child Movement

If we are to fight back, we need to ask why this is happening. Why this break in the compact between the generations which has sustained schooling and support for children for so long? There are many reasons for what is happening today.

The Reagan-Bush Legacy: The Legitimization of Greed

If one characteristic marks the changes which took place within the United States during the years of the Reagan-Bush presidencies, it is the legitimization of greed. One part of this greediness is seen in the massive tax cuts, "the voodoo economics" which decimated many federal programs while at the same time amassing more federal debt than all previous administrations from George Washington to Jimmy Carter combined. But the national greed went much further than federal tax policy. In the scandals of Wall Street insider trading to the looting of the nation's banks and savings and loan institutions, to the greed and ruthlessness of street-level crime, there seemed to be a general loss of social morality and restraint in an era presided over primarily by the genial and obviously rich presidents and their even richer friends who symbolized the age. Unfortunately, the election of Bill Clinton and the end of the Reagan-Bush era as done little to change the situation. While "national service" became a briefly popular theme in the early years of the Clinton administration, the new-style Democrat president showed little ability or inclination to challenge the fundamental ethos of the nation. While Republicans and Democrats argue over the size of tax cuts and the time-tables for balancing the budgets, the underlying economic divisions are going unchallenged.

Two Societies, Separate and Unequal

We also know that, as the census is now confirming, the children of this nation are increasingly nonwhite and from recent immigrant communities, while many of those who vote on taxes are white, older, and childless. We are becoming split apart. While many ask how people can care so little about the children who are the next generation of this country, the reality is that the majority of today's children are not the biological children of the majority of those who vote and set policy. In unprecedented numbers whites are having few children or remaining childless, while newer immigrants and people of color are highly represented among the nation's youth. This demographic divide between young and old, fueled by the nation's long heritage of racism, goes a very long way toward explaining the lack of concern for children which is so much a part of today's reality.

Racism, like greed, has also been legitimized in the America of the 1980s and 1990s. While the era of the Civil Rights movement may not have changed the beliefs of many whites, it did change the language. Overtly racist talk became unacceptable in many circles. But no more. The talk show host who says "They are not like you, and they are not like me. . . . They are something apart . . . a different species . . . "[18] leaves little doubt who "they" are. And this language is allowed. And more seriously, such language provides both fuel and permission for the combination of individual acts and social policies which further disenfranchise a substantial portion of the nation's citizens.

Lisa Delpit's extraordinary book, *Other People's Children: Cultural Conflict in the Classroom*, describes the reality faced by too many children of color in the United States at the end of the century.[19] They are taught by white teachers who far too often fail to understand or value their culture and their contribution to the larger society. But while Delpit vividly describes the split between the growing percentages of students of color and the still all too often all white teaching staffs, the issue at the level of social policy is even worse. School boards, state education agencies, and most of all voters fail to reflect the demographic changes among children and youth. There is a huge split between those who are in school and those who control school policies. It is truly a case of European Americans having undue influence in the education of "other people's children." And in too many cases, those with the power neither want to understand nor see a reason to appreciate the contribution of the others.

School's Responsibility: Having Claimed Too Much

Not all of the reasons for the lack of public support for public education can be placed on others, however. We who make our professional lives in this field must own our responsibilities also. Almost three decades ago, in the midst of a very different era in this nation's view of schooling, Charles Silberman wrote in his classic, *Crisis in the Classroom*:

> We will not be able to create and maintain a humane society unless we create and maintain classrooms that are humane. But if we succeed in

that endeavor—if we accomplish the remaking of American education—we will have gone a long way toward the larger task.[20]

In a sense, Silberman was merely restating vintage progressive educational
rhetoric from the turn of the century. But he was also catching the spirit of
the now much maligned 1960s, a time when many believed that the government could play a meaningful role in building a more humane society and
that public education was one of the important means to that end. Decades
later that vision has faded drastically. Silberman's rhetoric sounds hollow and
naive. Public confidence in all of society's institutions has declined drastically, but especially in the schools. This change too must be understood
before it can be reversed.

There are in fact many reasons for the significant shift in public attitudes.
For one thing, the educators of the 1960s claimed more for the schools than
the schools could possibly deliver. When Lyndon Johnson said that, "The
answer for all of our national problems comes down to one single word:
education," he claimed too much. But the claim was useful; it fit the spirit of
the times, and it certainly helped ensure growing educational budgets. These
budgets were important. From federal scholarships for graduate study to Head
Start, the Great Society programs did open schools to many who had always
previously been excluded. Unfortunately, the claims also guaranteed a reaction. When increased educational budgets didn't solve all of the nation's
problems, when poverty didn't go away, people began to wonder if the schools
could solve any problems.

A generation of scholars, led by Christopher Jencks, reviewed many of the
educational reforms of the 1960s and concluded that the "association between
one variety of inequality and another is usually quite weak, which means that
equalizing one thing is unlikely to have much effect on the degree of inequality in other areas."[21] Thus they questioned—and led many others who had
more mixed motives to question—if schools could be of much help in building a more egalitarian society.

At the same time, the last decades have not been kind ones for public
institutions of any sort. It should not be surprising in the decades after the war
in Vietnam, after Watergate, after Iran-Contra, that people do not trust large
governmental institutions. In these decades, schools in many parts of the
country have had their own Watergates. Stories of waste and outright corrup-
tion seemed to appear in many places, in the use of new federal funds and
in the continued use of traditionally raised tax moneys.[22] Building public
support when there is so little public trust is exceedingly difficult. No wonder

that those who see "restructuring" rather than new programs needing new funds, as the solution to many of the school's problems receive such a sympathetic hearing.

We who are concerned with improving education have also added to a public misperception of schooling. In cataloguing the failures of schools, which we must do, we have also contributed to a public perception that schools just don't work. Many who are concerned with education have been grateful for the light thrown on the school's failures by a generation of critics such as Jonathan Kozol whose first book, *Death At An Early Age,*[23] showed both the racism and the stifling of the human spirit which can happen in school. We have been glad also when critics have challenged the grandiose assumptions of those who have claimed that schools would solve all of our problems. We have, as we must, engaged in a public debate about schooling, and we should not apologize about that.

But now we do have a problem on our hands. We have criticized and hoped for change. Like David Tyack and his colleagues we have challenged the failures of schools to live up to their potential and now, "we are coming to feel rather like the railroad buff who complains about dirty cars, poor food, and bumpy roadbeds on Amtrak only to find others nodding and suggesting that passenger trains be abolished."[24] Whether it is through the strangulation of budget cutting measures, or through the more direct proposals to transfer resources away from schools, especially urban schools, we find our institution in a situation not too far from Amtrak's, with many wondering if the enterprise can or should survive. Clearly it is time for us to challenge this negativism quite directly.

Strategies for Fighting Back

In these bad times, it is essential not to give in to despair and discouragement. There are times when cynicism represents an accurate analysis, but there are more times when it is a refuge from commitment to the hard work of bringing about changes. There are many today who are working for change. There are many movements afoot which, if nourished and supported, will help to change the meanness of the times. No one policy will solve all of the problems facing today's children and their schools. But taken together, there are more than enough encouraging movements to give hope to those who are committed to educating the whole child in spite of the difficulties of the times. They need attention and support.

Reclaiming a Progressive Vision

In a very useful study, Patrick Shannon has traced the historical split which occurred soon after the beginning of this century within the progressive education movement between those who focused primarily on the child-centered school and those who gave primary attention to education as a means of social change. Shannon correctly notes that the inclusion of both a vision of social change and a focus on the child as the center of the curriculum has always been difficult to maintain, "and most progressive educators tipped the scales toward either the child-centered or community-centered schools."[25] Shannon's historical analysis is perceptive. But more important, his call for reuniting the two segments of progressivism provides an important agenda for late twentieth-century progressives.

A child-centered school with no social vision, as George Counts reminded us sixty years ago, can too easily be like "a baby shaking a rattle, we seem to be utterly content with action, provided it is sufficiently vigorous and noisy . . . .The weakness of progressive education thus lies in the fact that it has elaborated no theory of social welfare, unless it be that of anarchy or extreme individualism."[26] On the other hand, if we become merely advocates of social change without giving serious attention to the liberation of the students in our classes who have a primary claim on us as educators we have truly become the "voice crying in the wilderness." And we have cut ourselves off from the children who are our future. If we are to have an educational vision worthy of the name, we must focus on the education of the whole child—all children—and we must also remember that we are not effectively educating children if we prepare them only for the world as it is. We need always to maintain a larger vision and work for its fulfillment.

Education Should Build on Every Child's Strengths

Too much of education begins with a deficit model. When children are labeled—as the first act of preparing for their education—as in need of special education, in need of bilingual education, in need of other models to make up various deficits, something very important has already been lost.[27]

Perhaps it is in the realm of multicultural and bilingual education that this issue of a deficit model can be seen most clearly. In one of the most well-publicized of the national reports which appeared in the mid-1980s, the Report of the Twentieth Century Fund Task Force on Federal Elementary and Secondary Education Policy, challenged bilingual education programs. Out of a commitment that "students in elementary school learn to read, write, speak, and listen in English" (a commitment which very few would challenge), the task force recommended that "federal funds now going to bilingual programs be used to teach non-English-speaking children how to speak, read, and write in English." While avoiding a clear discussion of the implications of their recommendations, the task force seemed to recognize that it was essentially gutting a significant funding source which bilingual education programs have had and that the result of the recommendations would be the end of bilingual education as it has been known.

In the very next paragraph, however, the task force moved on to note that "young men and women with proficiency in foreign languages are sorely needed now that we are increasingly involved in competitive trade and investment with the rest of the world." They therefore made it clear that they wanted "every American public school student to have the opportunity to acquire proficiency in a second language." While some members of the task force used dissenting comments to note the contradiction between these two statements, the majority of the distinguished educators on this task force seemed comfortable with the obvious discrepancies in their two recommendations which appear only a paragraph apart.[28]

From an outsiders perspective, it seems that what the Twentieth Century Fund task force, and far too many other voices in education, seem to want is that every child who comes to the schools speaking another language be treated as having "a problem," and urged to forget that language and learn only in English as quickly as possible. At the same time the monolingual English-speaking student, who has a different deficit, should be urged to learn a second language with almost equal speed.

If schools are seen as the only source of knowledge, dispensing knowledge into the generally empty heads of passive students, then there is a certain logic to these odd recommendations. If, however, we view schools as one of many institutions which can help children learn and grow, then a very different logic takes over. Why not have bilingual programs which help students who speak another tongue learn English well while at the same time growing in their strength in the first language? Indeed, why not have schools such as the Rafael Hernandez in Boston which offer two-way bilingual programs in which the students who come to school speaking primarily a language other than English become teachers of the English-speaking children who want to gain a second language, while at the same time those with English as a first language also have the opportunity to teach and learn from their peers as well as from their teachers. The differences in these diverse models of bilingual instruction are not merely structural matters. They represent fundamentally different ways of viewing children as learners.

Paulo Freire stated this difference most dramatically when he wrote the now familiar words in *Pedagogy of the Oppressed* about the kind of education which becomes "an act of depositing, in which the students are the depositories and the teacher is the depositor. Instead of communicating, the teacher issues communiqués and makes deposits which the students patiently receive, memorize, and repeat." Freire contrasts this "banking" method of education with that of the "humanist, revolutionary educator," who must always be engaged with the students "in critical thinking and the quest for mutual humanization. . . . To achieve this, [the teacher] must be a partner of the student in his relations with them."[29] If teachers in the 1990s are going to challenge the mean-spiritedness of the times, then they are going to have to be "humanist, revolutionary educators," recruiting the children as our allies, treating them with respect as people who can be partners, not merely passive subjects.

It is only as children and youth are treated as full contributors to the school and the social good that democracy is real for them. Then, and only then, a different vision of the nation, and the contribution which every child can make to building the nation, can emerge. Antonia Darder is right:

> We are in search of America but not the America that for so long has been defined by Euro-Americans. We are in search of the true America— an America of multiple cultures, multiple histories, multiple regions, multiple realities, multiple identities, multiple ways of living, surviving, and being human. No where is this struggle for the true America more profoundly being waged than in the classrooms of public schools in the United States.[30]

And if the struggle can be won in the nation's classrooms, and in the way we view the children and youth who inhabit them, we will have come a long way towards envisioning that America in the rest of the society.

Ending Tracking

Perhaps the point at which schools most fail to build on the strengths which every child brings is in the persistent pattern of tracking which can be found in the vast majority of the nation's schools. There are few areas in education where theory and practice so thoroughly diverge as in the battle over tracking. For a generation, researchers and advocates have developed a significant body of literature showing the negative impact of tracking on those students slotted for the lower tracks while at the same time showing that the most advanced students also benefit from an untracked school. Very few voices have been raised in favor of tracking. Yet the vast majority of schools remain tracked. The unpublished folk wisdom of large segments of the teaching profession along with the fears of many parents continues to mean that tracking is seen by many as the only realistic means of instruction in most school situations.[31]

In the midst of this odd reality, Anne Wheelock's *Crossing the Tracks: How "Untracking" Can Save America's Schools* accomplishes two very important goals. First, Wheelock locates the struggle against tracking directly in the quest for democracy. Second, Wheelock challenges the folk wisdom that "it can't be done" by providing clear examples of schools across the country which have, in fact, moved to significantly different models of instruction.

At the outset of the book, Wheelock sets the work of those educators who are "untracking" schools in a democratic context. These are the people who are, "extending their thinking, talents, and time toward realizing deeply held convictions about democracy and schooling."[32] In a forward Jeannie Oakes elaborates on the theme. The battle over tracking, according to Oakes, is really a symbol for a larger struggle over the purpose of education:

Another norm that bolsters and legitimizes tracking is the American emphasis on competition and individualism over cooperation and the good of the community—a norm suggesting that "good" education is a scarce commodity available only to a few winners. Although the American system of public education was designed to promote the common good and to prepare children for participation in a democratic society, more recent emphasis has been placed on what a graduate can "get out" of schooling in terms of income, power, or status.[33]

In reality, the American system of education has always been torn between promoting the common good and selecting and nurturing a few winners who will be the leaders—and prime beneficiaries—of the society. Tracking is an ideal means of accomplishing the latter goal, for it identifies differences early and builds on them throughout schooling. A very different model is needed, however, if the other goal—the democratic goal—is to be central.

In her survey of schools from Massachusetts to California, Wheelock describes both the political context and the pedagogical methods of untracking.

A principal from Kentucky noted the first essential political move:

> You have to give parents the guarantee that their child is not going to
> be harmed. Parents ask, "Can you be sure my child is not going to be
> worse off?" I can say "She won't be worse off, and we hope she will
> be better off."[34]

This process, like all democratic processes, takes time. The schools where
effective untracking took place were schools which had long series of meetings over a significant time period. They were also schools where the evidence of successful heterogeneously grouped schools was presented and
reviewed. Parents know when they have real voice and when they are simply
being consulted after the fact. Only the former builds a lasting base for
change.

The pedagogical opportunities which came with heterogeneous groupings,
in the schools which did move toward them, were significant. Students were
engaged in new ways to pool their experiences and envision new possibilities. In the process new structures emerged as schools put into practice the
call for a relevant education of Jerome Bruner who said, "Let the skills of
problem solving be given a chance to develop on problems that have an
inherent passion—whether racism, crimes in the street, pollution, war and
aggression, or marriage and the family."[35]

Clearly all of this only works when there is a "climate of high expectations
and participatory learning for all," when there is support for "teachers' readi-
ness for change and willingness to take risks," and when there is a "rich,
high-level curriculum that reflects the goal of preparing students for a multiplicity of productive adult roles."[36] But then no educational reform works
without these resources. They are the prerequisites of a democratic structure
of education, and when they are present, as Wheelock amply demonstrates,
the radically democratic step of "untracking" works and works well.

Attacking Sexism

If we are to foster a democratic educational system which is inclusive of all
children, which builds on the strengths every child brings to school, the issue
of gender also needs careful attention. Far too often in our dialogue about
education the issue of gender has been separated from the discussion of the
building of a multicultural democracy. Progressive educators may be attentive
to both issues, but usually at different times and in different discourses.
However, we cannot afford that separation. As bell hooks has reminded us:

When feminism is defined in such a way that it calls attention to the diversity of women's social and political reality, it centralizes the experiences of all women, especially the women whose social conditions have been least written about, studied, or changed by political movements.

And she continues:

Sexist oppression is of primary importance not because it is the basis of all other oppression, but because it is the practice of domination most people experience, whether their role be that of discriminator or discriminated against, exploiter or exploited. It is the practice of domination most people are socialized to accept before they even know what other forms of group oppression exist.[37]

All of us who work with young children know this reality. We may not see overt race and class discrimination in our kindergarten classes (although we may), but we will certainly see sexism and sex role stereotyping.

In this case, researchers remind us of what early childhood educators already know. As Joanne Hendrick and Terry Strange's research shows:

By age four, both sexes were exhibiting these differing styles in one aspect of conversational behavior . . . [And] teachers were reinforcing that behavior by giving children subtle but consistent messages about what constitutes appropriate sex role behavior as they modeled submissive adult female behavior during conversation. The teachers taught this message to the boys by interrupting less when the boys were talking. Moreover, they made no attempt to balance the larger number of interruptions boys made as compared to those made by girls by encouraging the girls to speak up, or suggesting that the boys make "space" for the girls to join in.[38]

Whatever the causes of this reality, an inclusive democratic society cannot be built if it is ignored.

Too often we in education have accepted not only the split between boys and girls, but the split between the few who think great thoughts and the many who do the work of society. And few females have been included in the former class. As Charlotte Bunch has noted:

Certainly most women are not expected to take control, and, in consequence, are not encouraged to think analytically. In fact, critical thinking is the antithesis of woman's traditional role. Women are supposed to worry about mundane survival problems, to brood about fate, and to fantasize in a personal manner. We are not meant to think analytically about society, to question the way things are, or to consider how things could be different.[39]

It is this very matter of questioning the way things are and considering how things could be different that is at the heart of building a democratic society. If we are serious about this business, then we need to address it from the very beginning, in the ways we respond to very young girls, and very young boys, in our schools every day.

Educate the Whole Child:
Mind and Body/Thinking, Play, Work

Dividing people up by gender, by race, by class, and by learning style is not, however, the only way in which schools work against wholeness and health for children. Early childhood educators have long known what too many of their colleagues who teach older children seem to forget, that individual children cannot be divided between their minds and their bodies. Perhaps it is the origin of the kindergarten in the work of Friedrich Froebel which reminds us of his assertion, made over one hundred years ago, that it is play which "confirms, strengthens, and clears up in the mind of the child a feeling and perception deeply grounded in and important to the whole life of man— the feeling and perception of oneness and individuality, and of disjunction and separateness.[40] If all educators, at all levels, could continue to understand this essential role of play and fun in all of education, perhaps some of the deadly dullness which our enterprise sometimes takes on would be lifted.[41]

Education which begins to divide children up into their separate parts cannot be a form of education which prepares children, or their teachers, to engage in the struggle for a healthy world. Just as we cannot have some people who think about a democratic future and others who try to build it, we cannot divide individual children between work and play or between the life of the mind and the needs of their bodies. In another context, the philosopher of education, Walter Feinberg has reminded us that, "there is nothing contradictory between a liberal and a vocational education insofar as the vocational work provides a way for a student to try on different modes of being. There is only something wrong when the vocational work is taken up to preclude reflection and to reinforce an already limited field."[42]

The split between liberal and vocational—or intellectual and "hands on" learning—is coming earlier and earlier in schooling. Teachers of young children know the value of play and the reality that play and study are united in helping the student "try on different modes of being" and of growing. It is later in education—unfortunately not much later—when the testing and sorting begins, when some students are groomed for the intellectual life of thinking and reflection . . . for college . . . and others are tracked for the world of work, when vocational education becomes a means to "preclude reflection and to reinforce an already limited field." In this latter understanding of vocationalism students are prepared for a world in which their own contribution will be to take orders rather than to reflect critically. But taking orders without thinking is fundamentally contradictory to democracy, and if we are educators for democracy we must find other ways in which to envision the world of work and the preparation for it in school.

Finding better ways of linking the world of work to the classroom, without falling into a too easy tracking of students, some for work and some for intellectual pursuits, is an essential part of a meaningful democratic education. It also takes seriously the fact that human beings are whole creatures; that the individual's physical and mental pursuits are much more thoroughly linked than the curriculum of most schools would seem to admit.

The best forms of pedagogy already recognize this reality and help students engage in projects which build on their own interests. Thus Howard Gardner says:

> I often hypothesize that people probably learn more from the few projects they do in school than from hundreds and hundreds of hours of lectures and homework assignments. I imagine that many people end up finding their vocation or avocation because they stumbled into a project and discovered they were really interested in it.[44]

The time has come for a thorough revisioning of the structures of instruction so that all education is connected to the "real world" of student's interests. If this is done well, all education is vocational education in that it can play a part in helping children use the real world, the world of making things and accomplishing meaningful tasks—of making a contribution—in their school experiences even at the level of the earliest grades.

As we reflect on the lives of young children in America today, the statements made by George Counts sixty years ago come to mind once again:

Perhaps one of the greatest tragedies of contemporary society lies in the fact that the child is becoming increasingly isolated from the serious activities of adults. Some would say that such isolation is an inevitable corollary of the growing complexity of the social order. In my opinion it is rather the product of a society that is moved by no great commanding ideals and is consequently victimized by the most terrible form of human madness—the struggle for private gain.[44]

We do not have to be considering setting up machine shops in our kindergartens or sending five-year-olds off to work to argue that real play involves real things, and that an overly protected corner for young children separates them from the world of the future in most unfortunate ways.

Health

When we talk about educating the whole child, we are not only talking about issues of what is traditionally called pedagogy. We are also talking about being attentive to all of the needs of children, intellectual and physical. It has become very fashionable of late to talk about the need to free teachers from the mundane matters of attending to children's needs so that they can focus their work on the life of children's minds. While the complaint by overworked teachers that they are being asked to do too much is certainly understandable, these attempts to divide up the teaching profession ultimately divide up children. We call for one specialist for their minds, another specialist for their physical needs, and, of course, a therapist or a social worker for their psyches. The reality of children's lives is not, however, so easily divided.

Speaking of the problems facing urban educators at the beginning of the twentieth century, the late Lawrence Cremin wrote:

> The teachers of New York, for example, found themselves giving hundreds of baths each week. The syllabi said nothing about baths, and the teachers themselves wondered whether bathing was their charge. But there were the children and there were the lice![45]

We who teach at the end of the century can do no less than try to meet the equivalent needs of our students.

Smaller classes in which teachers could attend to the multiple realities of their children would serve education much more than the growing hierarchy coupled with the array of specialists who currently work in our schools. The old dividing line in which the teacher is responsible for the child until 3:00 p.m. when the social worker takes over just doesn't work. It never did, and in today's complex world it should be shed as quickly as possible. Such a change involves major changes in professional identity, especially for teachers and social workers, but also for those involved in educating professionals or setting school policy. It involves breaking down old professional walls and envisioning teaching in new and creative ways.

There are many ways for schools to respond to the many needs of their students. Indeed schools are usually the institution in the best position to respond. In New York City, at Franklyn K. Lane High School, serving one of the poorest neighborhoods in Queens, a student health center is being established to serve the health needs of a student body where, according to one school official, "On any given day, about 700 of the school's 4,000 students are absent and in need of medical care for 'acute or chronic illness.'" If we followed the recommendations of those who say that we must free teachers from the mundane matters of attending to children's needs so that they can focus their work on the life of children's minds, school officials would simply say that the health of the students is someone else's problem. "We are here to teach them—to serve their minds—the health of their bodies belongs to another department." But over-specialization of this sort won't work. Obviously, an unhealthy student will not learn well. A caring person must care for all aspects of a child's life. Thus, the *New York Times* cited David Kaplain:

> If you are going to reach kids at a time when intervention and prevention may have some impact, then you have to get to them early, and where they are. A school based health center is just an easy way to reach kids and address some of their issues.[46]

The logic is undebateable. Yet in spite of the valiant efforts of educators like those at Franklyn K. Lane, the general trend is in the opposite direction. In 1970 400 physicians worked in the New York City Public Schools. By 1993, as a result of two decades of budget cuts, the number had been cut to 23 and most of these were part-time.[47] This is for a public school system of a million students! If we are not addressing the issues which our students are bringing to us, including their health issues, we are not educating the whole person. Clearly we have a long way to go.[48]

Parent Involvement

When Elizabeth Peabody and Pauline Agassiz Shaw began the first kindergartens in Boston in the 1880s, their goal was a safe and caring environment for
children from the city's poorest neighborhoods. The kindergarten teachers
taught in the school for three hours a day and then spent the rest of their time
visiting in the homes of the children, working with their parents, and learning
about their needs. The kindergarten movement, for all of its incorporation
into the rest of the city's—and the nation's—educational systems, has always
maintained a part of this vision. Teachers in the higher grades have much to
learn from what the kindergarten movement has to offer.

At times, the early kindergarten leaders in Boston and in other parts of the
United States had a condescending attitude toward the homes from which their
students came which did not serve them well and which we cannot accept
today. In reaching out to serve the whole child—and the families of these
children—there must always be respect and mutuality. We need to encourage
parents to be much more involved with teachers if we are to succeed in building the bridges to the life of the child. Parents, and children, naturally resent
one who seems to know best. But if we can build meaningful ties, we can also
build a new base for the support of the educational enterprise.

The movement to involve parents has been strong in education for many
years now. The work of places like the Institute for Responsive Education,
and many other advocacy groups, is based on the notion that parents must be
central participants along with teachers and students in this business of education. As the National Coalition of Advocates for Students Board of Inquiry
noted in 1985:

> Most schools fail to draw on the resources of students, parents, and
> teachers in the immediate school community or of citizens in the larger
> community. Nor do existing practices encourage broad participation in
> the affairs of schools.[49]

If schools are to serve "the whole child," there needs to be a change in this
reality. Children whose families and communities feel that they have little or
no role in setting school policy are not going to be enthusiastic participants
in their own education. Communities and citizens who feel excluded from
their schools are not going to rally to the support of schools in hard times.
If funding for education is seen as merely the support of teachers as one more
"interest group" then we will fail. If, however, funding is seen as an invest-

ment in the future, a future to be designed and controlled by all, then we will succeed. As Don Davies so wisely said: "Parent and citizen involvement in school policy and planning is a way to improve students' education, and the right way to do business in a democratic society."[50] As advocates for an effective and democratic education, we can do no less.

School Governance: Let's At Least Give Real School Based Management a Try!

School governance is certainly one of the key issues which must be considered in an examination of the links between democracy and education. Schools which are to serve and prepare future citizens for a democracy must, obviously, be governed democratically. But what does that mean?

In 1917, Cora Bigelow, the president of the Boston Teachers Club, wrote, "We Americans preach democracy but after all we are loath to practice it in many ways."[51] This is still too often the case. Students, teachers, and parents all sometimes feel that the schools exist for someone else. They are not treated with respect as learners or as citizens. This is a tragedy.

Teachers, parents, and students can all give many examples of the times in which they feel undervalued and excluded. Unfortunately the times in which teachers feel appreciated for their enthusiasm and commitment are all too rare. The situation is more often one in which teachers feel undermined and ineffective and in which students and parents feel dissatisfied and underserved.

Today's teachers can certainly give many examples of these problems. One New York City teacher told the National Coalition of Advocates for Students Board of Inquiry of his experiences:

> A school such as ours is currently only an outpost of the distant bureaucracy. Good ideas occur to someone in an office far removed from the school and these ideas are filtered down through layers of bureaucracy to the principal.[52]

Many other teachers could certainly report similar experiences in which good ideas are constantly subverted as they wend their way through the bureaucratic maze. To complain that teachers are not energetic, creative, daring innovators in such a situation is cynicism of the worst sort.

The distinguished education psychologist Seymour B. Sarason has proposed a sweeping restructuring of school governance in his 1995 volume

Parental Involvement and the Political Principle: Why the Existing Governance Structure of Schools Should Be Abolished. Sarason begins with some obvious, but regularly ignored, statements regarding the appropriate means of making decisions in schools or anywhere else. He begins with a bedrock political principle for a democracy: "when you are going to be affected, directly or indirectly, by a decision, you should stand in some relationship to the decision-making process."[53] Such a statement should be obvious for any structure which depends on even a modicum of good will. It is essential for one which carries a mandate for building a democratic society. But clearly contemporary school governance does not meet the test. In the examples in this chapter, in Sarason's book, and in the experiences of most people who work with schools as students, teachers, or parents, the relationship to much of the decision making is tangential in the extreme.

Sarason asks a second seemingly obvious question of all governance proposals. How will they actually improve the quality of schools and do they include "an attempt to define the concept of quality education and to indicate how" the proposal—in this case parental involvement—will actually accomplish the goal?[54] Clearly much of what currently passes for the governance process of modern schools, especially in large bureaucratized city systems, fails to meet this test.

Thus Sarason concludes: "Boards of education are an anachronism with an ancestry going back to the one-room schoolhouse. Whatever virtues they may have had no longer are evident or even possible. They are now part of the problem, not the solution."[55] Such a strong judgment, from a person who has spent as much time studying schools up close and who has shown as much deep commitment to improving the educational experiences of children and youth, must be taken seriously. Perhaps the time is right for his book to provoke a much needed debate.

In a much earlier study, Sarason speaks to some of the same issues in a discussion of the resistance of teachers to many administratively designed changes. "The negative or lukewarm reactions of the teachers can be understood from several standpoints," Sarason insists, "but the one that can be easily overlooked—and it certainly is by administrative personnel—is the one that focuses on the role of the teacher in formulating, developing, and carrying out a program." In his case study of teacher resistance to the introduction of teacher aides, Sarason continues:

> In every such program I observed, the teachers were presented with a ready made program, and in some instances they learned about it in the

local newspaper. The advice of teachers was never sought, the problems that could occur were never discussed, teachers were given no role in formulating a training or selection program, and needless to say, teachers had no opportunity to express the professional and personal problems and questions they might have about the use of aides.[56]

And yet, school authorities were surprised at teacher hostility to the program!

Sarason notes that it need not be so. "When teachers are an integral part of the development of the program, have an important role in the training of aides, and come to know them before they are introduced into the program, the teachers and the aides not only find it a mutually productive experience but the gain to the children is great." Yet teachers seldom experience this sort of inclusion. Why is change so difficult?[57]

Parents experience a very similar reality. The National Coalition of Advocates for Students (NCAS) Board of Inquiry reported:

From parents we heard about school practices and policies that present barriers to their involvement. They told us of many ways in which schools make them feel unwelcome. We heard about daily conflicts which arise in the classroom or the principal's office, where parents seeking more input are stymied by teachers and administrators, who perceive that their autonomy, turf, and professionalism are being challenged. We heard about school officials who developed very effective techniques for deflecting parents' attempts at involvement.[58]

This is a tragic waste of a resource which could be serving to make schools more effective. It is also, in terms of the values of a democratic society, simply wrong.

There is also a long history of parents fighting back against these means of exclusion. The community control movement of the 1960s was only the most dramatic in a whole series of struggles in which parents sought to gain greater voice in their children's education. Community control has been painted as an antiteacher, antiprofessional movement, and at times it was. But such need not be the case. Parents and teachers, after all, share the same basic goals—the best means of education for the children in the schools. Parents and teachers are also often equally frustrated by their inability to make an impact on seemingly impersonal school bureaucracies.

The community control movement which flowered in New York City and was seriously considered in many other locations in the late 1960s deserves further study for its lessons in the means of empowering parents and the concerned citizens of local communities. Born out of the Civil Rights movement, the struggle for community control of schooling in a number of northern cities provided several short-lived but very important examples of restructured school governance. For all of the faults of the movement, community control was one of the few serious experiments in giving parents and local communities—including especially very poor communities and communities of color—real power in deciding the basic policies and programs of the schools where their children were learning. No wonder the experiment was attacked so quickly and so savagely.

There is much to be learned from the community control campaign that could be of benefit in planning more effective schools. Most parents do not want to be involved in the development of curriculum or in system wide policies. But they do want access and a voice in decisions effecting their own children. They do not want to be shunted aside when they have a complaint or a suggestion. And if they feel that their child is not being well educated they want—and have a clear right—to the means of changing the situation.

It is not only parents and teachers who experience a lack of control over schools. Many students feel excluded by their schools. They do not feel that their interests are respected or their due-process rights honored. A student also told the NCAS Board of Inquiry:

> The ideology behind the present school system is based on the idea that students aren't going to want to be in school, aren't going to learn, and therefore someone has to make them. If you base a system on control rather than on interaction, the results are apathy, alienation, and dropouts. This is not the kind of experience to prepare students for active democratic involvement either in school or in the larger society.[59]

This is also not a means of encouraging students to be active participants in their own education. Given this reality, it is ironic that some advocates of the standards movement have little patience with school based management and other efforts to democratize school governance. Do they think that students who experience school as a place which has no respect for their curiosity or their commitment to learning are really going to reach the high standards which are being proposed?

There is a need for radical change in the way schools are run if democracy is to be a reality in their administration or if the energy which can be released by teacher, parent, and student empowerment can be tapped as a means of school improvement. But long-term restructuring may be an essential means to improve the schools. The school improvement literature produced by Ronald Edmonds and others comes back to some very basic issues around empowering local school personnel including the principal, teachers, parents and students. As Edmonds never tired of telling audiences, the characteristics of an effective school are not hard to find, and when they exist even the most "at risk" group of students can succeed. Effective schools, "must have strong administrative leadership without which the disparate elements of good schooling can neither be brought together nor kept together." And, "Schools that are instructionally effective for poor children have a climate of expectation in which no children are permitted to fall below minimum but efficacious levels of achievement."[60] Schools with strong and visionary leaders, schools in which teachers have high hopes and high expectations for their students and a sense of empowerment that allows them to proceed are schools where students succeed. But how many of today's bureaucratized school administrations help create this sort of school? Clearly not only Seymour Sarason but large numbers of teachers and principals would answer "not many."

The school-based-management movement, like the campaigns for community control in the 1960s or the call for teacher councils at the time of the First World War, has the potential to radically democratize school governance and the equal potential to provide a veneer of democracy while maintaining the status quo. Indeed, it is hard to find an educator who opposes school-based management in the 1990s, but there are as many different definitions of school-based management as there are reformers using the term. Nevertheless, school-based management in its most radical form provides the potential for a much more democratic and community-based form of school governance. It can provide much of the radical reform which both Seymour Sarason and the advocates for community control of schools have called for for decades.

Real school-based management means that real power and budget freedom must be moved from school boards, superintendents, and central offices to the individual schools. School improvement happens at the level of individual schools not systems. This has clear implications:

1. Principals must be seen as the "educational leaders" of their institutions and given sufficient budget, personnel, and structural flexibility to allow them to make real changes. Without authority principals cannot be held accountable for the success of their schools. With authority they can and must be held accountable.

2. Ways need to be found to include teachers, parents, and at the high school level, students, along with representatives of the community at large in the development of school policy and procedures. Local councils with real authority devolving from the school board must function as the real board of education for each school. This is more than a matter of finding local ways to carry out the mandates of a central office. It means giving these councils the authority to decide the mandates which their school will meet and the goals which the teachers and principal of that school will be expected to achieve in their work with the students.

If these changes are made, then the central administration of each school system, including everything above the level of individual schools such as district offices, must be examined carefully to ensure that it serves only those functions which can best be served on a systemwide basis. It is a significant change from a "command and control" view of central offices to viewing them as the servant of the local schools, but it must happen. Generally this means that central administrations should be limited to two roles, providing necessary services and ensuring basic standards. Services would include a systemwide personnel policy and contract with the teachers union. Unions should not have to negotiate with smaller units and they would naturally oppose any changes which would move in that direction. Standards would include academic standards, desegregation of the system, a commitment to equity for all students—especially those with special needs—and effective student retention.

These are significant changes, but the problems facing our schools require significant change. Mistakes will be made in these schools but the potential for mistakes, even sometimes serious mistakes, is no excuse for not breaking down the numbing discouragement of the current large educational bureaucracies which now make more than their share of very serious mistakes. If the current structure of schooling in most cities and towns in this country accomplishes anything, it makes it virtually impossible to hold anyone accountable for failure, for too few people have the power to make real changes. If failures happen in truly decentralized school systems, at least they can be quickly identified and appropriate changes made.

Some of the most effective schools in the nation are small private schools with a limited number of students and teachers accountable to a board of parent and community representatives. Public schools may have something to learn from such examples. Parents must have access at the point they most want access, the experience of their own child in school. Teachers, at the same time, must have the freedom to design and carry out instructional plans without the creativity-numbing bureaucratic rules and regulations which too often plague our schools. Experiments with radically different kinds of schools must be available in every city.

On the other hand, these changes need not mean a move to neighborhood-based schools which would not be possible in many cities because of the needs to desegregate a school system in the face of a segregated housing pattern. If one looks at some of the best private schools, they draw students from a wide area, but the institutions themselves are relatively small, parents have a major voice, teachers are treated with respect, and policies are decided at the institutional level. Any school district could move in this direction without either privatizing any of the system or challenging the need for desegregation. It is a change worth exploring.

Quality schools are not created by school committees or by rules and regulations from headquarters, but rather by committed teachers and principals working closely with parents and students and communities to build a learning environment in which every child succeeds. If history teaches us anything about school structure it is that asking questions about the size and make up of the school committee or whether it should be elected or appointed is asking the wrong set of questions. It is time for us to turn our attention to the questions that do matter, questions of how we create meaningful learning environments at the school level and how we distribute power so that parents, teachers, and students are the primary players in school matters. Everyone else, from superintendent to school board to state and federal education agencies is support staff.

Teaching Democracy in our Schools

In the famous report of President Reagan's Commission on Excellence in Education, *A Nation at Risk*, the authors noted the link of schooling to democracy and "the honorable word 'patriotism.' " Having done so in the introduction, however, the authors also moved on to frame the whole report in terms of the nation's risk because "our once unchallenged preeminence in commerce, industry, science, and technological innovation is being overtaken by competitors throughout the world."[61] The resulting prescriptions for change were not surprising given this harsh assessment of the role of schooling— raise the standards and get tough with the students. This is not the kind of democratic education which is going to challenge the anti-child and anti-democratic sentiments which are abroad in the land today.

Samuel Bowles and Herbert Gintis have called for a new, and very different, theory of democratic education which

> must develop a conception of personal development in which schooling is treated as a means of rendering students capable of controlling their lives as citizens, family members, workers, and community members, and in which the educational process induces students to control increasingly substantial spheres of their education as they move from early to later levels of schooling.[62]

Here then is the split which we face today. Is the purpose of schooling only to produce a new generation of citizens capable of working hard enough and creatively enough to put this nation back on top of the world economy? Or are we talking about a new generation which—in their ability to control their own lives and give voice to their deepest aspirations—will lead the United States not only to prosperity but may also help lead this nation to be a voice for justice and democracy for all citizens of this country and for the people of this planet? Idealistic as this may sound, this must be the fundamental question in today's debates about school reform.

In the midst of the Great Depression, George Counts called on teachers to dare to build a new social order. He reminded the teachers of the 1930s "that the educational problem is not wholly intellectual in nature." Counts insisted that until we could enlist children themselves in a struggle for a better world, we were failing to offer them a proper education.

> Our Progressive schools therefore cannot rest content with giving children an opportunity to study contemporary society in all of its aspects. This of course must be done, but I am convinced that they should go much farther. If schools are to be really effective, they must become centers for building, not merely for the contemplation, of our civilization. This does not mean that we should endeavor to promote particular reforms through the educational system. We should, however, give to our children a vision of the possibilities which lie ahead and endeavor to enlist their loyalties and enthusiasms in the realization of that vision.[63]

That is a challenge for all of us. Too often, in our fear of promoting "particular reforms" or imposing our own values, we have conducted our schools as a valueless place where practical, but neutral, skills are imparted. We educators have too often absented ourselves from the struggle to shape a new world in the place where we have the most opportunity to do it, our own class-rooms. The result is that, as Counts warned us, we teachers seem to the outside world to be "moved by no great faiths; we are touched by no great passions." We need to hear again Counts' pleas:

> We cannot, by talk about the interests of children and the sacredness of personality, evade the responsibility of bringing to the younger genera-tion a vision which will call forth their active loyalties and challenge them to creative and arduous labors.[64]

This challenge, of projecting a vision which will call forth active loyalties, in ourselves and our students, is the one which we face today if we are to challenge the anti-child society in which we live. It is a calling we can no longer avoid.

Making Education an Experience in Democracy

Any discussion of the relationship of democracy to education which stops with the rhetoric of enlightened citizens has only scratched the surface of the issue. John Dewey noted the deeper issues three-quarters of a century ago when he wrote in *Democracy and Education*:

> The devotion of democracy to education is a familiar fact. The super-ficial explanation is that a government resting upon popular suffrage cannot be successful unless those who elect and who obey their gov-ernors are educated. . . . But there is a deeper explanation. A democracy is more than a form of government; it is primarily a mode of associated living, of conjoint communicated experience.[65]

Dewey is quite simply saying that for democracy to work well we must learn to live together and talk to each other. It is a simple enough idea, but its realization in a diverse and pluralistic society is exceedingly difficult. It is only with an education which provides both the tools of communication and the experience of building an inclusive community with differing peoples which can form a base for the success of this sort of democracy.

Certainly Dewey was correct that the belief that popular suffrage requires educated voters is a familiar but also a superficial explanation of the connec-tion between popular education and democratic society. Far deeper is the fundamental premise of democracy that power truly belongs to all of the people and indeed that "governments derive their just powers from the consent of the governed." This radical faith in popular power cannot be content with a form of acculturation in which schools help a diverse citizenry adjust to the values of a leadership class. On the contrary, a real democracy demands that the schools help all citizens engage in learning from each other and talking with each other so that common values and a common image of the good society can emerge. Schools, as George Counts said, must be not only democratically administered and must not only teach the values of a democratic society, they must—in the experience they offer their students— be vehicles for building a truly democratic culture in this country if they are to merit the term democratic schools. The immediate implications of such a faith for education are quite basic.

As a first step, it would seem obvious that schools in a democratic society should be run democratically. Yet this is hardly the case. Many commentators have noted the strange reality that schools, which are supposed to be our society's major vehicle for training youth for participation in democracy, are themselves one of the less democratic institutions in the society. As noted earlier in this chapter, schools seem to be run by impersonal bureaucracies with strongly hierarchical decision making by distant experts and administrators. Citizens, teachers, and students all find themselves treated as troublemakers when they attempt to be more than passive participants in decisions about public education.

The current structures under which schools are conducted are not new, but they are not the only options available. The bureaucratic, hierarchical system of educational organization began to emerge in the late nineteenth century when a new breed of professional administrators sought, with growing success, to displace both school boards and teachers as the real managers of public education. Under the banner of "taking the schools out of politics" these superintendents and their staffs have made themselves increasingly invulnerable to the demands of either public concern or the voices of teachers and students in their own institutions.[66] As Sheldon Wolin has noted, "Citizens cannot be expected to measure up to the demands of democratic political life if their formative experience in the workplace teaches hierarchy, subordination, discipline, and a fragmented experience."[67] Few workplaces teach hierarchy, subordination, and discipline more thoroughly than do the public schools, both to the teachers and their students.

This reality is far from being a theoretical issue. It is a day-to-day experience which both teachers and students find mind-numbing. The hierarchical model pervades both the structures of schooling and the ways most people think about schools. Seymour Sarason provides a dramatic example when he describes his own experience in leading a workshop for teachers which focused on their assumptions about appropriate classroom behavior.

> What I became aware of during the discussion was that these teachers thought about children in precisely the same way that teachers say that school administrators think about teachers, that is, administrators do not discuss matters with teachers, they do not act as if the opinions of teachers were important, they treat teachers like a bunch of children, and so on.[68]

In my own first year of teaching, many years ago, a colleague said to me, "You have to remember, Jim, the New York City Public Schools are run on the assumption that everyone at every level is a total idiot and only the level above will do things right." Unless not only the systems and structures of education but the very intellectual construct of school is thoroughly transformed and radically democratized, it makes no sense to talk of such things as empowering teachers or engaging students in active learning.

The most obvious victims of this shift in power have been the teachers themselves. Popular anger at the lack of accountability in schooling has spilled over to teachers as well as administrators. Many teachers have indeed internalized the sense that it is unprofessional to see themselves as accountable to a wider public of students, parents, or concerned citizens. But blaming teachers as a group only creates unproductive divisions among those who should be fighting for better public education. Teachers generally feel as excluded as other citizens when important educational decisions are made.

What is said of teachers can be said even more of students. Perhaps the most undemocratic note in the Commission on Excellence report is its closing word to students. Students are encouraged to give their best efforts to learning, and to seek to obtain knowledge and skills which will give them some control of their future destiny. There is no mention of controlling their present destiny or making important decisions about their immediate role as students and consumers in an educational system which often fails miserably to meet their immediate needs for significant and interesting experiences.[69]

This note about students leads immediately to the next question which must be faced in a discussion of democracy and education. It is not just the structure of the schools but the curriculum and the way we view the meaning and purpose of the institution which must be democratic if schools are to help fit the next generation for participation in a democratic society. Students cannot be asked to passively receive instruction for active future involvement in society.

Paulo Freire reminds us of the undemocratic nature of what he calls the "fundamentally narrative character" of much current educational practice. He warns of the danger of a curriculum in which, "Instead of communicating, the teacher issues communiqués and makes deposits which the students patiently receive, memorize, and repeat." Besides being ineffective most of the time—the communiqués are not being received well in the 1990s—this sort of education teaches the opposite set of values from those needed in a democratic society. In a truly liberating education, "Knowledge emerges only through invention and re-invention, through the restless, impatient, continuing helpful inquiry people pursue in the world, with the world, and with each other."[70] This is a conception of education which has been much maligned in recent times. Certainly it has been misused in the hands of lazy or incompetent people who allow mutual inquiry to become pointless conversation. But misuse does not discredit the basic assumption. Education which is top down in control or in pedagogical method is not education for a democracy. Education in which the student is only passive learner, and not active participant in the quest for knowledge, is not education which prepares citizens for their own role in society. A totalitarian curriculum may be appropriate for a totalitarian society, but not for a free one.

Of course, this idea is not new either. To quote Dewey again, seventy-five years ago he wrote of education not as "an affair of 'telling' and being told, but an active and constructive process. . . ."[71] With the optimism of his age, however, Dewey failed to recognize how difficult a change would be. Many are comfortable with hierarchy; many believe that they profit from it, and some do. But all discussions of democracy and education must take the democratic commitment to the heart of the educational process, to what the Commission on Excellence calls, "the very 'stuff' of education, the curriculum." If this is not dealt with democratically, nothing which follows will matter. The message to the students regarding ultimate values will already have been too clear.

It should not be surprising for people who do share a basic commitment to a radically democratic tradition, and who also care abut the future of public education, to find themselves turning to John Dewey's ideas. For all of his early-twentieth-century optimism, Dewey was quite clear that the link between democracy and education goes very deep. For a democracy, the commitment to education involves enlightening citizens, but far more it involves the continuous restoration and recreation of the idea of democracy itself as a powerful source of energy and vision.

It is as true now as it was in 1897:

> By law and punishment, by social agitation and discussion, society can regulate and form itself in a more or less haphazard and chance way. But through education society can formulate its own purposes, can organize its own means and resources, and thus shape itself with definiteness and economy in the direction in which it wishes to move.[72]

It is this very process of formulating and shaping the very nature and goals of society to which education must address itself. If this is done, then public education will be more than a training ground for jobs, it will be one of the places where fundamental discussions about the best shape of future economic policy will take place. If this is done, then public education will also be more than a training ground for voters, it will be one of the places in which people model what it means to live together and talk with each other with respect and with mutual commitments to a larger social good. All of this seems very far away at times, but it is a struggle worth the effort. In this sense, support for a truly democratic public school is support for a new way of ordering the nation's economic life, its political life, and its educational life

Children as Allies and Agents for Change

At this point, we have come full circle. Ultimately, the question is not serving the child, but enlisting the child as our ally, or, as Freire said, we must engage in "the quest for mutual humanization." Educating the whole child includes an assumption that the child is not just a passive recipient but an active partner in designing the goals of her or his own education and in shaping a yet to be more complete democracy. Indeed, there is no education worthy of the name in which the student can be passive.

Paulo Freire is far from the only one to recognize this. Part of American folk wisdom was expressed by a leader of the movement for the rights of the elderly who said, "Be careful of those who want to do something for you; they are likely to want to do something to you." The children of this nation, the children who are in our schools, and our human service agencies, and sometimes in our courts and juvenile justice centers are not merely the recipients of educational programs. As long as the nation's youth are seen as mere recipients of educational programs, their extraordinary energy and imagination will not be engaged in changing the schools or the larger society. Today's children and youth must be called on as the potential and necessary allies, or as George Counts said, they must be offered a vision, "which will call forth their active loyalties and challenge them to creative and arduous labors," if we are to make progress in addressing the greed of today and the injustices of history.

The hard times today are not just a shortage of cash for worthy programs. We seem also to lack great dreams and hopeful visions, among ourselves or as a heritage to give to our children. As Maxine Greene, a philosopher of education, has said:

> We live, after all, in dark times, times with little historical memory of any kind. . . . On the side streets of our great cities, in the crevices, in the burnt-out neighborhoods, there are the rootless, the dependent, the sick, the permanently unemployed. There is little sense of agency, even among the brightly successful; there is little capacity to look at things as if they could be otherwise.[73]

Unless we instill in the children we are serving, the dreams and visions to build a better tomorrow; unless our children regain the capacity "to look at things as if they could be otherwise," we will have failed in our quest to educate the whole child. Spirit and dreams and hopes are every bit as much a part of our children as their needs for skills learned in schools or healing of the psyche offered through counseling.

This is a difficult task. Educators who take as their goal revisioning the very nature of the democratic tradition will be labeled as dangerous radicals or dismissed as utopian dreamers with little to offer to the pressing needs of the classroom. But to do less is to abandon the consideration of the purposes of education and to give up the "capacity to look at things as if they could be otherwise." A democratic education must always begin with the extraordinary resources of the citizens themselves, including especially the young citizens who inhabit the nation's schools.

CHAPTER FIVE

Technology, Democracy, and School Policy

> It would be heartbreaking to look into the future only to see this wonderful network of access to knowledge for some people while others were excluded, or to see that education had become even more than in the past a breeding ground for intolerance and hatred . . . The only rational choice I see is to forge ahead in the encouragement of educational diversity with a dedicated commitment not only to expanding its benefits to all who want them but also to making sure that those who choose not to want them are making an informed choice.
>
> Seymour Papert, *The Children's Machine*

In the last decade, the computer has burst on the scene in American public education as the tool which will, in many people's minds, transform the nature of schooling. While national boards have met and national policy groups have debated the merits of one reform proposal or another, local school boards and superintendents have been in the process of buying an enormous amount of new technology—computer hardware and software— which has transformed the work environment of most teachers far more than the recommendations of the most publicized reform coalitions. Many of the children and youth in the schools have developed their own enthusiasm for computers, whether they find them in school, at home, or in the arcades and traditional neighborhood hangouts. Nintendo has replaced both television and pool for many. Seymour Papert is right, "Across the world children have entered a passionate and enduring love affair with the computer."[1]

This is not the first time technology has been greeted with amazing enthusiasm by some of those who would reform schools. In 1913, Thomas Edison predicted, "Books will soon be obsolete in the schools . . . Schools will soon be instructed through the eye. It is possible to touch every branch of human knowledge with the motion picture."[2] More recently, Seymour Papert, one of the best-known proponents of the use of computers in schools has predicted, "There won't be schools in the future. . . . I think the computer will blow up the school. That is, the school defined as something where there are classes, teachers running exams, people structured in groups by age, following a curriculum—all of that."[3] Clearly for some, the computer is the reform of the future for schooling. And like any reform available today, the primary question to be asked about the use of computers—or any other educational technology—is to what extent does it foster the expansion of democracy, in the classroom and in the larger society? The answer, in this case, must always be some variation of "It depends." There are many possible uses of computers and many different computer based pedagogies available today. The very complexity of the computer itself, linked to the variety of possible uses, can lead to considerable confusion. The essential starting point for gaining clarity regarding this very powerful new element in American education—the computer—and its potential impact on school policy and ultimately democratic education must be, the question of democracy itself.

Paulo Freire defines the educational task as fundamentally a dialogue, a dialogue in which all participants bring their own voice and their own expertise to make the whole richer. Freire has often been misunderstood at times by those who want to claim that there are no experts, that all voices are of similar worth on all topics. Nothing can be further from the truth. What Freire really says, indeed insists on, is that many different kinds of expertise must be shared if real education is to take place, if really important new knowledge is to be generated. A truly liberating educational dialogue takes place, Freire tells us, in the "restless, impatient, continuing helpful inquiry people pursue in the world, with the world, and with each other."[4] In the 1990s this focus on a "restless, impatient, continuing helpful inquiry," has been dismissed as romantic by some. There are those who argue that we must "be practical," and being practical means focusing education on ensuring the nation's continued economic dominance. And in that quest, the computer can be used in certain quite specific ways. From another perspective, however, one can insist with Douglas Sloan, "The central question is not whether one is for or against computers in education, but to define the human and educational criteria and priorities that can make a truly human use of the computer possible."[5] The test of whether we are using computers in truly human ways is quite simple: do they give voice to all students, especially those who too long have been silenced by the forms of pedagogy used in our schools; do they build up the common sense of humanity and community among all students, among all participants in this venture of education? That is the test by which all of us who call ourselves educators must measure all of our work.

The Great Divide: Critics and Advocates

Beginning with a bias for democracy and then turning to the field of computers in the school, the first and most dramatic thing to be seen is that there are really two quite distinct, and almost totally unrelated, conversations going on. The use of computers in education seems to be discussed on two parallel and generally unconnected tracks. There are, on the one hand, a significant number of critics of the use of computers in schools who are worried about what they see as the increasing inequity in our schools brought about by many changes, but also exacerbated by the use of computers. There are also, on the other hand, a growing number of experts in this field, people who are—often to their own surprise—embracing the possibilities of the computer as a powerful tool in improving the quality of instruction and the opportunities for critical inquiry among the students in our schools.

The Critique

As Rosemary E. Sutton has reminded us, we are talking about a very new field. "In 1975, the first microcomputer was developed. By 1981, the majority of secondary schools owned at least one microcomputer, and, by 1985, more than 90% of all public schools owned at least one microcomputer."[6] The critique of computer use was almost as quick to develop as was the ownership of the machines. In 1979, Michael Apple, who has done so much to frame the educational debates of the last two decades in the larger social, cultural, economic context, began to raise serious questions about the impact of computers in the nation's classrooms in his *Ideology and Curriculum.*[7] Other scholars joined in giving the use of computers in schools critical reviews. In the summer of 1984, the *Teachers College Record* devoted an entire issue to examining the use of computers in education from a critical perspective.[8] Throughout the 1980s, critical voices amplified their ideas on several fronts.

In the 1990s, as the use of computers and related technology became ever more commonplace in schools, more voices also joined the chorus of concerns. Neil Postman, known to many teachers for his 1979 classic, *Teaching as a Subversive Activity*, joined the fray with *Technopoly: The Surrender of Culture to Technology* in 1992 followed in 1995 with *The End of Education*.[9] While *Technopoly* represents a far-ranging examination of the changes in society wrought by the computer revolution, *The End of Education* includes the computer as one of "the gods that failed" in the transformation of the school. At the same time, Kirkpatrick Sale, a contributing editor of *The Nation*, published *Rebels against the Future: The Luddites and Their War on the Industrial Revolution: Lessons for the Computer Age*. For Sale, the Luddites who attacked the machines of early industrial era England have much to teach those who are concerned with the technology of the late twentieth century. Specifically Sale, who draws heavily on the work of Lewis Mumford, argues that we need to learn to ask the right questions and to frame the right debate.

The political task of resistance today, then—beyond the "quiet acts" of personal withdrawal Mumford urges—is to try to make the culture of industrialism and its assumptions less invisible and to put the issue of its technology on the political agenda, in industrial societies as well as their imitators. . . . This means laying out as clearly and as fully as possible the costs and consequences of our technologies, in the near term and long, so that even those overwhelmed by the ease/comfort/ speed/ power of high-tech gadgetry (what Mumford called technical "bribery") are forced to understand at what price it all comes and who is paying for it.[10]

Clearly the computer and its attendant technology is not arriving in the school or the larger society uncontested.

For Apple the large scale introduction of computers into the nation's schools threatens to reinforce some of the most serious issues of inequality which already exist.

There is evidence of class-, race-, and gender-based differences in computer use. In middle-class schools, for example, the number of computers is considerably more than in working-class or inner-city schools populated by children of color . . . These more economically advantaged schools not only have more contact hours and more technical and teacher support, but the very manner in which the computer is used is often different than what would be generally found in schools in less advantaged areas. Programming skills, generalizability, a sense of the multitudinous things one can do with computers both within and across academic areas—these tend to be stressed more (though simple drill and practice uses are still widespread even here). Compare this to the rote, mechanistic, and relatively low-level uses that tend to dominate the working-class school. These differences are not unimportant, for they signify a ratification of class divisions.[11]

In Apple's view, it is not just a matter of access to computers in schools but also the differences in the use of computers, once they are available, among different groups of students which makes the machine an agent of inequity. As others have also noted, growing inequity in our schools is not just a matter of what is being done in the computer lab; it is a characteristic of far too much of what has been done under the name of reform during the last decade.[12]

The issues of inequality in access and pedagogy is not the end of Apple's critique of the widespread use of computers in the nation's schools, however. He also worries, with considerable reason, about the impact of the advent of computers on teachers. "One of the major effects of the current (over)emphasis on computers in the classroom may again be the deskilling and disempowering of a considerable number of teachers. . . . Instead of teachers having the time and the skill to do their own curriculum planning and deliberation, they become isolated executors of someone else's plans, procedures, and evaluative mechanisms."[13]

The complaint that computers in the classroom have the potential to downgrade the role of teacher has a familiar ring for those who have studied other "reform" movements in American schools in the last century. Reflecting on much of what was passing for reform in turn-of-the-century Chicago, Ella Flagg Young warned in 1901 that if the direction of the reform movements did not change teachers would soon "fall into a class of assistants, whose duty consists in carrying out instructions of a higher class which originates method for all."[14] We run the risk, Apple and others are telling us, of using the introduction of computers into the classroom as one more in the long line of plans to develop teacher-proof curricula and to ask teachers, as Margaret Haley warned at the beginning of the century, "to carry out mechanically and unquestioningly the ideas and orders of those clothed with the authority of position and who may or may not know the needs of the children or how to minister them." From the teacher activists of the turn of the century to the critics of the 1990s, there is clearly a well reasoned tradition within the teaching profession for being cautious about the impact of any new reform, including the advent of the computer, on the role of teachers.[15] This caution is not reduced when one of Seymour Papert's most recent books proclaims on its cover, "Educators with a vested interest in the status quo will hate this book. It is about their demise."[16] The statement is good enough if applied only to those with a vested interest in the status quo. But even the teachers most committed to fundamental changes in the schools cannot help wondering if their demise is not also part of the agenda.

Larry Cuban has listed four stages in the response to any new kind of technology in the classroom—from motion pictures in the 1920s to computers in the 1980s:

1. "Claims predicting extraordinary changes in teacher practice and student learning, mixed with promotional tactics.

2. "Academic studies to demonstrate the effectiveness of a particular teacher aid as compared to conventional instruction (marred only by a few complaints from teachers)

3. Surveys documenting teacher use of the particular tool as disappointingly infrequent.

4. Criticism of administrators who left costly machines in closets to gather cobwebs, or stinging rebukes of narrow-minded, stubborn teachers reluctant to use learning tools that studies had shown to be academically effective.

As Cuban notes, few scholars, policymakers, or practitioners ever questioned the claims of boosters or even asked whether the technology should be introduced. Seldom did investigators try to adopt a teacher's perspective.[17]

Others have also looked at the larger social questions brought on by the advent of the computer. Apple is far from the only one asking the obvious question about whose interests are served by the sudden advent of all of this new technology. Indeed some sort of questioning should emerge from any thoughtful look at this revolution. As Douglas Sloan has noted, "It does not take a flaming Bolshevik, nor even a benighted neo-Luddite, to wonder whether all those computer companies, and their related textbook publishers, that are mounting media campaigns for computer literacy and supplying hundreds of thousands of computers to schools and colleges really have the interests of children and young people as their primary concern."[18] Research subsequent to the time when Sloan wrote has supported his concern. In the 1992 *Review of Research in Education,* Tony Scott and his colleagues have noted:

> One of the most critical characteristics of the deployment of information technologies into education has been its commercial dynamic; that is, the manufacturers of computers, the publishers of software, and the middlemen, reseller, dealers, and system integrators have had the most to gain by understanding U.S. school systems as a marketplace. Not to appreciate the significance of the economic motive in the sale and distribution of hardware, software, collateral print materials, computer courses, and the services of the cohort of experts who provide the training and guidance for the use of these technologies is to miss the central driving force behind the technology revolution in education.[19]

The question, "whose interests are being served," can never be far from the minds of any who would study any proposed reform in education. In terms of the use of computers, it raises a worrisome note.

Scholars from the Laboratory of Comparative Human Cognition at the University of California, San Diego summarize their own research by concluding that:

> the net effect of the microcomputer "revolution" in primary education has been to reinforce and exacerbate previously existing inequalities of educational achievement. Instead of realizing a long-standing dream of general increases in basic literacy as a result of children's involvement with microprocessors in their classrooms, we seem to be witnessing a case where the rich are getting richer and the gap between them and the poor is widening."[20]

Clearly the issue of equity must be attended to if the advocates of expanded computer use in the schools are going to have a right to a meaningful hearing.

Yet the issues of equity and the rights of teachers are not the whole of the critique. For many critics, using computers in schools breaks down cohesion and creates not a potentially democratic classroom but rather a set of increasingly individualized students each living in his or her own world, devoted to their own individual project, and needing little in the way of intellectual stimulation from either peers or teachers. Thus Postman worries that the focus on social cohesion among some computer advocates, including Seymour Papert, is not likely to be the norm.

Nevertheless, like the printing press before it, the computer has a powerful bias toward amplifying personal autonomy and individual problem-solving. That is why, Papert to the contrary, most of the examples we are given picture children working alone. That is also why educators must guard against computer technology's undermining some of the important reasons for having the young assemble in school, where social cohesion and responsibility are of preeminent importance.[21]

While Postman may be accused of overstating the success of traditional schools in achieving meaningful social cohesion, his concern must be addressed.

While Postman and Papert may debate this issue and argue about when and how computers may be effectively used to foster social cohesion, there are many besides the sometimes romantic Postman who worry that the very structure of the machine is part of the problem. Paul N. Edwards, for one, worries that the very success which computers have in being able to hold and fascinate students for long periods of engaged learning are also part of the danger. If computers draw students, and others, into a microworld such as Papert's Mathland,[22] they will likely learn math more effectively, but what else will they also learn?

Computer simulations are thus by nature partial, internally consistent but externally incomplete; this is the significance of the term "microworld." Every microworld has a unique ontological and epistemological structure, simpler than those of the world it represents. Computer programs are thus intellectually useful and emotionally appealing for the same reason: they create world without irrelevant or unwanted complexity.[23]

The problem, of course, is the degree to which the child who dwells in such worlds for any length of time, finds him/herself resisting the return to the complexity of the world full of real live contending human beings. Important learning takes place for any child in the fantasy world where things can be made simple and all endings can be made happy. But fostering a retreat into this world, and creating a machine which allows children and young adults to continue to live large portions of their lives in such worlds, has the danger of fostering the separation and isolation which so much of today's society seems to foster in any case. It is not a model calculated to build an engaged, diverse, and vibrant democratic discourse.

If what has been said so far is the whole story, there is not much left to be done. If computers are simply a tool for an undemocratic inequality, should we not simply remove the machinery from our classrooms and return to earlier means of instruction? It may be important to study the social impact of computers, but from a safe distance. There are some—certainly Postman comes close to this camp—who argue that we should do just that. But there is more to be considered. The critique of the use of computers in schools, as important and compelling as it is, is not the whole story. If computers have the potential to oppress they also have the potential to liberate, and it is to that potential that we must now turn our attention.

The Advocates of Computer Use

If Michael Apple and Neil Postman, in quite different ways, have emerged as among the strongest critics of the use and misuse of computers in schools, Seymour Papert has certainly become one of their strongest defenders. Papert's great contribution to education is his development of a new pedagogical methodology and his simultaneous articulation of a new philosophical and psychological understanding of the learning process. In a world where theory and practice are so often kept far apart, Papert has bridged the gap with amazing skill. The Logo program which enables children to engage in the exploration of a wide range of ideas through the control of their own computer provides teachers and their students with immediate entry into a powerful new pedagogical system.

At the same time, Papert, building on and moving beyond the work of Jean Piaget, argues for a much more interventionist approach to children's development which enables children to "concretize" formal operations at a much earlier age than Piaget would expect while doing so with much more pleasure than has been the case for children moving through the traditional educational processes which have emerged in Europe and North America during the last century. In Papert's view, computers allow children to be engaged in education in new ways and given a new form of both confidence and comprehension. As he argues, "The new knowledge is a source of power and is experienced as such from the moment it begins to form in the child's mind."[24] Artificial intelligence, as envisioned by Papert, is thus far from being a neutral tool, it is a means of liberating children's minds for much deeper and more fascinating forms of inquiry.

If he has done nothing else, Papert has identified the philosophy underlying the terrible dullness which characterizes so much of what takes place in school. Anyone familiar with schools is familiar with the underlying assumptions regarding passive students being fed—sometimes force-fed—bits of information by teachers who receive both the information and the means and order of instruction from yet higher authority. As Papert says:

> A caricatured hierarchical theory of knowledge and school might run something as follows: Knowledge is made of atomic pieces called facts and concepts and skills. A good citizen needs to possess 40,000 of these atoms. Children can acquire 20 atoms per day. A little calculation shows that 180 days a year for 12 years will be sufficient to get 43,200 atoms into their heads—but the operation will have to be well organized, for while some overrun on time can be absorbed, as little as 10 percent would make it impossible to achieve the goal. It follows that the technicians in charge (hereafter called teachers) have to follow a careful plan (hereafter called the curriculum) that is coordinated over the entire 12 years.[25]

This is, after all, what Paulo Freire called banking education. The teachers making deposits in the passive minds of the students. Papert, to his credit, has not only recognized the problem, he has—like Freire—proposed a completely different educational structure in which the student becomes the one in charge of making meaning of the world, while the teacher and the educational structures stand in the service of the student's enterprise. Not only that, but he has proposed ways in which both students and teachers can have fun along the way. No wonder Papert's ideas, and the computer as a learning tool, have become so popular so quickly.

A central role for computers in the process of schooling—novel only a few years ago—has become one of the major components of most contemporary discussions of the changing nature of education in the United States. In the introductory issue of the *Apple Education Review*, published by Apple Computers, Joanne Koltnow speaks of change and asserts that:

> The perception of teaching and learning is changing. . . . [The future] requires that students become engaged in constructing their own knowledge and understanding, and that teachers facilitate and coach their students—rather than just dispense information.

Also on Koltnow's list for the future is the fact that:

> Technology is becoming more available for education—and more appropriate. Computers and other technologies are moving into the schools,

both because they're seen as a part of modern life that students should know about, and because educators are finding ways to use them to enhance learning.[26]

Building on, but also often departing from the work of Papert, a whole generation of specialists in this new field of computers in education has now emerged, designing a wide range of pedagogical possibilities for today's youth.

To the surprise of many critics, the language of computers proponents such as Papert or Koltnow is taking on a surprisingly liberatory ring. They are not talking about using computers for rote, mechanistic learning. On the contrary, when Papert speaks of knowledge as a source of power to be experienced as such or when Koltnow speaks of changing the role of teachers from dispensers of knowledge to facilitators, they are beginning to take on a distinctly Freireian ring. It is, after all, the Brazilian educator who says that, "Education is suffering from narration sickness. The teacher talks about reality as if it were motionless, static, compartmentalized, and predictable." For Freire, the only solution is a new kind of engagement on the part of teacher and student; an engagement leading to real communication, for "only through communication can human life hold meaning. The teacher's thinking is authenticated only by the authenticity of the students' thinking. The teacher cannot think for his students, nor can he impose his thought on them."[27] The words sound quite similar. The question must be raised, are they all saying the same thing? Are Koltnow's call that teachers "coach their students—rather than just dispense information," and Freire's insistence that, "The teacher cannot think for his students," pointing to a similar understanding of the process of education?[28] To explore that question, we must look at some specific examples.

It should not be surprising that one of the most popular areas in which computers have been used effectively for instruction is in mathematics. As Tony Scott and his colleagues remind us, "in the years before World War II, the word computer referred to a person who computed numbers." They also note that well into the early 1980s, the use of computers in schools was focused almost exclusively in the field of working with numbers.[29]

Judah L. Schwartz has, perhaps more than anyone else, moved forward the use of computers in the teaching of math. As he argues, "I believe that students have a right to be challenged to create in every field they study in school. . . . In some subject areas such as English composition and art, students, their parents, and society have come to expect schools to offer the challenge of creating. In mathematics this is rarely the case." Schwartz has devoted the last decades to remedying that situation. Through the development of a number of computer tools which he calls "intellectual mirrors" which "provides a setting and an occasion for conjecture and creativity for both student and teacher in the mathematics classroom."[30] Schwartz's belief is that through work of this sort students develop "an appreciation of the fact that mathematics is a live and lively discipline that continues to grow and evolve."[31] As any teacher knows, this is a significant accomplishment in any field, all the more so for many students in mathematics.

The use of computers in education, while it has dramatically enriched the teaching of mathematics and related subjects, has also moved far beyond math instruction. Sylvia Weir is one of many who is convinced that through the use of computers in schools, a much richer pedagogy can emerge. Thus she says of Papert's Logo system that "Logo activities are designed to respect the need for learners to be actively involved in the construction of their own knowledge." Not only do students take on a new level of problem solving skill, but "[t]he teacher can concentrate on looking at what students actually do, rather than checking on their ability to reproduce the expected answers."[32] In a world of schooling still far too limited to top-down instruction and the search for the "right" answer, this level of interaction is truly revolutionary.

Everyone who is realistic about the enterprise of schooling knows that a high level of student ownership of their own instruction, aided by teachers who orchestrate a rich variety of activities, is not easy to achieve. As Weir also notes, "To realize this goal, the teacher must understand the pragmatic knowledge the student has developed during interactions with the computer, in order to link it to more formal knowledge, without depriving the student of a sense of identification with and ownership of that pragmatic knowledge."[33] This requires a teacher who is both very well versed in a diverse range of "formal knowledge" while at the same time highly skilled in the resources available through the use of a computer. It is a tall order for any teacher. Much of what has gone wrong with the use of computers in schools is because of a lack of teacher expertise. Indeed, far too many of all of the failures in education come not from ill will but from a simple inability to do the job with excellence. Expertise must therefore be an essential goal, and programs which support the use of computers in education need to keep a level of expertise at the center of the enterprise. The result, when successful, can be a much more liberating form of education in which, "in addition to internalizing social knowledge from the adults around them, students suddenly find themselves the producers of knowledge their teachers and parents do not yet have. This ownership is sweet indeed."[34]

Perhaps nowhere else has the extraordinary potential for computers to give students new means to produce information and give themselves voice been so amply demonstrated as in special education. In a column in *The Computing Teacher*, edited by Joan Thormann, Linda Laverty has summarized the incredibly liberating potential of the computer for students with severe special needs. "It is part of the human condition," Laverty says, "to participate in and enjoy competitive and creative activities. In the past, many assumed that the very nature of physical disabilities excluded those individuals from competition and creativity." That no longer need be the case. "The technology is there; it just needs to be used."[35]

The role of the computer in school is clearly here to stay; and it seems likely to expand. For many this is clearly a breakthrough of the first magnitude. As former U.S. Secretary of Education Terrel H. Bell and Donna L. Elmquist have written:

> Current technological advances such as computers, laser discs, high speed printers and satellite or fiber optic telecommunications can help American education make the transition into an era of individualized learning. Those responsible for educational reform need to push to bring to our classrooms the potential of the technological advances of recent years. By using existing methods of electronic instruction, the capacity exists to revolutionize the work of both students and teachers. Children today live in a world of visual images and high technology. But when they enter the classroom, they leave behind their high-tech world to spend their school days cloistered in classrooms virtually devoid of any technology—even telephones. Clearly, the world of education needs to join the new technological era and move beyond teacher talk, the printed page and chalkboards.[36]

It seems evident that the era of mere "teacher talk, the printed page and chalkboards," will be left behind in the very near future.

The Needed Dialogue

There is a problem here. Clearly the right use of computers has enormous potential to improve the education of all children. At the same time there are significant dangers that the misuse—or the unthinking, uncritical use—of computers will exacerbate many of the most significant problems present in our schools today. However, a dialogue between advocates and critics of computer use in schools, which is badly needed, is not taking place. More and more is being written on these themes, but repeated assertions by proponents of each position does not constitute a dialogue. The question which must be posed at the beginning of the dialogue is: What if they are both right? At base, we know, almost intuitively, that there is something that rings very true in the assertions of each position. Access to, and the use made of computers in schools varies dramatically depending on the socioeconomic status of the school district and the race and gender of the students involved. And the use of computers in instruction opens opportunities previously closed off for many students from learning disabled to the most gifted. The question before us is can we engage in a Freirian dialogue, a kind of "restless, impatient, continuing helpful inquiry," which leads to a new and much more focused and more liberating use of computers in our schools?

We know that American education is segregated and unequal. To ignore that reality is to perpetuate injustice, and it should therefore be no surprise that any new technology which is adopted supports that status quo. For all the talk about a democratic system of education, American education remains deeply undemocratic—it is segregated by race/class/gender and it serves to perpetuate inequality. It is also not geared to make the majority of students critical intellectuals. Given this sad reality, it should be no surprise that advocates of a new means of instruction, especially a means as powerful as computers, should find themselves, wittingly or unwittingly, in the service of the "sorting machine."[37] What else could one expect?

One of the fundamental issues in a democratic system of education is the matter of voice for all citizens, or as Marie Clay has called it, "the child's fundamental drive to make meaning of experience,"[38] which is at the core of literacy. Is it surprising then that a tool as powerful as a computer should be a potential major help in the process, providing new ways to make meaning, new entrances into literacy, especially for those for whom older methods have not worked well? In so doing, the computer can be a powerful tool for a more democratic education. The question here is not the machine, it is how it is used.

Perhaps Melvin Kranzberg is right when he describes "Kranzberg's First Law [which] reads as follows: Technology is neither good nor bad, nor is it neutral. This refers to the fact that technology's interaction with the social ecology is such that technical developments frequently have social and human consequences that go far beyond the immediate purposes of the technical devices themselves."[39] In the case of that system of social ecology called the school, it is our responsibility as educators to be sure that the social and human consequences of the computer are not bad or merely neutral, but part of a badly needed revolution which leads schools to finally live up to the democratic ideal with which they have been justified for two centuries.

In 1929, discussing an earlier technological innovation in schools, John Dewey wrote:

> The radio will make for standardization and regimentation only as long as individuals refuse to exercise the selective reaction that is theirs. The enemy is not material commodities, but the lack of the will to use them as instruments for achieving preferred possibilities.[40]

The question before us as educators in the 1990s is not fundamentally different from that of the 1920s, do we have the will to make the latest material invention an agent of the democratic process in our schools? In order to begin to explore ways in which the computer can assist with that question, I believe that there are a number of other questions which must be explored.

Critical Questions for the Dialogue

In order to facilitate a dialogue between the differing perspectives on the use of the computer, between the critics and the proponents, there are some questions which may help facilitate the conversation, the answers to which will help us move toward a truly democratic use of computers in the classrooms of tomorrow. Three questions especially deserve our attention.

1. Equity: How do we ensure equity across the great divides of race, class, gender in access to the use of computers in schools? How do we make sure that the computer is not used for rote learning for one group of students and critical inquiry for another?

We must begin our look at the use of computers in the schools with the question of equity: How do we ensure that all children have access to the best? Any teacher in this field who is saying, I am doing the best I can for the children in front of me, and who is working in a rich school district with rich—and often male—students, is part of the problem, not part of the solution. A significant part of democracy is access and all students must have access not only to the best materials but the best use of these materials.

Clearly we are a long way from guaranteeing equality in access or equality in pedagogy in the field of computer education. Many have noted the tendency of computers to increase inequality in schools. The simple cost of the equipment makes it unlikely that computers will be as available in poor districts as in affluent ones. Perhaps more serious is the research which shows, quite conclusively, that computers are used differently with different groups of students. Rosemary Sutton's work provides an excellent overview of both kinds of research.

While Sutton notes that there may have been some improvement in access during the decade of the 1980s as more and more schools, even in poor districts, gained some access to computers, "Four national surveys conducted during the 1980s comparing access to computers by pupils of different social class background and different ethnic origins showed consistent and predictable inequalities: Poor and minority children had less access to computers both at home and at school."[41] The situation does not seem to have improved in the 1990s. One report on "Technology in Public Schools, 1994–1995" found that the national average was twelve students per computer. When one looked at the poorest school districts in the country, the range was from 13.9 to 1 to 23 to 1. And wealth is not the only factor. The same study also found, "In general, the more ethnically diverse a school's population, the less access individual students have to personal computers."[42] Clearly, at the most fundamental point of access, both wealth and race make a significant difference. While different surveys used different sets of questions to approach the issue, all resulted in the same conclusion. Relatively well off, white, male students had much more access to computers than students who were less well off, of color, or female.

In the discussion of equity in the use of computers in schools, access is far from the only issue. Again Sutton's research is helpful in describing the problem. "Whereas type of computer use changed over time, inequalities remained consistent: minority and poor students spent more time on drill and practice and less time on programming than did high-SES [socioeconomic status] and White students."[43] And when the question turned to male/female differences, "whereas school-related gender differences in overall access were relatively small, differences in type of use were larger. Becker and Sterling (1987) found that girls were underrepresented at the elementary, middle, and high-school levels in elective programming, game playing, and before/after school use. The only area in which girls were overrepresented was in high-school word processing."[44]

While computers as static machines may be neutral, their use in schools can be far from neutral. Thus K. A. Whooley notes, "There is a dearth of software designed to attract girls. Girls. . . . do not like games which are violent or fast-paced. They prefer to have clear instructions and time to reflect on solutions."[45] Many girls also prefer a different content to the interaction. Thus a group of Canadian scholars who have conducted some careful research about girls' interest in computers report, as one example, an interview in which:

> Nine-year old Sandra explained that she did not find video games fun because all you do is jump on guys and kill them. Her idea for a game would be about people on an adventure. These people would travel from city to city and meet different people. These people could be relatives or friends and the object of the game was to deliver packages to people in other towns. She also suggested there would be certain obstacles like ditches, wolves and bears. In order to get by the animals without them eating you, it would be necessary to give the animal a certain kind of food.[46]

Clearly, at least in this example, there is no thrill to killing the animal. The issue is only partially one of attracting girls as well as boys to the use of computers. It is also one of mirroring the kind of society in which we want girls and boys to live. As another commentator has noted, "If we don't seriously question the [computer] games and, more to the point, the culture that designs them, our lives could become one endless round of Space Invaders."[47] There must be a better alternative.

Tony Scott and his colleagues also note, the culture carried by a computer program is not just one of gender:

> There is a fact, not often enough acknowledged, that computer hardware carries cultural content: Computers can be adapted to work in Spanish, but they are designed in English . . . The menu structure, the design of icons, and the styles of problem decomposition and solution together construct the computer-human interface. So whatever communicative processes can be created within and between ethnic minorities, insofar as they are mediated by computer, they are also mediated by Anglo culture.[48]

This is a sobering reminder of the depth of mainstream cultural imperialism; of the degree to which sexism and racism pervades every aspect of our current educational enterprise.

Those who note the current disparity in the use of computers also provide important examples of the ways things can change. K. A. Whooley, while noting the current sex bias in the use of computers, also believes that when computers are used in ways which build on the strengths which all students bring to a class, "males and females can and do experience success in their own way." Thus while noting the different learning styles exhibited by boys and girls after years of schooling she concludes:

> If girls working with boys learn to be more confident in their application of trial and error strategies, a strategy which relies heavily on intuition for success, and boys learn from girls to cooperate in their problem solving, then each party to the interaction will have gained new ways to meet the challenges of troubles on or off computers.[49]

The potential for mutual gain is there.

Computers have also been used to foster a more effective multicultural curriculum, especially across the barriers of language. They have literally allowed students to cross boarders and the barriers of language. Thus Scott and his colleagues cite one study in which students who, when given the freedom to speak English or Spanish in a computer mediated context, improved in both. They also describe an experience in which, "through the use of telecommunications," it was possible "to set up a cross-border project involving students from half a dozen institutions of higher education (three American, three Mexican) and in that context pursue a common purpose and a common syllabus.[50] The possibilities are real. But so are the pitfalls.

If Seymour Papert has a fatal flaw, it is his failure to see the misuses to which not only computers but his own programs for computers can be put. To be fair, Papert vigorously advocates using computers in only the most creative and engaging ways for all students. He is as critical as any computer critic of those schools which having invested heavily in computers are "using them for other purposes—perhaps for drill and practice, perhaps for 'computer literacy.' "[51] Clearly he has something quite different in mind. One must also have some sympathy for Papert's frustration that those who advocate the use of computers are held to a higher standard than those who advocate business as usual. He is right, it is not fair or sensible to give up "real advantages in exchange for the pretense of equality."[52] It is certainly the case that the computer-free schools of the first three quarters of this century did not reflect the equity for which the computer's critics call. The Neil Postmans of this world must always beware of a nostalgia for an egalitarian past that never was.

Having said all of this, however, there is still a problem with which Papert and other computer advocates have yet to contend. While Papert and others have proposed ways to use technology to radically restructure schools in ways which will serve students far more effectively and equitably than they are served in today's schools, the status quo is strong. The bureaucracies, the overtired and overbusy teachers, the parents anxious for immediate benefit for their child, all of these things can conspire to undermine the technology's potential. It is only when the computer advocates have dealt with these realities that they can be seen as truly effective advocates for a more democratic school.

Noting the possibilities is also a long way from seeing them implemented. Scott and his colleagues are clearly sobered by the reality that, "when minorities do have equitable access to computing resources, one observes 'low-quality usage' in which drill-and-practice programs are used in place of enrichment activities, styles of classroom organization and management are adopted that reduce effectiveness of computer use, and telecommunications activities are pursued exclusively in English."[53] Anyone familiar with the history of education in the United States in this century knows that the opportunity to wipe out barriers of sex, race, and class does not mean that the opportunity will be grasped. But the work of researchers like those noted here proves that it is possible to use computers in ways that break down the old barriers; that truly serve all of the nation's children. The challenge, then, is to ensure that these possibilities become reality, not just for a few but as the expected norm.

2. Voice: How do we ensure that the forms of computer-assisted instruction which we adopt actually give students increased voice in their own education and in their approach to the world? Are we teaching for technical mastery or for empowerment?

Teaching skills, even very important skills, is not sufficient for a democratic education. Democracy means voice for all citizens, including students. A democratic education not only ensures equity (though it must do that), and it not only teaches democratic values (though it must also do that), but it models the nature of democracy, giving voice and power to all of the participants in the schools (students, teachers, parents, community) and to all of the students in the class. Studies clearly show that computers are used in some classrooms, and with some groups of students, for rote learning and in other classrooms, with other groups of students, for critical inquiry. How do we ensure voice for all? How do we ensure rigorous critical intellectual activity in the use of computers for all? This is not a matter of the machine but of how it is used.

In a devastating critique of what goes on in too many of today's urban schools, Michelle Fine has described the process of silencing which takes place for many students, especially those in low-income areas:

> Silencing provides a metaphor for the structural, ideological, and prac-
> tical organization of comprehensive high schools. . . . Although the press
> for silencing is by no means complete or hermetic (that is, ripples of
> interruption, resistance, and outright rebellion are easy to spot), low-
> income schools officially contain rather than explore social and eco-
> nomic contradictions, condone rather than critique prevailing social and
> economic inequalities, and usher children and adolescents into ideolo-
> gies and ways of interpreting social evidence that legitimate rather than
> challenge conditions of inequity.[54]

Silencing can be a metaphor for what many students experience in school. It
is also a quite specific day-to-day reality. Computers can be as effective in
aiding the silencing effort as they can in giving voice.

In an educational world too often characterized by silencing, the onus is
on those who advocate the use of computers in schools, especially low-
income schools, to ensure that this tool is used as a means of changing the
reality Fine describes. The goal must be one of giving voice to students who
understand all too well "prevailing social and economic inequities," and who
can, with the right tools, describe that reality for the world even as they begin
to take action to change it. As described in the preceding section, there have
been many victories on this front. But all of us who care about education for
democracy must be continually on guard. The alternative is to drop the veil
of silence even further over the institution which is supposed to be a vehicle
for voice.

In addition to students from historically oppressed communities, students
from all kinds of communities who have been labeled as in need of special
education have been consigned to a world of silence. Based on the expectations of their teachers and the larger culture, based on difficulty with traditional modes of communication, special education students—especially students
with more intensive needs—are often among the most silent. And among
these students, the experience with computers as a new means of voice is
truly extraordinary.[55]

As one specific example, Linda Laverty reports on a new set of competitive games which she and others have designed and also a program for doing
art work under which one of her students, by using "a head switch, this child
created his very first picture under his own initiative."[56] If this is not giving
a democratic citizen voice, what is?

Sylvia Weir has said, "Perhaps we should learn from the 'special need'
to interact among students who have, in the past, so often been silenced

through the designation of 'in need of special education.' In interesting ways, the computer as an instrument of interaction becomes a means of engaging students with a variety of different working styles."[57] The fundamental nature of the democratic dialogue has thus been expanded through new technology.

For a computer to be useful in giving students—and teachers—a more effective voice in school and society it has to be available. My colleague Alan Cromer has pointed out the failure of the computer industry to be helpful on this front. As he says, "Technology can rapidly become so complex that it defeats its own purpose." School-based technology is rapidly approaching this defeat at every level from elementary school to higher education. "It is easy to fall in love with high-tech gizmos—I've done it myself—and to lose sight of the ultimate objective: the education of a student. . . . Funding agencies have come to equate technology with the complex and the expensive, thus promoting research in that which is, by definition, unsuitable for mass utilization in schools." For Cromer there is a clear road not taken but still available:

> In the early 1980s, I had expected the price of computers to fall as had the price of calculators. Instead, computer manufacturers kept their prices roughly constant while dramatically increasing the functionality of their product. In the process, they discontinued their older models, instead of selling them for a lower price. The calculator manufacturers, on the other hand, reduced the prices of their basic and scientific calculators as they marketed more expensive programmable and graphic calculators. Had the computer manufacturers done the same, we would have the equivalents of an Apple II+ or a Mac II selling for under $200.[58]

And this alternative is still available. A relatively simple and affordable computer would allow teachers to master the technology and students to have it. And the development which Cromer calls for, a low cost standardized computer for all schools, would be a powerful new tool for giving voice to many.

There is a great reservoir of silenced people in this country, people who have never been given voice in our schools. Now it is clearly the case, as we have been shown by people as diverse as Alan Cromer, Rosemary Sutton, and Michael Apple, that computers have often been a means of silencing some and giving voice to others. The same machine is made available to one set of students in the form of a rote skill to be mastered while their more well-off counterparts have used the computer as a tool of self-expression and intellectual engagement. But what if we were to make that situation change?

What if we were to insist that we must find ways to use computers to give a new kind of voice to those usually left voiceless in schools?

The novelist James Baldwin reminds us that, "there are in this country tremendous reservoirs of bitterness which have never been able to find an outlet, but may find an outlet soon." Giving voice, in school and in the larger society, is not a safe or easy process. As Baldwin continues

> It means, in brief, that a great price is demanded to liberate all those silent people so that they can breathe for the first time and tell you what they think of you. And a price is demanded to liberate all those white children—some of them near forty—who have never grown up, and who never will grow up, because they have no sense of their identity."[59]

The issue of voice is fundamental to a healthy identity. Silence is unacceptable. Talking about expression is talking about very powerful stuff; and this is the stuff of democracy.

Now I do not mean to imply that the right use of computers in our schools is suddenly going to turn around the injustices of the larger American society, injustices perpetuated far too much in our schools. I do not believe that using computers more effectively to help people be better writers is going to give voice to all of the "inarticulate and dangerous rage,"[60] which so many students have today or that we, as instructors, would know what to do with it if we did help to unleash it. But I do believe that the right use of computers can liberate the voices of some of those who are voiceless. This machine does have the potential to help teachers get out of the role of instructor and into the role of coach for the inarticulate but powerful longings which are in so many of our students. If that happens it can lead to some very powerful speech which this society badly needs to hear.

We live in times when far too many are silenced, when conformity pervades too much of our public life. If the use of the computer can give voice to the voiceless and release the critical imaginations of the silenced, we will have made a significant step in the direction of a better world for us all. When students are supported to gain both skills and freedom to think creatively about their use, computers can be one significant tool in moving forward the agenda described by Maxine Greene:

> In "the shadow of silent majorities," then, as teachers learning along with those we try to provoke to learn, we may be able to inspire hitherto unheard voices. We may be able to empower people to rediscover

their own memories and articulate them in the presence of others, whose space they can share. Such a project demands the capacity to unveil and disclose. It demands the exercise of imagination, enlivened by works of art, by situations of speaking and making. Perhaps we can at last devise reflective communities in the interstices of colleges and schools. Perhaps we can invent ways of freeing people to feel and express indignation, to break through the opaqueness, to refuse the silences. We need to teach in such a way as to arouse passion now and then; we need a new camaraderie, a new en masse. These are dark and shadowed times, and we need to live them, standing before one another, open to the world.[61]

Clearly the use of computers in schools, under the right circumstances, has demonstrated the potential for the computer to "free people," people long denied any voice, "to express indignation." Linda Laverty describes using computers in schools to help students exercise their imagination. In doing so, she is helping move all of us in the direction Greene speaks of when she calls for a society, "enlivened by works of art, by situations of speaking and making." These are not the uses normally thought of for the use of computers in the classroom. They were most certainly not the uses intended by those who first designed a new higher order calculator, "designed to work out ballistic firing tables," in the great battles of World War II.[62] But it is a use to which we can turn this new tool, if we have the will and the imagination. Then we will have indeed found a way to fight against the dark and shadowed times in which we live.

3. How do we ensure that all students not only learn how to use computers but learn about the social impact of computers in the American social, political, economic context?

Neil Postman begins *Technopoly* with a reminder that people are inclined "to be tools of our tools."[63] It is certainly the case that the only way to avoid that trap, to master the computer rather than serve it, is to be thoroughly reflective about it—about the uses and misuses which can be made of this powerful tool.

An article in the *Newsnotes* of the Center for Law and Education describes the familiar tendency of traditional vocational education programs to sort students and consign far too many to an education which will only prepare them for a permanent place "on the bottom rungs of the economy." However, it goes on to tell of the little noticed but very far reaching changes taking place in the field of vocational education as a result of the 1991 revision of the Carl D. Perkins Vocational and Applied Technology Education Act which require all students in vocational education programs to be exposed to "all aspects of the industry." As the editors say:

> This new focus allows students to understand and participate in changing the economic, social and technological forces that shape their lives, their workplaces, their communities, and their opportunities. It can overcome the tracking of disadvantaged students away from high-level academics, and the division of students into those who will eventually understand that big picture plan, and decide, and those who will spend their work lives carrying out other people's decisions.[64]

If one of the great fears about the use of computers in the schools is that it divides students by race/class/gender and divides them far too much between those who are taught basic word processing versus those who are taught to understand and apply the larger world of computers, then there may be much in the recent Perkins Act and the activity it has spawned in vocational education from which to learn. If the use of computers in schools truly includes a study of "all aspects of the industry," then all students and their teachers will have to move beyond technical mastery to sociological—and ultimately ethical—reflection.

Vocational education, like too many computer classes, has suffered from being on the bottom end of the sorting process in American education.[65] Like the computer class which teaches only word processing for future secretaries, vocational education has been the place where students who were deemed as "less successful" were shunted while their counterparts were given the academic opportunities to prepare them for leadership. But in the last generation, the voc ed community has fought for significant changes in the perception of the field. The latest Perkins Act legislation, requiring a knowledge of "all aspects of the industry," requires that students in vocational education programs gain not only skills, but the social and economic understanding of their industry which will give them the potential for a meaningful role in shaping the future of the society in which they will live. We can ask no less of all computer programs.

Students who do study "all aspects" of the computer industry will learn some interesting facts about the role of the computer in the changing American economy. The use of computers in schools is popular with the general public, in part, because of the perception that much of the nation's economic future is tied to the computer revolution and therefore students who gain skills with computers in school will have increased opportunities for quality employment in the future. But students who truly learn all aspects of the computer industry will have important reasons to question some of these assumptions.

In 1984 Douglas Noble was asking why computer literacy was being advocated so strongly as a means of ensuring future employment for future graduates when "recent studies using Bureau of Labor Statistics data, however, challenge these assumptions by showing that very few of tomorrow's jobs will require any familiarity with computers."[66] And even the term "familiarity with computers" can mean many different things. For every job which requires significant training and skill, many more computer-related jobs are at the low end of the scale in computer manufacturing or in service industries where the work has been "deskilled" by computers.[67] Given these economic realities, Noble and others have begun to question if the introduction of computers into schools is not simply one more part of the end-of-the-century reality in which the rich have gotten richer and the poor poorer and the divide between the two more impenetrable. Given the split of the American economy into the 20 percent who will be the highly skilled and highly paid "symbolic-analysts" and the other 80 percent whose skill levels and salaries are dropping rapidly, such fears need to be taken very seriously.[68]

Many thoughtful people have reviewed in detail the computer's potential to "reinforce and exacerbate previously existing inequalities of educational achievement."[69] If that is true, then we must ask some very basic questions about the use of computers in schools: Whose interests are being served? What vision of education and the good society is being promulgated in the use of computers? Or as Larry Cuban has warned in his study of the use of technology in schools throughout this century, "Before we give the schools over to the requirements of the new technology and the corporation, we must be very certain that it will benefit all of us, not primarily those who already possess economic and cultural power."[70] Clearly it is important to challenge the agenda of those who believe that students must simply be prepared for a new economic reality with the important question, "Who will define that reality?"

In pursuing the answers to these questions, we cannot ignore the origin of the computer in the military or the link of the computer to the military-industrial complex.[71] We need not hand a tool as powerful as the computer over to the military-industrial complex, but we must be ever mindful of the pitfalls. It is incumbent on those who believe that computers can be part of a liberating education to envision the kind of society in which this would happen as well as the methods of instruction which open new opportunities for individual students—every individual student.

The battle over the use of technology in schools is part of a much larger struggle. To what extent do schools need to be radically restructured and to what end? What is the larger social good, the vision of the good society, which schools should serve? These questions must be at the heart of the educational debate—at the level of national education policy and equally at the level of classroom discourse. Neil Postman is right that too much of the contemporary educational debate focuses on technical questions, "Should we have national standards of assessment? How should we use computers?" What is needed is a more fundamental conversation. The questions under consideration too often have in common, the fact "that they evade the issue of what schools are for. It is as if we are a nation of technicians consumed by our expertise in how something should be done, afraid or incapable of thinking about why."[72] But the larger questions must be asked. And, in fact, the classroom is the ideal place to begin asking exactly these questions.

What if, we must ask, in the name of studying "all aspects of the industry," that is the computer industry, we began to develop a school curriculum around the fundamental debates which Kirkpatrick Sale raises in his study of the Luddites. What if, at the same time that students were engaged in new and creative ways to learn mathematics in Papert's "Mathland," they also engaged in a study of the social changes brought about by technology? To do this they would have to look at the split, as Sale describes it, between those who are optimistic and those who are pessimistic about technology in the society. "These neo-Luddites are more numerous today than one might assume," Sale tells us, "techno-pessimists without the power and access of the techno-optimists but still with a not-insignificant voice." Indeed, hearing and responding to both voices is at the heart of critical thinking and a democratic dialogue. This is not a matter of merely "teaching the debate." It is a more fundamental process of inviting students and teachers into the debates, as partisans and as activists.[73]

In the process of this dialogue, students would also have to wrestle with the lessons Sale believes we should learn from the Luddites including:

1. Technologies are never neutral, and some are hurtful.

2. Industrialism is always a cataclysmic process, destroying the past, roiling the present, making the future uncertain.

3. "Only a people serving an apprenticeship to nature can be trusted with machines."

4. The nation-state, synergistically intertwined with industrialism, will always come to its aid and defense, making revolt futile and reform ineffectual.

5. But resistance to the industrial system, based on some grasp of moral principles and rooted in some sense of moral revulsion, is not only possible but necessary.

6. Politically, resistance to industrialism must force not only "the machine question" but the viability of industrial society into public consciousness and debate.

7. Philosophically, resistance to industrialism must be embedded in an analysis—an ideology, perhaps—that is morally informed, carefully articulated, and widely shared.

8. If the edifice of industrial civilization does not eventually crumble as a result of a determined resistance within its very walls, it seems certain to crumble of its own accumulated excesses and instabilities within not more than a few decades, perhaps sooner, after which there may be space for alternative societies to arise.[74]

One need not agree with all of the points which Sales and the Luddites or their twentieth century successors might want to make to agree public consciousness and debate are essential elements in a democratic system of education. Without public consciousness and public debate any change is, by definition, mindless. And mindlessness is the ultimate enemy of education— as opposed to mere instruction or training.

This great debate can be at the heart of a critical and thoughtful educational process. There is no reason why questions such as these cannot be—should not be—at the heart of the computer education curriculum every bit as much as questions about how to use technology or how it will enhance other forms of learning. Papert is right, "The only rational choice I see is to forge ahead in the encouragement of educational diversity with a dedicated commitment not only to expanding its benefits to all who want them but also to making sure that those who choose not to want them are making an informed choice."[75] Indeed, to engage in the use of computers in schools and not also engage in this kind of dialogue about the values and costs of computers in school, in the day-to-day instructional process, is to engage in an educational enterprise which is limited, partial, and fundamentally both anti-intellectual and undemocratic. The larger enterprise, difficult and threatening as it can be, is the only one worthy of being included in a democratic education or a democratic society.

Conclusion

This chapter began with a look at Paulo Freire's understanding of the nature of dialogue. But Freireian dialogue is never an end in itself. For Freire, dialogue is a part of the larger process of liberation. And dialogical education is always part of a political process of liberation.[76] It is not surprising then that I find myself, in conclusion, coming to the issue of political action, for it is in that much misused word politics that the fundamental test of the use of the computer in our schools must be made. Are we, in our work with computers, agents of liberation or protectors of the status quo? That is the ultimate test of all of our work.

Ultimately the key is to politicize the field of computers in education. When I say politicize I mean it in the broadest sense, to situate the conversation about the use of this machine not in a technical but in the largest social context; to situate it in the dialogue about the nature of education for the good society. If we continue two parallel, unconnected sets of conversations, we are not going to achieve the needed breakthroughs in placing the use of computers in our schools at the service of a democratic education and a democratic society. We run the risk of a kind of unthinking Ludditism on the part of the critics and an even more dangerous uncritical enthusiasm on the part of proponents. It is only through the dialogue that we will achieve the positive potential of this new media. It seems to me that there will, of necessity, be at least four elements in democratic computer use:

1. Every student will have the ability to use computers and access to the machines so that this ability can both be learned and used repeatedly, the skills are important.

2. Every student will be challenged to use computers to give voice to his/her own thoughts . . . not merely a skill to be mastered but a tool for basic critical inquiry and conversation.

3. Every student will understand the role of computers in the sociopolitical context of the United States at the end of the twentieth century.

4. Every teacher will have the resources to use computers as a tool for creative teaching, not the delivery of programs mandated by others.

If we wrestle with these questions, if we guarantee these uses of computers in our schools, then we will have turned one of the great tools of the twentieth century to the service of a better world.

In the last analysis, the use of computers in the classroom must be evaluated—as must everything else in school—by the degree to which it fosters the growth of free and independent students and citizens and the degree to which it fosters the growth of a more just and open society. As my teacher, the late Lawrence Cremin has written:

> John Dewey liked to define the aim of education as growth, and when he was asked growth toward what, he liked to reply, growth leading to more growth. That was his way of saying that education is subordinate to no end beyond itself, that the aim of education is not merely to make parents, or citizens, or workers, or indeed to surpass the Russians or the Japanese, but ultimately to make human beings who will live life to the fullest, who will continually add to the quality and meaning of their experience and to their ability to direct that experience, and who will participate actively with their fellow human beings in the building of a good society. To create such an education will be no small task in the years ahead, but there is no more important political contribution to be made to the health and vitality of the American democracy and of the world community of which the United States is a part.[77]

To the degree in which we are able to direct the use of computers in education to the creation of that kind of education—which helps human beings live lives to the fullest while helping to build a good society—to that degree the computer will have become a powerful tool for a more democratic education. We can ask no less.

CHAPTER SIX

Preparing Teachers
for Democratic Schools

> To educate as the practice of freedom is a way of teaching that anyone can learn. That learning process comes easiest to those of us who teach who also believe that there is an aspect of our vocation that is sacred; who believe that our work is not merely to share information but to share in the intellectual and spiritual growth of our students.
>
> bell hooks, *Teaching to Transgress*

The Context for Change

In September, 1996, the National Commission on Teaching and America's Future released its long-anticipated report. Chaired by North Carolina Governor James B. Hunt, including some of the nation's most distinguished educators, and funded by the Rockefeller Foundation and the Carnegie Corporation of New York, the commission was well placed to attract public notice. And the report which was issued, *What Matters Most: Teaching for America's Future*, written by a team led by Linda Darling-Hammond of Teachers College, Columbia University, made a series of clear and dramatic recommendations including a call for states and school districts to "get serious about standards, for both students and teachers," and for a thorough restructuring of teacher preparation, recruitment, and professional development. Finally, the report called for encouraging and rewarding teacher skills and for ensuring that schools are structured for success.

In offering the media a combination of dramatic examples of current failure—over one-third of mathematics teachers have not had a major or a minor

159

in the field, the majority of teacher education institutions are not accredited—and in calling for sweeping change, the report generated immediate notice. Ironically, neither the publicity around the report nor the report itself gave significant attention to the fact that this was one of many in a series of reports stretching over two decades which made similar calls. While the authors of *What Matters Most* do make respectful reference to some of the most influential reports of the past decade, they are hardly central to the argument. No wonder that some of the more experienced, or perhaps jaundiced, of observers have been asking, what is different this time?[1]

Nevertheless, while cynicism can come easily, it is essential that those who are committed to a more democratic system of education attend seriously to *What Matters Most* and the reports which have come before it. These reports, and the publicity, conferences, and calls for reform which surround them, do point to real problems. And more important, the public discussion of the reports offers new opportunities for committed democratic educators to make badly needed changes in teacher education and ultimately in the whole structure of public education. The issue is not a question of either uncritically embracing or rejecting these reports. It is a matter of using the opportunities that they present in thoughtful and critical ways. There is much to be learned from the possibilities of some of the best noted of the last generation of such reports which should influence the reaction to *What Matters Most* and its inevitable successors.

In the spring of 1986, two education reports appeared almost simultaneously which taken together—as they almost always were—redefined teacher education in the United States. *A Nation Prepared*, the report of the Carnegie Forum on Education and the Economy, and *Tomorrow's Teachers* from the Holmes Group of Education Deans in 1986, both of which called for a significant restructuring of teacher education programs throughout the United States, set the agenda for nearly all debates about teacher education in this country for the decade which followed their publication.[2] By the time the Holmes and Carnegie reports were published in 1986, the nation and especially the nation's educators were well used to reports criticizing some aspects of the nation's schooling. Since the publication of *A Nation at Risk* in 1983, there had been a plethora of reports about the problems of American education. But these new reports, the so called "second stage reports," were different. They moved from critique to proposing solutions.[3]

In making this shift, the two reports managed to capture the attention of educational leaders and policy makers throughout the nation. They have also dominated almost all debates about teacher preparation among scholars in the decade since their publication. Whether the writers are supporters or opponents of the reforms outlined in Carnegie and Holmes—and there are plenty of each—the authors of those two reports have set the terms of the debate about teacher preparation.[4] For many of us in the field, implementing the recommendations of the reports has also dominated our professional lives as we have sought to shape the process, holding on to the best of the recommendations while resisting other parts of the agenda.

Carnegie and Holmes: What They Said and What Happened

The reports, now thoroughly familiar to almost everyone in the field of education, are amazingly similar in the basic reforms which they call for. The basic list, as summarized in the Carnegie report, includes the following:

- Create a National Board for Professional Teaching Standards . . . to establish high standards for what teachers need to know and be able to do. . . .

- Restructure schools to provide a professional environment for teaching. . . .

- Restructure the teaching force, and introduce a new category of lead teachers. . . . [The Carnegie report offers more detail in its call for a hierarchy within teaching led by Lead Teachers, with a large number of "professional teachers" supported by aides and interns. The Holmes group calls for a similar hierarchy led by "Career Professionals, with Professional Teachers, and at the lowest level Instructors rounding out the picture.]

- Require a bachelors degree in the arts and sciences.

- Develop a new professional curriculum in graduate schools of education leading to a Master in Teaching degree, based on systematic knowledge of teaching and including internships and residencies in the schools.

- Mobilize the nation's resources to prepare minority youngsters for teaching careers.

- Relate incentives for teachers to school-wide performance. . . .

- Make teachers' salaries and career opportunities competitive with those in other professions.[5]

While the pages of scholarly journals have been filled with debates about these recommendations, the recommendations have dominated the discussion. The options in teacher education seem too often to be limited to either the complete implementation of the Holmes and Carnegie proposals or to casting a critical eye on the reform efforts in a way which—given the absence of alternative reform visions—actually supports the maintenance of a status quo which should be satisfactory to no one.

At the same time as this debate is going on, however, many of the proposed reforms have been implemented at breakneck speed. It is one thing for self-selected national boards to call for major changes in teacher preparation, it is quite another for change to actually happen. Indeed, the history of education reform movements in this country has been one of much national rhetoric and little action at the local level. The reforms of the 1980s it seems have been different. An amazing number of states and individual institutions have become involved in changing at least some parts of their systems for preparing teachers. Within the first two years of the publication of the Holmes and Carnegie reports, the majority of the fifty states had made some kind of change in their certification laws. This speed in actual implementation of reform proposals stands in sharp contrast to the success of many reform efforts conducted earlier in the twentieth century.[6]

As has always been true in educational reform, there has been a wide diversity of specific changes implemented under the Carnegie and Holmes banner, and it is not always easy to know from a national perspective exactly what is happening. Two states may use the same language—especially when certain reform language is especially popular—and end up with quite different meanings. However a review of state activity yields some startling results.

Courtney Leatherman's review of the changes in teacher preparation regulations in the first two years after the publication of the reports indicates changes in several areas:

- "Twenty-six states have stiffened the requirements for admission to teacher education programs. Of those states, 17 require people who want to enroll in teacher-education programs to take a basic skills test. Six states have increased the minimum grade point average for prospective teachers."

- "Thirty-two states have revised the curriculum for students who plan to become teachers. Some have abolished the undergraduate degree in education and now require prospective students to major in an academic subject area. . . . Other states have increased the number of courses in pedagogy that teacher education majors must take."[7]

In the time since Leatherman wrote, the momentum has scarcely slowed. Indeed, the 1996 *What Matters Most* report would not have been possible without this base upon which to build. At the same time, the Carnegie Corporation has continued to build national base for institutionalizing the proposals through its funding of the National Board for Professional Teaching Standards, chaired by former North Carolina Governor James Hunt, which has now issued its first certificates for "Board Certified Teachers." With Carnegie support, the Carnegie Forum on Education and the Economy has also been transformed into the National Center on Education and the Economy, now an independent advocacy agency based in Rochester, New York. Clearly one of the advantages a foundation the size of the Carnegie Corporation of New York is that it can both propose major reforms and simply pay for the implementation of at least some of its recommendations.[8]

At the same time, the Holmes group of education deans has also continued its discussions, and the work of reforming the teacher preparation curriculum on many campuses. Two more reports have followed the original report. *Tomorrow's Schools* (1990), focuses much more on the role of teachers, as opposed to university-based professors, in the preparation of their successors, while *Tomorrow's Schools of Education* (1995) calls for a significant shift in the primary location of teacher education to professional development schools.[9] Much of the criticism leveled at the original Holmes report, in this paper and elsewhere, has been dealt with in the later Holmes reports which attend to issues of racism and political disenfranchisement quite seriously. However, it was the original Holmes report, linked closely with its counterpart from Carnegie, which set much of the tone for the changes which followed in teacher education. Whatever the differences from state to state in putting the Holmes and Carnegie reforms into practice, the authors of those reports seem to have set the terms of teacher preparation for the next decade, as *What Matters Most* may for the decade ahead. While there are important differences between the 1986 reports and their 1996 successor, this analysis of Holmes and Carnegie raises questions which will need to be applied to the Report of the National Commission in the years ahead.

The problem with the current state of affairs in teacher education as with the use of computers in the schools is that a debate in which all parties line up either as enthusiastic proponents or harsh opponents misses much of the complexity and possibility which is present in the current moment. The reality is that while some of the Carnegie and Holmes proposals are very problematic, others are excellent. They offer an opportunity to improve the education of the teachers of the future seldom seen in American education. The lack of critical engagement with the details of the proposals offered by

the reports has resulted in a lack of careful judgments about individual proposals or clear practical alternatives to the recommendations, which has
impoverished the educational debate. As with the use of computers, so in
teacher education, a debate has taken place in which people on two sides fail
to learn from each other and in which progressive critics, because of their
substantive reservations about proposed changes, run the risk of defending an
unacceptable status quo. Something much more engaged and sophisticated is
required of us.

Educating Teachers for What?
Education in a Democratic Society

One of the most significant problems with the Holmes and Carnegie reports,
and one which has properly overshadowed all others in much of the debate
about their recommendations, has been the vision which they offer of the
purposes of education in a democratic society. Many would argue that there
needs to be a quite different vision of the purposes of public education than
those enunciated by the authors of the Holmes and Carnegie reports. While
the authors of the reports follow the norm in 1980s and 1990s reform rhetoric
and talk of competition, of "securing America's place in the world," critical
theorists talk more of community, of building a new culture—in the United
States, but ultimately in the world.

Maxine Greene speaks for many when she calls for the projection of new
visions and new dreams:

> This is a moment when great numbers of Americans find their expec-
> tations and hopes for their children being fed by talk of "educational
> reform." Yet the reform reports speak of those very children as "human
> resources" for the expansion of productivity, as a means to the end of
> maintaining our nation's economic competitiveness and military pri-
> macy in the world. . . . But the world we inhabit is palpably deficient:
> there are unwarranted inequities, shattered communities, unfulfilled lives.
> We cannot help but hunger for traces of utopian visions, of critical or
> dialectical engagements with social and economic realities.[10]

We have far too few dreamers today. But we are fortunate to have the Maxine
Greenes who remind us that, "we might begin by releasing our imaginations
and summoning up the traditions of freedom in which most of us were reared."[11]

More recently, bell hooks has talked of her own commitment to teaching which is rooted, in "the traditions of freedom," in part her own high school experience with school desegregation. "Remembering this past, I am most struck by our passionate commitment to a vision of social transformation rooted in the fundamental belief in a radically democratic idea of freedom and justice for all." For bell hooks, the root is in both the radically democratic idea and in the passion of the commitment. A teacher education program which lacks this commitment and this passion has already condemned itself to being a tool for the production of technicians rather than a means of engaging and mentoring progressive educators.

For hooks it is essential to keep alive a notion of teaching—and by extension of teacher education—which challenges the whole of the contemporary status quo.

> The classroom, with all its limitations, remains a location of possibility. In that field of possibility we have the opportunity to labor for freedom, to demand of ourselves and our comrades, an openness of mind and heart that allows us to face reality even as we collectively imagine ways to move beyond boundaries, to transgress. This is education as the practice of freedom.[12]

Imagine a system of teacher education focused on preparing future practitioners in this kind of classroom and for this kind of classroom!

As hooks and Greene and others remind us, there are alternative visions of the potential of education available today. The visions nurtured by the Civil Rights movement, by generations of progressive educators, of a schooling which builds free citizens and a new sense of community, not human resources for the maintenance of an economic hegemony in the world's market economy, need to be nurtured and expanded.[13]

But there is a missing piece in today's arguments. While the vision continues, however much it may at times seem dimmed or marginalized, the ideas for putting that vision into practice are sadly lacking.[14] Where Dewey had his laboratory schools and the Civil Rights movement spawned freedom schools and the movement to desegregate public education, there has been few comparable proposals for new institutional arrangements in today's schools by those who are the heirs of Dewey and King, Jane Addams and Septima Clark. We are all victims of Greene's lament, "There is little sense of agency, even among the brightly successful; there is little capacity to look at things as if they could be otherwise."[15] But those of us who hunger for a different and better world must move beyond a pedagogy of resistance, powerful as that can be, and toward a pedagogy of engagement, in which we too have our proposals and strategies for changing schools and schooling and specifically teacher education.

Today's progressive educators do not yet have a program. Those who have found themselves highly critical of the proposed reforms have also found themselves moved significantly to the margins. While the pleas of critical education theorists may dominate the pages of some academic journals, they have had little impact on the public policy debates and less on public practice. In part, this lack of impact is because there is a lack of sufficient specific program proposals coming from those who are critical of proposals like those offered by the authors of Holmes and Carnegie or the National Commission.

Henry Giroux and Peter McLaren have noted one of the major reasons why those with a critical perspective have done little about specific institutional changes:

> We believe that one major reason lies with the failure of leftist groups and other educators to move beyond the language of critique. . . . The agony of this position has been that it has prevented left educators from developing a programmatic language in which they can theorize for schools.[16]

This problem is not new. As Lawrence Cremin has noted, there has long been a preference for journalistic exposé among American progressives.[17] But at this point in history, theorizing for and with schools and school people is exactly what is needed if the opportunities which are available in the "contested terrain"[18] of contemporary education are to be seized.

In this chapter, I will argue that the current reform era does indeed provide a unique opportunity for people with a variety of perspectives to be more than sideline critics; to move from "theorizing about" reform to being active players. The current range of reforms under discussion offers the opportunity to do two important things:

1. To place all specific reform efforts in a larger ideological perspective, and to argue for a quite different ideology than the one which governs much of the reform literature;

2. To pick and choose among the reforms, supporting some as vigorously as we must oppose others to design a quite different reform program.

The results, I argue, is that while certain of the proposals currently under consideration—especially the testing of teachers and the creation of a fixed hierarchy within the profession—must be rejected, the majority of the current reform efforts can be both embraced and reshaped into a program for teacher education which will move forward a progressive vision of the purposes of education in a democratic society. Specifically, I would argue that there are four elements in the Holmes and Carnegie reports which can still be at the heart of a progressive approach to teacher education a decade after they were first promoted:

1. The replacement of the education major with an arts and sciences major

2. The recruitment and retention of people of color in the teaching profession

3. The empowerment of teachers

4. The expectation of a clinical experience much more substantive than current student teaching.

Far from being objects of critique, these four proposals should be a central part of any strategic efforts to build a progressive program for educating future teachers. Of course, a great deal depends on who is implementing any specific reform. In the wrong hands, all of these reforms can support an undemocratic profession in an undemocratic society. But in the right hands, these proposals can be the basis for a broad-based reform effort which will help move the process of teacher education in much more progressive directions than either the status quo or the changes being adopted by others.

The Need for an Arts and Sciences Major

Critical theorists speak of the need for teachers to be "transformative intellectuals"—that is critical thinkers who are also engaged in the process of transforming the society in which they live. Both the Holmes and the Carnegie reports call for requiring all future teachers to complete an arts and sciences major as part of their professional preparation.[19] They may or may not be discussing the same thing. I would argue that, given the right conditions, the arts and sciences major can be an important means to the end of empowering all teachers as critical intellectuals. Indeed, when Henry Giroux and Peter McLaren argue that "our central concern is in developing a view of teacher education that defines teachers as transformative intellectuals and schooling as part of an ongoing struggle for democracy,"[20] they could be arguing for a very specific kind of arts and sciences major.

Of course, an arts and sciences major does not guarantee critical inquiry. For almost a millennium the arts curriculum has been caught between those who see its primary purpose as defending a given culture—more or less uncritically—and those who see it as transforming culture. Indeed, there are many today who see the primary purpose of the liberal arts as preserving the culture as it is. It takes a specific perspective for the liberal arts major to be a means of transforming inquiry. But it is within the arts curriculum that this debate is joined. Providing future teachers with the opportunity to study a single discipline or field of study in meaningful depth, while not a guarantee of anything, opens up possibilities which are simply not there in a smorgasbord curriculum, however well conceived or offered.[21]

In order to be critical intellectuals—and not just mediators in a "banking" process of education—teachers must be able to understand the construction and deconstruction of knowledge. If teachers are the people who "distribute" knowledge in this society, they need to understand how knowledge is socially constructed in the different disciplines and indeed to deconstruct that knowledge, to take ideas apart and consider other ways of putting ideas together.

The need to know how knowledge is put together is the primary argument for asking every teacher to know a specific discipline in considerable depth. The issue here is not just learning material so that it can be taught to others. The issue is to understand the nature of the construction of knowledge, including knowing the political, economic, cultural, and sociological issues involved in the development of knowledge in a given society and in a given field of study.

This business of constructing and deconstructing knowledge is not merely a matter of gaining new intellectual mastery of material. It is fundamentally, as Maxine Greene has noted, a matter of envisioning a much wider way of looking at the world: "To speak of the liberal arts today, and particularly in relation to professional studies, is to summon up visions of multiple doorways opening on landscapes in many ways unexplored." These visions, Greene continues, "feed my notion of liberal education offering openings in consciousness, expanding our freedom by extending our naming of our worlds."[22] To understand the way knowledge is made and shared is ultimately part of the process of self-empowerment and of expanding freedom and "extending our naming of our worlds," and teachers in a democratic society must do no less at whatever level they are teaching.

As Susan Laird has noted recently, there is a special irony in the reality that preparation for a profession which is still made up overwhelmingly of women also involves little or no consideration of the issues of gender in the creation of knowledge or in the structure of schools as institutions. Of course issues the role of gender in the creation and transmission of what is considered the dominant culture could theoretically be considered in many parts of the curriculum, just as issues of race and class can be. But it is essential that these issues receive attention at the heart of a student's field of greatest concern, not just as marginal interests. It is in the thorough study of at least one field that students are provided with the best opportunity to consider all of the social issues—including issues of gender, race, class—which go into making that field what it is in contemporary culture.[23]

Theresa Perry has proposed four stages through which programs move as they attempt to come to terms with the inclusion of issues of race in shaping the curriculum for programs which will prepare future teachers. In the first two stages, issues of race are dealt with in a separate course that "purports to provide one with the knowledge, sensitivities, and background to work with children of color." At first, the course is an elective, then later a requirement. At the third stage, Perry insists that, as part of reconceptualizing teacher education, "a liberal arts major is required; distribution requirements include courses that allow students to study in the canonical literature, life, history, cultures, and traditions of people of color," but the "overall framework is not altered, the inclusions of information and the perspectives of people of color does not push one to reconceptualize the course." It is only in the fourth stage, one which few if any teacher preparation programs in the country have reached, that "the liberal arts majors are reconceptualized to include significant study of people of color . . . and [this allows] the lives of the historically oppressed to critically influence the shifting of frames, the reconceptualization of work in their discipline areas."[24] It is probably true that few if any colleges or universities in the United States have reached Perry's fourth stage. It is exactly this stage which should be the hallmark of any arts and sciences curriculum which truly purports to give students a liberal education, that is, one which engages him or her in understanding the very fabric of a discipline—how knowledge is created, tested, and understood in that field of study.

It is obviously the case that many of today's college students complete the requirements for a major in many different fields without ever beginning to think about how knowledge is created in that field of study—the construction of knowledge in that field—much less considering the possibility of deconstructing knowledge and building it in new and different ways, or the impact of race, class and gender in the definition of important knowledge. Many different studies have well documented the way all parts of the college curriculum can be merely the passing on and memorizing of received knowledge. But if there is any place in the current college curriculum where the nature of the creation of knowledge, the political context in which knowledge is formed and reformed, is considered, it must be at the point in the curriculum where students study one subject in depth—in their major.[25]

Henry Giroux and Peter McLaren speak to the importance of this level of depth for future teachers when they say:

> Under the shadow of the present neo-conservative assault on education, the esteemed model of the teacher has become that of the technologist, technician or applied scientist. There is little talk within this view about the need for teachers to make critical and informed judgments with respect to both their own practice and what they consider to be the meaning and purpose of education. What is missing from neo-conservative discourse is the image of the teacher as a transformative intellectual who defines school as fundamentally an ethical and empowering enterprise dedicated to the fostering of democracy, to the exercise of greater social justice, and to the building of a more equitable social order.[26]

Teachers will not be encouraged to be transformative intellectuals until teacher preparation programs are dramatically altered from a structure which seems to be geared to the creation of unimaginative technician handing on received knowledge without having thought about its construction in a specific context.

As Maxine Greene has also reminded us, "No matter who our students are, it seems to me, we need to do what we can to help them break out of enclaves, out of the narrow cubicles of specialization, no matter how practical, how technical that specialization may be. We need to release them for wondering, for pondering, and for critique."[27] Until the liberal arts major, and the whole teacher preparation process, truly releases students "for wondering, for pondering, and for critique," it will not be serving tomorrow's teachers no matter how strong the technical mastery of content or methodology is.

To be truly empowering, majors for future teachers—for all students— should include study of the subject in detail, an opportunity to conduct research in the field, to make their own contribution, however small, to the development of the field as a means of understanding how a field grows and changes, and an opportunity to consider the political and cultural issues involved in the creation of knowledge in that field in a given society.

On today's college campuses, an academic major can mean many different degrees of depth. Far too often a major simply means a collection of 10– 15 courses in the same field. But a meaningful liberal arts and sciences major should have a coherent curriculum which allows a student to know the field in depth, which requires the student to conduct meaningful research in the field, and ultimately to make his or her own contribution to the field as a means of understanding how knowledge is constructed in the specific discipline. With such a major, a college graduate will have a much clearer sense of the role of intellect in society and thus be well prepared to begin to function as a transformative intellectual, whatever professional course is pursued.

It is very important that those who argue for an arts and sciences major for all teachers not defend it primarily in terms of the knowledge base it gives those who will teach a certain subject. Obviously it is important that people teaching in a certain field know that field. The logic of history teachers majoring in history and biology teachers majoring in biology has long been recognized, and most state certification requirements expect such a concentration for high school teachers. But whether high school or elementary school teachers are under consideration, there is another quite different, but even more important reason for teachers to know one field of study well. It matters significantly less what the specific discipline is.

Unfortunately, many well-meaning people argue that while arts and sciences majors make good sense for future high school teachers who will teach in a specific field, elementary teachers, who teach in many subject matter areas, need a different major—one in which they are exposed to the breadth of subjects which they will teach rather than a single subject in depth. Indeed, there is a growing body of literature which purports to demonstrate that the arts and sciences major is not, in fact, the best preparation for future teachers at the elementary level. But there is a fundamental problem here. Who defines the good teacher? If the best teacher is one who passes on undigested a cultural heritage which has been given to her/him, then it is possible that a vocational major might serve quite well. If however, the goal of teacher preparation programs is empowering teachers as transformative intellectuals, intellectuals who are capable of "wondering, pondering, and critique," then it would seem obvious that an intellectually rigorous major which included sufficient depth of study, would be an essential prerequisite to any further work in preparing for teaching at any level from kindergarten through high school.[28]

Certainly it is true that the nature of elementary teachers work requires them to teach in many fields, to have sufficient knowledge to be able to teach in diverse fields including history, English, the sciences, math, art and music, and so on, and they need all of the possible support for that difficult task. Teachers at all levels should complete a rigorous general education requirement as one means of ensuring sufficient knowledge to cover these fields. Other means of guaranteeing breadth, especially for elementary teachers, must also be found. But knowing a little of this and a little of that cannot be sufficient preparation for teaching at any level if teachers are to play a transformative role in schools and not merely function as passive dispensers of knowledge passively received.

Future elementary teachers, as well as their middle and high school counterparts, must know something well—whether they are ever going to teach that specific field of knowledge or not. They must achieve an in-depth understanding of one field, as outlined above, as a means of understanding the nature of knowledge, the nature of disciplines, the nature of the process of constructing and deconstructing knowledge. Henry Giroux and Donaldo Macedo are right when they argue that "we need to embrace the democratic ideal of defining liberal arts education as a form of public service dedicated to creating a public sphere of critically-minded citizens. We should cut the claims of the logic of narrow individualism and specialization which combined with the underlying desire for technical mastery to produce an education that is measured merely by its skills currency."[29] To deny this level of depth is to deny teachers a professional preparation which will allow them to be truly critical intellectuals in the name of a "relevant" professional preparation which defines relevant knowledge as preparation to be cogs in a larger educational wheel rather than active participants in the making and transmission of knowledge.

Too often in the past aspiring teachers have been relegated to a curriculum which focuses almost exclusively on "how to" methods courses with little attention to critical thought or a critical cultural perspective. Thus it is true that "in mainstream schools of education, teaching practices and methods are all too often linked to a menu of learning models which are to be employed in the context of particular stipulated conditions. . . . Within this model of teacher training, 'performance at a prespecified level of mastery is assumed to be the most valid measure of teaching competence . . . the desire to have teachers critically reflect upon the purposes and consequences in terms of such issues as social continuity and change are not central."[30] Obviously this must change. And if late-twentieth-century progressive educators, in their rightful opposition to some of the Holmes and Carnegie recommendations, fail to embrace the need for a liberal arts major for future teachers, an important opportunity will have been missed.

It is also important to note that all of the arguments in this article in favor of an arts and sciences major should not be construed as opposition to education courses, at both undergraduate and graduate levels. It is true that many education methods courses have been poorly conceived and offered. So have many arts and sciences courses. Too many education courses have been organized to make teachers mere technicians. But the problems with such courses, like the problems with liberal arts courses, should not deflect progressive educators from finding the means of transforming the courses and the programs in which they appear. It is simply not the case that a solidly educated person—the recipient of the best in the breadth and depth of the liberal arts— is ready to enter a classroom.[31] There are issues of child development, classroom management, and the means of shaping the school curriculum to include diverse cultures which must also be included in the preparation of teachers from the earliest possible levels of the baccalaureate curriculum.

Indeed, it is best if future teachers can begin to study in the field of education, and have field opportunities to observe and teach in real classroom settings, as early as possible in their college careers, even during the freshman year. Such opportunities provide the students with the chance to engage in action/reflection models from the earliest days of college . . . to try ideas and methods, and critically reflect on the results. On a more practical level, they also offer students the chance to see if public schools, and the children and youth who inhabit them, are a congenial work setting. But it does not require an education major to offer such opportunities. A limited number of courses and field experiences, perhaps the equivalent of a college minor or less, is sufficient to meet these important needs. The breadth and depth of the arts and sciences curriculum, including a liberal arts major, must be the heart of the undergraduate experience for all who would teach in democratic schools.

Recruiting People of Color to the Teaching Profession

While the original Holmes report is virtually silent on the issue of recruiting people of color to the teaching profession,[32] the Carnegie report makes an eloquent plea for a new commitment to a diversified profession and outlines the seriousness of the current decline in the numbers of minority teachers.[33]

In addressing this issue, the authors of the Carnegie report are responding to a growing crisis in the nation's schools. A report from the New York State Department of Education summarizes the problem as well as any:

> Data show that the percentage of minorities in the teaching field has been declining nationally while the percentage of youngsters from minority backgrounds has been rising. National data reveal that 30 percent of the urban school age population is minority; that percentage is expected to climb to 49 percent by the year 2000. Statistics show that only 6.9 percent of public school teachers is Black although Black students account for 16 percent of public school students. Similarly, 1.9 percent of public school teachers is Hispanic while 9.1 percent of public school students is Hispanic.[34]

Unfortunately, the Carnegie report, while long on description of this problem and the need for solutions, is fairly short on the kind of procedures and organizational arrangements which will lead to real change. Effective minority recruitment must include attention to the many barriers which limit the entrance of people of color into the teaching profession and thus make the issue so critical.[35] As we know from the long history of the Civil Rights movement, it takes much more than simply saying that an issue like minority recruitment should be a priority in order to make change happen.

Minority Recruitment: Why a Goal?

The first critical question which must be answered as part of any campaign to recruit more people of color to the teaching profession is the most obvious one—why is it important to have teachers of color? Failure to ask the "why" question, to proceed with a campaign to recruit people of color to teaching without asking why it is important, is likely to yield the same dismal results as most other campaigns for reform in education which fail to ask fundamental questions. After a short time, failure is announced while the public focus moves on to other things.

The usual reason given for recruiting a diverse group of teachers—that minority youth need role models among their teachers—is certainly significant. An all white teaching staff does give African American, Latino, or Asian descent students little encouragement to believe that they might some day be professionals. And in schools where the majority of students are from disempowered groups in this society, having a teaching force which includes few if any representatives of the communities which the schools are supposed to serve creates power relationships which reinforce the disempowerment. But there are other, even more important, reasons why increasing the numbers of people of color in the teaching profession is critical.

It is not only children who need a diversity of role models. White teachers also need to experience working with people of color as peers and receiving supervision from people of color. If all of a white teachers' experiences with people of color is in relationships where the white person is a helper or leader, an important opportunity is missed. As Willis D. Hawley has argued,

> The most effective way to combat racism is to undermine the assumptions upon which it rests and to arm persons with the skills to overcome its consequences. These objectives can be achieved by placing persons of different races or ethnic backgrounds in situations where they have the opportunity for recurrent interaction involving cooperative and rewarding activities.[36]

Such a statement seems self-evident once it is said, but the idea is almost totally lacking from the current dialogue about recruiting people of color to teaching. It is only as teachers of different races have the experience of working together and teaching together that white teachers learn to treat people of other races as equals. The importance of this experience for teachers in terms of their relationships with parents, community leaders, and ultimately with their own students cannot be overstated.

Even more important than providing role models for students or other teachers, however, there is another fundamental reason why more people of color are needed in teaching. Hawley begins to point to this issue when he insists that "significantly increasing the proportion of minority teachers is important to the racial and ethnic integration of American society."[37]

There are two fundamentally different views of the relationship of the different cultures and races to each other in the United States among those who argue for multicultural curricula or for a diverse teaching force. On the one hand, there is the all too easy assumption that the dominant culture properly defines the content of the culture and the curriculum, and that affirmative action programs are needed in order to invite representatives of other groups to enter into that culture. It is quite a different matter, however, to recognize that what is needed in the United States is a commitment to build a new, and as yet unrecognized, culture in which all citizens—Native Americans and immigrants from Africa, Asia, Europe, Latin America, and the Pacific Islands—make their own contribution and play their part in the design of new cultural assumptions; in which the current mainstream culture is but one of the many represented.

If one believes the latter view, then having representatives of different cultures and races on the teaching staff of any single school becomes an essential step towards building a new culture in that place.

Lisa Delpit has issued a significant challenge to those who would teach "other people's children," especially white teachers working with students of color. Delpit has provided example after example—all familiar to anyone who has worked in schools with a diverse student and teacher population—in which teachers fail their students by imposing inappropriate cultural assumptions. As Delpit says, the problem is often not individually bad teachers. "They do not wish to damage children; indeed, they likely see themselves as wanting to help. Yet they are totally unable to perceive those different from themselves except through their own culturally clouded vision."[38] In America at the end of the twentieth century, it is no wonder that many people—teachers and others—have a "culturally clouded vision." The racism, the fear, the hatred are all around us, maiming the culture itself as well as so many citizens. Thus Delpit poses a fundamental set of questions for anyone who cares about democratic schools or a democratic society:

> Why do the refrains of progressive educational movements seem lacking in the diverse harmonies, the variegated rhythms, and the shades and tone expected in a truly heterogeneous chorus? Why do we hear so little representation from the multicultural voices which comprise the present-day American educational scene?[39]

The answers to Delpit's questions lie in the fundamental structure of American society. But the restructuring of society, and answering Delpit's questions, can begin in a single school, if it can achieve a truly diverse faculty. If the "heterogeneous chorus" exists in one faculty, the possibility exists to create in that school a microcosm of a new culture and a new set of opportunities for envisioning a truly progressive education. But the chorus cannot exist if the representatives are not there. Recruiting people of color to the teaching profession, ensuring a truly diverse profession, is thus fundamentally essential to the development of a democratic system of public education in the United States. It is a goal which simply cannot be ignored.

Recruiting People of Color: Strategies for the Agenda

The fact that there are several very important reasons for recruiting people of color to the teaching profession does not change the fact that the strategies and struggles necessary to make a significant increase in the racial diversity of today's teachers—and candidates for the profession—will be long and difficult. The essential first step in addressing this issue involves dealing directly with racism: the poor schools, lowered expectations and dropout rates which make the pool of college students and graduates of color so small. Obviously this is a long-term issue, but unless the long-term problems which so severely limit the pool of available college student candidates for teaching are addressed, no other solutions will make a significant difference.

At the same time as the larger issues of institutional racism must be recognized, steps must also be taken to do the immediate, short-term things which can begin to change the institutional reality. To err too much on either side is a serious mistake. There are those who treat minority recruitment as simply a matter of technical readjustments in the structures of the profession. This failure to deal seriously with the long-term issues of racism virtually guarantees that the most difficult institutional realities will be overlooked. On the other hand, the complexity of institutional racism can become a reason why the more immediate steps which can be taken are constantly postponed. Too many today are saying, "affirmative action is a very difficult issue," and thus excusing themselves from any immediate action. A multipointed strategy—including both immediate action and long-term strategic thinking—is the only one which has a chance of being successful.

There is no one magic solution to this problem. Patience and many strategies are needed. While no one strategy is likely to solve the problem, no possibility should be dismissed because it does not reach the full goal. On the contrary, many different programs must be linked in moving forward the long-term agenda of building a multiracial teaching staff to serve the schools of the new multicultural society in which we will all live in the very near future. As part of a multipointed strategy, the following steps are essential elements:

Simplification of Certification Requirements. Among the things which can be done immediately to recruit more people of color to the teaching profession one of the most important is streamlining the certification requirements. One of the greatest barriers to recruiting many people of color to the teaching profession—indeed, one of the greatest barriers to recruiting many qualified people to the profession—is the rigidity of the certification requirements. Most of the recent reform proposals have called for greater flexibility in the paths to certification, especially for experienced adults who already have a baccalaureate degree. Under current certification requirements in most states, such candidates would have to return to college for at least a year and often longer in order to complete student teaching and the course work for certification. And many with limited financial resources or families to support, which includes the vast majority of people of color, simply cannot engage in such a protracted process.

In Massachusetts, for example, one of the important changes brought about by the adoption of the recommendations of the Commonwealth's Joint Task Force on Teacher Preparation in 1987 was the creation of a two stage certification process in which the first-level, provisional certification, could be reached much more easily than the old certification, while the standards were raised for full certification.[40] There are many people today, including many people of color, who would like to be teachers and are well qualified. There are many, indeed, who already have baccalaureate degrees, some of whom have had successful careers in other fields, who would be interested in the teaching profession. People with this sort of education and experience do need some additional preparation before entering the classroom as teachers. But programs and requirements could be dramatically simplified so that after a summer or a semester's preparation a candidate could be qualified to begin actual teaching—with full salary—and appropriate supervision and support for continued professional growth.

In the summer of 1990, Wheelock College in Boston, Massachusetts began a program which moved in just this direction. The college offered a new Summer Provisional Certification Program in which twenty-five students and six faculty members spent eight weeks covering the requirements for provisional certification under the new Massachusetts state regulations for provisional teacher certification. In beginning the program the college made a commitment to ensuring that at least half of the faculty and half of the students in the program were people of color, and that the focus of the curriculum was urban education, specifically in Boston. This link of accelerated programs for postbaccalaureate professionals with a commitment to recruiting people of color to teaching needs to be duplicated many times over.[41]

Ironically, many today recognize that there is such a pool of qualified applicants for the profession and have sought the means to help them become teachers. Some of the nation's most prestigious universities have begun programs for "mid-career professionals" so that they can become teachers. Many states have changed their certification requirements or developed special apprentice programs to help such candidates for the profession move in easily. But almost no one has linked such measures to the campaign to recruit people of color to the profession. It is indeed a mark of the racism of the society that minority recruitment and the search for mid-career professionals and others with baccalaureate degrees and some preparation for teaching have been kept so separate. Few, if any, policymakers have recognized the existing pool of minority candidates who could enter teaching through this route and few of the prestigious university programs for mid-career professionals have any effective track record or plans for recruiting people of color. But institutions of higher education and state departments of education which are serious about the issue of minority recruitment could begin to make such a recognition and initiate policies for special programs specifically aimed at recruiting people of color with baccalaureate degrees and experience into teaching.

Avoidance of New Barriers.   One of the great ironies of the Carnegie report is that while it dramatically calls for increased minority recruitment into teaching it also proposes other steps which will narrow the pool of people of color who are able to consider teaching. Specifically in the proposals for required fifth-year or master's degree programs and for competency testing, steps are proposed which will make it even more difficult for people of color to become teachers.

Five-year Programs.   As is noted elsewhere in this article, five years of study prior to an initial appointment as a teacher—and the opportunity to begin to earn a salary—is not necessary in order to improve the quality of teacher education. A masters degree should, indeed, be an eventual goal for all teachers, but an on-the-job master's degree program makes the most sense, both economically and pedagogically. Four-year programs which include an arts and sciences major and an education minor—or short-term post-baccalaureate programs which offer the equivalent of an education minor to people who are already college graduates—combined with a masters degree to be earned on the job provide much better means of quality instruction and an opportunity for novice teachers to learn, reflect, and receive supervision at the point where the learning is most beneficial, where it can already be tested in lived experience in a classroom. Yet in spite of this reality, many states are following the lead of the Carnegie and Holmes reports and requiring a fifth year or more of preparation prior to first certification and the opportunity to earn a salary. Such barriers will only reduce the number of people who have had trouble paying for four years of college in teaching and shift teaching into a profession for the children of the upper middle class. And given the low correlation of upper middle class youth and youth of color, such moves will have a devastating impact on minority recruitment.

Competency Testing. Competency testing for teachers is an even more popular "quick fix" for the problems of today's schools. Many states have begun testing teachers prior to entry into the profession, and some have begun testing those already well into their careers as a means of supposedly weeding out incompetent teachers. The fact there is virtually no correlation between success in tests and success in the classroom, and the even more clearly documented fact that any test available today has considerable race, class, and gender bias in it, makes such testing proposals foolish at best and deliberately racist at worst. Tests for admission to programs are especially foolish; they ignore the possibility of significant learning in the programs themselves. Progressive educators must argue for high standards for the teaching profession. Lowering standards, or special standards for people of color, feeds the worst elements of racial stereotyping in the United States. The Carnegie task force is right when it asserts, "The issue is how to produce enough minority candidates who can meet the high standards."[42] But standards must be meaningful standards, which truly measure a candidates fitness for the work to be done, and competency tests have clearly failed to meet that requirement.[43]

Early Recruitment of Youth of Color for Teaching.   While it is essential not to place new barriers in the way of those who seek to enter teaching, more positive steps must also be taken to ensure that much larger numbers of youth of color enter teaching in the years ahead. One of the most effective steps which can be taken is to identify youngsters who might be good teachers at an early stage, preferably at the middle school level. If such youth are contacted, offered support, and encouraged to stay in school, enroll in and complete college, and enter teaching, the numbers of minority teachers will begin to change dramatically. To wait and look at the numbers of college students or college graduates of color—to allow the current dropout rates among high school students of color to take their toll—is to ensure that the pool of available teachers of color will be too small.

In a number of areas, plans have been made to intervene at this early stage in the career selection process. For example, in 1994 the Boston Teachers Union included in a new contract with the city's schools a commitment to a program in which area colleges, in cooperation with public school teachers would work with high school, and even middle school students, to help them complete high school, find college placements and scholarship support, and ultimately find jobs as teachers in the Boston Public Schools. "Teach Boston" now includes students at several of the city's high schools for whom their school-to-career option is the teaching profession. Lesley College in Cambridge, Massachusetts, and the Rindge School of Technical Arts have begun a "Careers in Education" program which attracts high school students, especially students of color, to teaching. The program offers high school students the opportunity to join a Lesley student teacher in one of the city's elementary schools while also taking a high school course focused on issues of teaching. The course familiarizes students in the program with college campus life and students from the program will be able to enter college with credits from the course towards their baccalaureate degree. Programs of that range and seriousness exist and many more are needed.[44]

Affirmative Action and Support in Colleges of Education.   The small percentage of students of color in virtually any collegiate teacher preparation program in the United States is an embarrassment to American higher education.[45] Colleges and universities which, at least since the 1960s, have worked hard to increase their enrollments of African American, Latino, Asian, and Native American students have very little to show for their efforts when it comes to teacher education programs. There are many reasons for this problem.

Undergraduate admission offices which have long been used to specialized recruitment of students of color in many fields have simply not given the same efforts to their education programs. Too often teaching has continued to be a program for suburban and rural students who wish to return to suburban and rural school systems.[46] In addition, many current programs have internal barriers to student's success. While admission to most professional programs may not ensure a student success in the program, it usually does ensure a clear path and some measure of faculty support. Many teacher programs include what is virtually a second admission process—special barriers which must be conquered prior to placement in student teaching. And far too often these barriers are designed in ways which discriminate significantly on the basis of race and class. Any special limitations—grade point average, recommendations, and so on—prior to beginning student teaching must be monitored very carefully to ensure that they are not a special barrier for students of color.

Schools/colleges/departments of education—and the state agencies which evaluate them—must give a high priority to an examination of their own internal regulations and support systems so that they will be successful in both recruiting and graduating people of color in significant numbers. In 1989 the Massachusetts Board of Regents and Board of Education Task Force on the Recruitment of People of Color to the Teaching Profession recommended:

> The Department of Education should require an "affirmative action plan" for the recruitment of students and faculty of color as a component of the teacher preparation program approval process and should expect significant and measurable progress in meeting affirmative action targets when programs are considered for reapproval. The Board of Education must give serious consideration to ending the approval of programs which continue to serve an essentially white student body and do not provide evidence of aggressive outreach efforts.[47]

Almost a decade later college and university administrators, and state departments of education, should demand no less of their teacher preparation programs.

Mentoring and Support through the First Placement.   Some of the nation's school systems are now engaged in vigorous affirmative action programs, some have court mandated targets for minority teacher hiring, while other school systems have at best a laissez-faire attitude toward the recruitment of teachers of color. But whatever the range of hiring procedures faced by the newly certified teacher of color, the reality of the placement can be quite different from the promises offered by the personnel office. Many minority teachers find themselves isolated in all-white schools. Many find themselves in situations where the passive—or active—racism of peers makes every step from the lunch break to playground or hall supervision a time of tension. Mentors and university supports, when they are available, do not always have the training or the desire to be supportive of teachers of color. Much more must be done to make entry into the profession a good experience for teachers of color.

In part this issue will only be addressed as the racism of the larger society—reflected in the attitudes of many white teachers and administrators—is changed. But much can be done in the meantime. Colleges and universities can provide postgraduation support and mentoring for their graduates, and be sure that those mentors assigned to novice teachers of color are themselves people of color or at least people with a clear understanding of the issues faced by a novice teacher of color. School systems can make sure that they hire a critical mass of teachers of color so that the lone teacher is not isolated in an all-white world. Teacher unions and other professional associations can develop support groups so that teachers in different schools and even different school systems can support each other.[48]

Efforts like those proposed here, and others which can be designed by thoughtful people can make a significant difference in the numbers of people of color who are teaching in the nation's schools. But in spite of all efforts, the odds are that for at least a generation, the majority of children of color will be taught—during most of their classes—by white teachers. In addition, there will be many white children who will have few, if any, teachers of color throughout twelve years of public schooling, especially if they live and attend school in many of the suburban and rural areas of the nation. It is therefore essential that future white teachers receive a much better immersion in multiculturalism than their predecessors have received. A token course in the study of cultural differences or even worse a "social problems" course is not the solution. All college students, as part of a quality baccalaureate education, must be provided with a much better understanding of the cultural diversity in the United States and the world. Equally important, the underlying assumption in all studies of cultural diversity must be that the goal is mutual learning and the building of a new common culture, not that there is a properly dominant culture which may tolerate certain differences along the way.

One final word is needed in this section. There have been those who argue for keeping the standards for teacher preparation programs low because, "after all, we have to attract minorities." That sort of racism must be rejected. The key steps in minority recruitment involve providing the kinds of support and mentoring so that students of color, like others, can meet tough standards for teachers while also removing the false barriers such as racist testing requirements or overly expensive programs which really do discriminate.

Only with a willingness to experiment, to try many different methods, and to put institutional resources behind the commitment, will the goal be met of diversifying the nation's teaching profession. It is a goal worthy of the work involved.

Empowering Teachers

Perhaps the best known of the Holmes and Carnegie recommendations have to do with empowering teachers. As the Carnegie authors state so clearly:

> Professional autonomy is the first requirement [for fulfilling the report's goals]. If the schools are to compete successfully with medicine, architecture, and accounting for staff, then teachers will have to have comparable

authority in making the key decisions about the services they render. Within the context of a limited set of clear goals for students set by state and local policymakers, teachers, working together, must be free to exercise their professional judgment as to the best way to achieve these goals.[49]

This is not a point of view with which any progressive educators should disagree.

Indeed, Henry Giroux and Peter McLaren seem to make almost exactly the same point when they write about the problems faced by teachers and students who "work in overcrowded conditions, lack time to work collectively in a creative fashion, or are shackled by rules or sets of institutionalized scruples that disempower them . . . "[50] Teacher empowerment, it seems, is an issue about which all sides agree thoroughly. But the issue is more complex than first appears to be the case.

Giroux and McLaren certainly seem to follow the same thinking as the Holmes and Carnegie authors when they criticize policies which tend to define "teachers primarily as technicians, that is, as pedagogical clerks who are incapable of making important policy or curriculum decisions."[51] However, the critical theorists also expand very significantly beyond the definition of teacher empowerment contained in much of the current reform literature when they continue to insist on "the need for teachers to make critical and informed judgments with respect to both their own practice and what they consider to be the meaning and purpose of education."[52]

In a simple clause, Giroux and McLaren have dramatically expanded the definition of teacher empowerment in ways which would make many of their more cautious contemporaries very nervous. It has become the conventional wisdom of reform efforts of the 1980s and 1990s that teachers must be allowed to, indeed must be encouraged to make "critical and informed judgments with respect to . . . their own practice." While institutional resistance certainly continues in many places to proposals for decentralizing educational decision making and trusting teachers at the school level, most reform efforts now include the shift of much authority over the best means of the delivery of the curriculum to teachers.

This power over the delivery of the curriculum is only the first step, however. As Michael Apple has been pointing out for some years now, at the same time as the reform language talks of giving teachers more power, the development of new technologies has actually reduced the power teachers have over much of the content of the curriculum. Thus, "considerable pressure is building to have teaching and school curricula be totally prespecified and tightly controlled for the purposes of 'efficiency,' 'cost effectiveness,' and 'accountability.' In many ways, the deskilling that is affecting jobs in general is now having an impact on teachers as more and more decisions are moving out of their hands and as their jobs have become even more difficult to do."[53]

A second, far more important step must also be included when teachers are asked to "consider the meaning and purpose of education." Teachers can be empowered to consider different means of delivering a predetermined curriculum and a stagnant view of American culture. Teachers can also be empowered to reconsider the very nature of the curriculum and their own work, and to take a critical approach to the nation's culture. Herein lies the crux of many of the differences among those who call themselves reformers in today's schools. Both sides speak of empowering teachers, but they are talking of empowering teachers for quite different ends. For one side, the professional status to make curricular and management decisions regarding the best ways to prepare students to find their place in today's competitive market economy, albeit a place in which they can contribute and be productive citizens, is the goal. For others, however, empowerment is for quite different ends; ends that include teachers becoming, and recruiting their students to join them, as transformative intellectuals, ready to attack much in today's economy and able to "play a central role in the fight for democracy."[54]

The debate about empowering teachers—and the definition of empowerment—is not new. In the early years of this century many reformers, led by Chicago's Ella Flagg Young, proposed teachers councils as a means of empowering teachers, of giving them a greater say in the decisions regarding their schools. Young saw these councils as an essential step in asserting teacher's democratic rights. If such moves were not made, she warned, "In a short time the teachers must cease to occupy the position of initiators in the individual work of instruction and discipline, and must fall into a class of assistants, whose duty consists in carrying out instructions of a higher class which originates method for all."[55] In Young's vision, these councils would provide a means for teachers to play a major role in the development and implementation of the curriculum at the local level, but also the councils were meant to give teachers a voice in the higher levels of school policy development. In other words, they were to follow Giroux and McLaren's call for "teachers to make critical and informed judgments with respect to both their own practice and what they consider to be the meaning and purpose of education."

And as at the end of the century, so in the early years of the century, the councils were embraced at the curriculum delivery level and rejected at the policy level. Thus in 1919, John Dewey wrote:

There isn't a sinister interest in the United States that isn't perfectly willing to leave in the hands of the teaching body the ultimate decision on points of that particular kind which come to be known as "pedagogy" and "pedagogical methods." There is no certainty, there is no likelihood, however, that the views of the body of teachers, in most cities and towns of the United States, will at the present time have any real, positive, constructive influence in determining the basic educational policy of the schools of their communities, so far as a more general aspect of education is concerned. As to things that in the long run affect the life of the community, that affect the relations of capital and labor and so on, the discussions and deliberations of these purely pedagogical bodies are, as we know, practically impotent.[56]

The question of allowing teachers to address the "relations of capital and labor," or "the need for teachers to make critical and informed judgments with respect to . . . what they consider to be the meaning and purpose of education"—to impact the content as well as the delivery of the curriculum—remain as much a matter of contention today as when Dewey wrote over seventy-five years ago.

Significant empowerment of teachers in teacher education programs also involves a shift from a traditional top-down to a very different style pedagogy in these programs. "In mainstream schools of education," Giroux and McLaren charge, "teaching practices and methods are all too often linked to a menu of learning models which are to be employed in the context of particular stipulated conditions. . . . Within this model of teacher training, 'performance at a prespecified level of mastery is assumed to be the most valid measure of teaching competence . . . the desire to have teachers critically reflect upon the purposes and consequences in terms of such issues as social continuity and change are not central concerns."[57] As long as the curriculum of the schools, or the curriculum of college programs for preparing teachers is viewed in the traditional way of pouring ideas and methods into the next generation, all of the language of empowerment will mean little. Only when the curriculum of the schools and colleges, like the institutional structure is changed will empowerment have significant meaning.[58]

A word of warning is also needed here. As Theresa Perry has pointed out, it is important to ask why teacher empowerment has become so popular just at the moment when the teaching force is increasingly white and both the children and parents in urban schools, and the people being elected/appointed to school committees are increasingly people of color.[59] To raise this issue is not to be opposed to teacher empowerment vis a via principals and even more distant (and also mostly white) school bureaucracies. It is, however, to recognize that the equation is complicated, and that it is essential to empower both teachers and other key actors, especially parents at the same time.

As Michael Apple has noted in his plea for "facing complexity":

> Of course, all this is not to say that one should uncritically accept teachers' positions on everything of importance simply because it is a group of people whose work is being restructured and intensified who hold such beliefs. Given teachers' contradictory class position, there *will* be times when they will take less than democratic stances. Rather, it is to say that without a thoroughgoing analysis of the long history of gender as well as class struggles and strategies in teaching, we would not know what stance is progressive in what specific arena in the first place.[60]

The debate about teacher empowerment cannot be allowed to fall into a simple minded discussion that assumes teachers will always make the right—or the wrong—decisions. Reality, and human nature, is indeed more complex. But a democratic schooling must give substantial power to those whose lives are most affected by decisions, and that must include teachers, parents, and students.

Parents and teachers are not, after all, natural antagonists. It is essential, however, to recognize that there are times when they have different perspectives and different concerns. This is especially true when schools are located in communities of the disempowered, and parents and teachers represent different class and racial perspectives. Any conversation about the relative power of teachers, parents, and the larger community must take into account the race and class differences among the groups. It is one thing to consider these issues in an all white suburb or small town when teachers, parents, and the larger community reflect similar cultural identities. It is quite another thing to have the same conversation in a large city, other rural areas, or an Indian reservation when the cultural clash is profound. In the latter case, Delpit's reminders are essential:

> The clash between school culture and home culture is actualized in at least two ways. When a significant difference exists between the students' culture and the school's culture, teachers can easily misread students' aptitudes, intent, or abilities as a result of the difference in styles of language use and interactional patterns. Secondly, when such

cultural differences exist, teachers may utilize styles of instruction and/
or discipline that are at odds with community norms.[61]

The solution to the problems brought on by differences between teachers and
parents is not empowering one at the expense of the other, but rather by
providing the best means for mutual understand and resolution of differences.
This is not an easy process. Cultural assumptions are often deeply held and
seldom easily examined. The "underlying attitudinal differences in the appropriate display of explicitness and personal power in the classroom," which
Delpit describes—the tendency for a white middle-class teacher to ask "Would
you like to sit down now?" when the African-American teacher may say, "Sit
down, be quiet . . . NOW!"—come from a lifetime of experience which is
not easily reconsidered.[62] Yet it is in the process of just this kind of self-
examination and mutual consideration that groups of teachers and teachers
with parents will come to be truly effective educators.

The basic unit for the resolution of these issues, indeed the basic unit for
all education, should be the individual school, not the whole school system.
With the focus on individual schools, parents would have access at the point
they most want access, the experience of their own child in school. Few
parents want access to the system as a whole. Their focus is their own child
and her/his school. Such a focus also allows parents to interact with teachers
on a face to face basis, and around the issues which most matter to both.
Especially at a time when in many urban areas, the majority of parents are
people of color and the majority of teachers are white such contact is essential. There will always be differences, but the local school is the unit at which
these differences need to be resolved. If that is done, then the goals of empowering teachers and giving parents the role they need in their children's
education will not be in unresolvable tension with each other.[63]

The choice remains as clear today as when Ella Flagg Young wrote in 1901
that either teachers were to be cogs in a machine and schools, "a mere mill,
grinding uniform grists," or the teachers were to play am much more significant
role, having "the power of initiative and execution."[64] A reform movement
worthy of being called progressive must clearly be in the latter camp.

Providing a Meaningful Clinical Experience

When the authors of the Carnegie report say that there is a need to develop,
"a new professional curriculum in graduate schools of education leading to

a Master in Teaching degree, based on systematic knowledge of teaching and including internships and residencies in the schools," they raise a wide variety of interesting options.[65] Progressives are naturally, and quite rightly, wary of the language of professionalization and extended graduate programs. Too often such language, and such programs, have been used to create a small elite unaccountable to the majority of citizens. Extending the number of years of required schooling has long been a means of excluding poor and working class candidates from any profession, with law and medicine as the outstanding examples.[66]

A generation of historians such as Burton J. Bledstein have warned that:

> the culture of professionalism required amateurs to "trust" in the integrity of trained persons, to respect the moral authority of those whose claim to power lay in the sphere of the sacred and the charismatic. Professionals controlled the magic circle of scientific knowledge which only the few, specialized by training and indoctrination, were privileged to enter.[67]

Bledstein has caught much of the tone of contemporary "reform" efforts in education. Too often the discussions of differentiated staffing leads to what many fear would be the creation of a small elite, Holmes' and Carnegie's "career professionals," who would be the few who would control the magic circle of the scientific knowledge of pedagogy, while the amateurs, including both the majority of classroom teachers, as well as parents would have to simply "trust in the integrity of trained persons." This is not the democratic vision which a critical approach to education warrants.

The dangers of this professional elitism are exacerbated by the ways in which the contemporary economy separates the professional elite from the rest of society. We cannot ignore Christopher Lash's reminder that the nation's emerging elite "arc far more cosmopolitan, or at least more restless and migratory, than their predecessors. In effect, they have removed themselves from the common life."[68] If this is what is happening in America at century's end, if the top 20 percent of citizens, Reich's "symbolic analysts" are receiving most of the rewards but withdrawing from any meaningful participation in the larger society, the question must be asked: Will students and schools be well served by including teachers in the new elite?

On the other hand, it is a mistake to ignore the opportunities which are present in proposals such as those in the Carnegie and Holmes reports for extending the graduate-level training of teachers. It is not a tenable position to simply argue that the teaching profession requires only limited preparation with no review of professional standards or consideration of appropriate graduate programs. Perhaps it is possible to use teaching to develop both a new kind of graduate professional program and a new professional model—more egalitarian, more rooted in both practice and community, and more democratic.

If we are serious about strengthening the undergraduate experience of teachers in the arts and sciences, in developing an arts and sciences major which is strong in both content knowledge and critical inquiry, then time must be found somewhere else for more extended professional training. If the baccalaureate experience is going to focus on breadth and depth in a new arts curriculum which includes attention to diverse cultures and to the construction of knowledge itself, then master's level programs are the logical place for further professional development. And if the empowerment of teachers is a serious part of the agenda, then one piece of that empowerment must be a much larger role for veteran teachers in the education of future teachers. Proposals for "internships and residencies in the schools," if properly implemented, can be a significant step in accomplishing these goals. Indeed, such models can link new teachers must closer to their predecessors and to the communities in which they will serve.

Finally, and most important, graduate programs if properly constructed, if deeply immersed in the actual practice of the profession of teaching, can be a very effective means of creating opportunities for action and reflection to lead to a new level of critical understanding. Such an interactive form of education, in which the student is as active a participant in the learning process as the teacher, is the opposite of traditional education. Too often teacher education, like the rest of American education, follows the traditional "banking" model, as Freire calls it, in which education professors "deposit" knowledge in the minds of novice teachers so that at some future day it can be "withdrawn" by their own students in the public schools. This must not be the norm in the future.[69]

The critical issue then is not whether or not to have graduate programs in teacher preparation—and a requirement of graduate-level work for all future teachers—but rather how to design such programs so that they will further the ongoing process of helping teachers to be fully empowered critical intellectuals, able to understand the nature of knowledge and the process of passing knowledge on in the specific cultural context of the schools in which they teach.

In order to be effective, graduate programs in teacher education need to be marked by two characteristics.

First, graduate-level teacher education programs must be firmly based in schools and communities giving their students the opportunity to be responsible educators themselves while receiving the support and mentoring of experienced professionals. Graduate education courses at the university campus at which more traditional pedagogy is both modeled and taught are not what is needed. On the contrary graduate programs for teachers need to be designed to maximize the opportunity for responsible action in teaching and sustained critical reflection on that experience.[70]

Keeping the heart of graduate-level teacher education in the schools also increases the opportunity for experienced teachers to play a meaningful mentoring role in the master's degree program. Mentor teachers have years of experience to offer. If the language of empowering teachers means anything, it must mean that they should have the power to support those entering the profession after them. Today's cooperating teachers are given far too little recognition, remuneration, or power within the teacher preparation program. The mentor teacher must be a fully equal member of the college faculty in designing and evaluating the novice teachers master's degree curriculum.[71]

Secondly, effective graduate programs for teachers must also be financially available to everyone. It is easy to say that this should be done through generous financial aid, but that aid is too seldom forthcoming and is highly unlikely to be sufficient to allow novice practitioners to maintain a reasonable life. A different approach is to designate novice teachers as real teachers to be paid a full salary as members of the profession. Such a step guarantees sufficient financial support for those entering the profession, whether or not financial aid programs are well funded in any given year. Indeed, a salary is the only means of ensuring the necessary financial support and professional recognition which will keep the profession of teaching open to people of diverse class backgrounds and diverse resources to pay for their education. And even more important a salary formally recognizes the novices role as a real teacher engaged along with more senior colleagues in the practice of the profession—learning through critical reflection on real experience—rather than merely preparing for some future responsibility.

It is at the point of the internship or clinical experience that the whole pattern of a critically reflective practitioner will, or will not, develop. The opportunities for the novice teacher to act and reflect must be real opportunities, which means that the novice teacher must have the role and authority of a teacher. It is ironic that current regulations in most states require a specified level of preparation before certification but no active reflection on practice once one has the certificate which gives the authority to practice. In the name of protecting the children, student teachers are given very little real authority. Yet suddenly at the moment of certification, a teacher is deemed to be a finished product, ready for full authority, and no longer required to continue in the study of pedagogy or subject matter. Such a reality simply does not reflect the way human beings learn. There is no substitute for real work as the basis of ongoing reflection about that work. It is only in the process of acting and reflecting—with the full authority to act as well as the time to reflect—that people grow in their professional judgments.[72]

Creating graduate programs of the sort proposed here is not difficult. Many states have already moved towards requiring a masters degree or having a two stage certification process in which a provisionally certified teacher must do some extended work—such as earning a graduate degree—in order to achieve final certification. A graduate program which is based on a meaning-ful internship in the schools is certainly consistent with the Carnegie report's call for, "a new professional curriculum in graduate schools of education leading to a Master in Teaching degree, based on systematic knowledge of teaching and including internships and residencies in the schools." At the same time a program of this sort is ideally suited to creating a learning environment in which novice teachers are given badly needed support and opportunities for critical reflection on the daily experience of teaching and thus chances to grow in their professional and personal critical consciousness.

In calling for a program of mentoring, and the appointment of mentor teachers, great care must be given to avoid moves toward a permanent core of master teachers, a fixed elite within the profession. Both the Carnegie and the Holmes reports fail to take this care in their calls for an hierarchical profession. The stratified, hierarchical profession proposed in reform sugges-tions for "differentiated staffing" must be rejected. Such divisions have no relationship to real quality. A temporary apprenticeship is one thing. A per-manent low level as both Holmes and Carnegie imply is quite another. At the other end of the spectrum, mentor teachers (classroom teachers who tempo-rarily take on special duties) are quite different from a permanent elite as the Holmes "Career Professionals" or the Carnegie "Lead Teachers with Board Certification." It is essential that progressives in education avoid the models used in the reform of medicine earlier in this century. The future must not involve a profession in which there are a few highly paid equivalents to the surgeons, and the vast majority of teachers relegated to the "direct service" role to which nurses have long been consigned.[73] Mentor teachers should emerge from and return to the profession which, more than most, can cel-ebrate its egalitarian nature.[74]

The nature of the apprenticeship or intern experience as a location for critical reflection on the pedagogy and the politics of education is essential to the development of a truly critical teacher education which will help produce transformative intellectuals among tomorrow's teachers. The problem with current student teaching is that the student teacher lacks status, responsibility, or time, to be truly engaged in the teaching experience. S/he is in a position of needing to give constant deference to both cooperating teacher and education professor, both of whom hold the candidate's professional future in their hands. At the same time, the whole experience is too short in duration—a semester at most—and too lacking in authority, to provide a meaningful base of professional experience from which to engage in thoughtful critical reflection. Under such circumstances, the goal must be to survive, make few mistakes, and heed well the idiosyncrasies of specific supervisors. This is not a set of circumstances likely to breed critical inquiry.

At the same time, a more extended, formal apprenticeship, also has its dangers. Apprenticeship in other trades has often been marked by a commitment to the status quo. The apprentice learns very well to practice the trade exactly as it is practiced by the master. It may be a good means of instruction, but it is not one which will yield critical, transformative inquiry. The apprentice teacher must have much more freedom, including the freedom to fail, to try new ventures, and to question existing assumptions. Indeed, the questioning of "the way things have always be done," must be one of the central marks of the apprentice's curriculum.

The core of the experience of a novice teacher must be based on Paulo Freire's notion of dialogue in which both novice and experienced teacher are allowed to give voice to their experience, reflections, and visions of the future—and both are respected in the process. Only in this way will the apprenticeship experience yield the kind of critical reflection necessary for ensuring tomorrow's teachers are transformative intellectuals.

Giroux and McLaren make one point that is essential to the kinds of specific structural changes in teacher education which I propose when they speak of the process of critical analysis which includes "its potential to open the text to a form of deconstruction that interrogates it as part of a wider process of cultural production; in addition, by making the text an object of intellectual inquiry, such an analysis posits the reader, not as a passive consumer, but as an active producer of meanings."[75] This is an essential issue in all parts of teacher education but especially in the clinical internship.

More than in most fields, there is still the assumption that candidates for teaching need to consume great amounts of information—usually presented in "how-to" methods courses, before they can do anything in the classroom. Thus the normal progress in teacher preparation programs is from several courses in education (sometimes up to half of the undergraduate curriculum), to one semester of student teaching, to lifetime certification. The fact that candidates for teaching need to gain experience and bring that experience to the ongoing dialogue of their own education, indeed that there should be a dialogue, instead of merely passive consumption of materials and ideas, is yet to be part of the norm in teacher preparation programs. Changing this is one of the essential attributes of any structural set of changes that will allow candidates for the profession to be critical intellectuals, not passive consumers and later dispensers of knowledge.[76] A meaningful clinical experience will be a long step in the right direction.

Conclusions

For all of my attempts to outline a kind of reconciliation, a new opening between different factions within the education reform movement, there are also areas where no agreement is possible, and it is essential to be clear on the differences. Most important of all, progressive people must militantly reject the language which views children as human resources for the expansion of competitiveness and insist that the purpose of education remains the creation of a more humane, more just, more democratic society. Our vision must be—and we must always be clear about this—not the development of schools which will help us compete more effectively with Japan, but rather the development of what W. E. B. DuBois called for in his plea for an education which would produce "young women and young men of devotion to lift again the banner of humanity and to walk toward a civilization which will be free and intelligent, which will be healthy and unafraid."[77] Indeed, until we ourselves are unafraid of being branded romantics for using such language, the essential vision which will guide all of our other work will remain unattainable.

If the purpose of schooling is to defeat the Japanese, the Germans, and the Koreans in worldwide competition, if it is to develop a skilled elite of managers and engineers and a pool of low-level workers for the computer and service industries who are only relatively better off than their counterparts in the Third World, then one set of methods and school models will be appropriate. If, however, the aims of education, are to protect and expand democracy, if the goal is to empower teachers, but also students and their parents, and to encourage teachers, parents, and students as empowered citizens, then the goals and the methods will be quite different.

There are obviously many problems with many of the proposals being supported in the name of reforming teacher education today. At the same time, I want to argue that progressive educators must avoid the marginalization of critics who refuse to engage in the world of institutional change. To abdicate responsibility for what is happening in the current era of changing school structures is to leave the definition of reform to others or worse to give a kind of support the status quo defended by some who seem to believe that we have already achieved perfection in teacher education programs. Progressives, those with a critical perspective, cannot afford to be this kind of bystander. We must play an essential role in today's debates about the future course of teacher preparation programs and the debate should focus at the fundamental questions regarding the aims of education.

We must nurture our own vision, as Maxine Greene reminds us, "because it is only through the projection of a better social order that we can perceive the gaps in what exists and try to transform and repair."[78] We must be clear regarding this basic choice, but also very wise in the step-by-step methods which will turn it into reality. Both parts of the equation are essential. In holding to the vision of the purposes of education as the building of a more just and democratic society, there can be no compromise. At the same time, in the means of accomplishing that vision, in the means of structuring schools, and specifically teacher preparation programs, the greater the level of common ground which can be achieved among the broadest segments of society, the greater the chances of success in the reform efforts and ultimately in the development of the whole vision.

NOTES

Preface

1. George S. Counts, *Dare the School Build a New Social Order?* (Carbondale, IL: Southern Illinois University Press, 1978; original edition, 1932).

2. Donaldo Macedo, *Literacies of Power: What Americans Are Not Allowed to Know* (Boulder, Colo.: Westview Press, 1994), p. 173.

3. Manning Marable, *The Crisis of Color and Democracy: Essays on Race, Class and Power* (Monroe, Maine: Common Courage Press, 1992), p. 12.

1. Education Reform

1. The National Commission on Excellence in Education, *A Nation at Risk: The Imperative for Educational Reform* (Washington, D.C.: U.S. Government Printing Office, 1983), p. 5.

2. Carnegie Forum on Education and the Economy, *A Nation Prepared: Teachers for the 21st Century: The Report of the Task Force on Teaching as a Profession* (New York: Carnegie Forum on Education and the Economy, 1986), p. 11.

3. Stanley Aronowitz and William DiFazio, *The Jobless Future: Sci-Tech and the Dogma of Work* (Minneapolis: University of Minnesota Press, 1994), pp. 13–14.

4. Kevin Phillips, *Boiling Point: Democrats, Republicans, and the Decline of Middle-Class Prosperity* (New York: Random House, 1993).

5. For an excellent analysis of the impact of Sputnik and the Cold War on school reform efforts in the 1950s and 60s, see Joel Spring, *The Sorting Machine Revised: National Educational Policy since 1945* (New York: Longman, 1989).

6. Bennett Harrison and Barry Bluestone, *The Great U-Turn* (New York: Basic Books, 1988). See also Robert B. Reich, *The Work of Nations: Preparing Ourselves*

for 21st-Century Capitalism (New York: Vintage Books, 1991, 1992), p. 196ff., and Aronowitz and DiFazio, p. 4. See also Harrison and Bluestone's earlier work, *The Deindustrialization of America* (New York: Basic Books, 1982).

7. Reich, p. 7.

8. Reich, p. 208.

9. Reich, p. 282.

10. Reich, p. 171.

11. Reich, p. 172.

12. Reich, pp. 174–80.

13. Andrew Kopkind, "Bobby's in the Basement: Doctor Reich's Economic Rx," *The Nation*, August 17–24, 1992, pp. 166–68.

14. John Dewey, lecture notes: political philosophy, 1892, pp. 44–45, Dewey Papers, "Moral Theory and Practice" (1891), in *Early Works*, 3:105–6, cited in Robert B. Westbrook, "Schools for Industrial Democrats: The Social Origins of John Dewey's Philosophy of Education," *American Journal of Education* 100. (August 1992): 409.

15. Reich, pp. 198–202.

16. Reich, p. 282.

17. Stephanie Coontz, *The Way We Never Were: American Families and the Nostalgia Trap* (New York: Basic Books, 1992). See also Pat Burdell, "Teen Mothers in High School: Tracking Their Curriculum," in Michael W. Apple, ed., *Review of Research in Education 21* (Washington, D.C.: American Educational Research Association, 1995), pp. 163–208.

18. Stanley Aronowitz, *The Politics of Identity: Class, Culture, Social Movements* (New York: Routledge, 1992), pp. 219–222.

19. *Contract with America* (Washington: The Republican National Committee, 1994), p. 91.

20. Reich, pp. 55–57.

21. Aronowitz and DiFazio, p. 23.

22. The run up to the October, 1995 election for president of the AFL-CIO has led to a new focus on exactly this question of organizing the unorganized, among the candidates, among many of the current rank and file in today's unions, and among a few observers of the election debates. See, for example David Bacon, "Upsizing Labor," *The Nation*, 18 September 1995, pp. 259–60.

23. Aronowitz and DiFazio, p. 99.

24. Aronowitz and DiFazio, p. 279.

25. Aronowitz, *The Politics of Identity*, p. 237.

26. Bacon, *The Nation*, p. 260.

27. Aronowitz & DiFazio, p. 269.

28. *New York Times*, 26 October 1995: Steven Greenhouse, "New Fire for Labor: John Joseph Sweeney," pages 1 and D25; Peter T. Kilborn, "Militant Is Elected Head of A.F.L.-C.I.O., Signaling Sharp Turn for Labor Movement," p. D25.

29. Daily Labor Report [Online], Nexis Library, News file: DLABRT.

30. Eric Alterman, *Sound and Fury: The Washington Punditocracy and the Collapse of American Politics* (New York: HarperCollins, 1992), p. 203.

31. Seymour Melman, *Our Depleted Society* (New York: Holt, Rinehart and Winston, 1965), pp. 3–4.

32. David Halberstam, *The Fifties* (New York: Fawcett Columbine Books, 1933), pp. 616, 396.

33. Deborah W. Meier, "Get the Story Straight: Myths, Lies and Public Schools," *The Nation*, 21 September 1992, pp. 2712.

34. Reich, p. 321. ["The Afterword" is an addition in the 1992 version of *The Work of Nations*.]

35. See, for example, Aronowitz and DiFazio, especially pp. 63–80; Maxine Greene, *The Dialectic of Freedom* (New York: Teachers College Press, 1988) and, of course, John Dewey who, in 1915, reminded us that "a democracy is more than a form of government; it is primarily a mode of associated living, of conjoint communicated experience," *Democracy and Education* (New York: Macmillan, 1916), p. 87.

36. James D. Anderson, *The Education of Blacks in the South, 1860-1935* (Chapel Hill: The University of North Carolina Press, 1988), p. 1.

37. The federal government has issued a number of publications describing the process and the content of Goals 2000. See for example the pamphlet, "National Goals for Education" (Washington, D.C., U.S. Department of Education, July 1990), and "Building the Best: Summary Guide, The National Education Goals Report, 1993" and "Building a Nation of Learners: The National Education Goals Report, 1994" (Washington, D.C.: National Education Goals Panel, 1993, 1994).

38. *Contract with America*, p. 79.

39. Michael W. Apple, "Do the Standards Go Far Enough? Power, Policy, and Practice in Mathematics Education," *Journal for Research in Mathematics Education* 23.5 (1992): 412.

40. Ibid., p. 413.

41. Boston Public Schools, *Boston Public Schools Promotion Policy 1-12* (Boston: Boston School Committee, 1983).

42. I am grateful to David Stratman, who first raised this question with me. See his *We Can Change the World: The Real Meaning of Everyday Life* (Boston: New Democracy Books, 1991).

43. Reich, p. 247.

44. Reich, p. 227.

45. See Stratman, pp. 59–81.

46. For a discussion of the work of Deborah Meier and her colleagues, see Deborah Meier, *The Power of Their Ideas* (Boston: Beacon Press, 1995) and also Deborah Meier and Paul Schwartz, "Central Park East Secondary School: The Hard Part Is Making It Happen," in Michael W. Apple and James A. Beane, *Democratic Schools* (Alexandria, Va.: Association for Supervision and Curriculum Development, 1995) and James Traub, "It's Elementary," a book review in *The New Yorker*, 17 July 1995, pp. 74–79.

47. Aronowitz and DiFazio, p. 303.

48. Apple, "Do the Standards," p. 428.

49. Adria Steinberg, *Real Learning, Real Work: School to Work As High School Reform* (New York: Routledge, forthcoming).

50. Malcolm X, *The Autobiography of Malcolm X* (New York: Grove Press, Inc., 1964), p. 36.

51. Reich, p. 226.

52. Ibid.

53. Dewey, *Democracy and Education*, p. 307.

54. Reich, p. 227.

55. Ibid.., p. 227.

56. Reich, p, 228.

57. Dewey, *Democracy and Education*, p. 312.

58. Reich, p. 247.

59. Ibid.., p. 247.

60. See Larry Rosenstock and Adria Steinberg, "Beyond the Shop: Reinventing Vocational Education," in Apple and Beane, *Democratic Schools*; and also Steinberg, *Real Learning, Real Work.*

61. *Serrano v Priest*, 5 Cal, 3d 584, 96 Cal Rptr. 601, 487 p. 2d 1241 (1971), cited in David Fellman, ed., *The Supreme Court and Education* (New York: Teachers College Press, 1976), p. 283.

62. "Mr. Justice Marshall Dissenting," in *San Antonio School District v. Rodriguez* 411 US 1 (1973), cited in Fellman, p. 295.

63. For a discussion of this issue, see *Barriers to Excellence: Our Children at Risk* (Boston: National Coalition of Advocates for Students, 1985), especially pages 69-89.

64. Jonathan Kozol, *Savage Inequalities: Children in America's Schools* (New York: Crown, 1991), pp. 236–37.

65. James Traub, "It's Elementary," *The New Yorker*, 17 July 1995, p. 77.

66. See, for example, Ronald Edmonds, "Effective Schools for the Urban Poor," *Educational Leadership*, October 1979, pp. 15–24. Edmonds contribution to current thinking about schools is described in more detail in chapter 4.

67. Reich (1992), pp. 317–23.

68. *Contract with America* (New York: Times Books, 1994), specifically, pp. 83, 91, 106.

69. See David Corn, "A Frank Talk on the Budget," *The Nation,* March 24, 1997, pp. 23–24.

2. Defining Democratic Education

1. Horace Mann, "Twelfth Annual Report" (1848), in Lawrence A. Cremin, *The Republic and the School: Horace Mann on the Education of Free Men* (New York: Teachers College Press, 1957), pp. 89–90.

2. Malcolm X, " 'See for yourself, listen for yourself, think for yourself,' A Discussion with Young Civil Rights Fighters from Mississippi, January 1, 1965," in Steve Clark, *Malcolm X Talks to Young People: Speeches in the U.S., Britain & Africa* (New York: Pathfinder Press, 1991), p. 49.

3. Jonathan Kozol, *Savage Inequalities: Children in America's Schools* (New York: Crown, 1991), p. 3.

4. Ibid, p. 233.

5. Arthur M. Schlesinger, Jr. *The Disuniting of America: Reflections on a Multicultural Society* (New York: Norton, 1992), pp. 127–28.

6. Jane Addams, cited in Lawrence A. Cremin, *The Transformation of the School: Progressivism in American Education, 1876–1957* (New York: Vintage Books, 1961), p. ix.

7. Manning Marable, *The Crisis of Color and Democracy: Essays on Race, Class and Power* (Monroe, Maine: Common Courage Press, 1992), pp. 247–28.

8. Manning Marable, *Race, Reform and Rebellion: The Second Reconstruction in Black America, 1945–1990* (Jackson: University Press of Mississippi, 1991), p. 197.

9. Eric Alterman, *Sound and Fury: The Washington Punditocracy and the Collapse of American Politics* (New York: HarperCollins, 1992), p. 226.

10. See Antonio Gramsci, *Selections from Prison Notebooks*, ed. and trans. Quintin Hoare and Geoffrey Nowell-Smith (New York: International Publishers, 1971).

11. Alterman, p. 2.

12. John Dewey, *The Public and Its Problems* (New York: Henry Holt, 1927), p. 157.

13. See Jonathan Kozol, "Corporate Raid on Education: Whittle and the Privateers," *The Nation*, 21 September 1992, pp. 272–78.

14. Thomas Jefferson, "A Bill for the More General Diffusion of Knowledge" (1779), cited in Gordon C. Lee, *Crusade against Ignorance: Thomas Jefferson on Education* (New York: Teachers College Press, 1961), p. 83.

15. Horace Mann, "Twelfth Annual Report," p. 90.

16. Barbara Finkelstein, "Education and the Retreat from Democracy in the United States, 1979–198?," *Teachers College Record* 86 (1984): 280–81.

17. Langston Hughes, "In Explanation of Our Times," *Selected Poems of Langston Hughes* (New York: Vintage Books, 1959), pp. 281–83.

18. James D. Anderson, *The Education of Blacks in the South, 1860–1935* (Chapel Hill: University of North Carolina Press, 1988), p. 1.

19. Ibid, p. 280.

20. See Robert Gooding-Williams, editor, *Reading Rodney King: Reading Urban Uprisings* (New York: Routledge, 1993).

21. *Report of the National Advisory Commission on Civil Disorders* [the "Kerner Commission"] (New York: E. P. Dutton, 1968), p. 1.

22. Michael Apple and James A. Beane, *Democratic Schools* (Alexandria, Va.: Association for Supervision and Curriculum Development, 1995).

23. See J. A. K. Thomson, trans., *The Ethics of Aristotle* [*Nicomachean Ethics*] (New York: Penguin, 1953).

24. Jefferson, "A Bill for the More General Diffusion of Knowledge" (1779), pp. 83–92.

25. Abigail Adams to John Adams, Braintree, 31 March 1776, in L. H. Butterfield, Marc Friedlaender, and Mary-Jo Klein, eds., *The Book of Abigail and John: Selected*

Letters of the Adams Family, 1762-1784 (Cambridge, Mass.: Harvard University Press, 1975), pp. 120–21; Langston Hughes, "Freedom's Plow," in *Selected Poems*, pp. 291–97.

26. Jefferson, "Bill for the More General Diffusion of Knowledge," (1779).

27. W. E. B. DuBois, *Black Reconstruction in America: An Essay toward a History of the Part Which Black Folk Played in the Attempt to Reconstruct Democracy in America, 1860–1880* (1935, reprint Cleveland: World, Meridian Books, 1962), pp. 641–49, cited in Anderson, *The Education of Blacks in the South*, p. 6.

28. See especially Anderson, *The Education of Blacks in the South, 1860–1935*, pp. 4–32, 277–85.

29. John Dewey, *The School and Society*, (Chicago: University of Chicago Press, 1899, 2nd ed., 1915), p. 29.

30. Alexis de Tocqueville, *Democracy in America*, ed. Richard D. Heffner (New York: New American Library, 1956).

31. W. E. B. DuBois, "The Meaning of Education (1944?) in *Against Racism: Unpublished Essays, Papers, Addresses, 1887–1961*, ed. Herbert Aptheker (Amherst: University of Massachusetts Press, 1985), pp. 249–52.

32. Paulo Freire, *Pedagogy of the Oppressed* (New York: Seabury Press, 1970), p. 33.

33. Paulo Freire, American Educational Research Association, Chicago, April 1991.

34. Marable, pp. 258–59.

3. The School and Multicultural Democracy

1. Theresa Perry and James W. Fraser, *Freedom's Plow: Teaching in the Multicultural Classroom* (New York: Routledge, 1993), p. 3.

2. John Dewey, *Democracy and Education* (New York: Macmillan, 1916), p. 2.

3. James Crawford, *Bilingual Education: History, Politics, Theory, and Practice* (Trenton, N.J.: Crane, 1989), p. 19.

4. Diego Castellanos, *The Best of Two Worlds: Bilingual-Bicultural Education in the U.S.* (Trenton, J. J.: New Jersey State Department of Education, 1983).

5. See U.S. Commission on Civil Rights, *The Excluded Student: Educational Practices Affecting Mexican Americans in the Southwest*, Mexican American Education Study, Report 3 (Washington, D.C.: GPO, May 1972).

6. Crawford, pp. 21–30.

7. For an excellent analysis of the nation's changing ethnicity and the impact of these changes on today's youth, see Shirley Brice Heath and Milbrey W. McLaughlin, eds., *Identity and Inner-City Youth: Beyond Ethnicity and Gender* (New York: Teachers College Press, 1993).

8. *A Nation Prepared: Teachers for the 21st Century: The Report of the Task Force on Teaching as a Profession*, (New York: Carnegie Forum on Education and The Economy, 1986), p. 79.

9. Maxine Greene, "In Search of a Critical Pedagogy," *Harvard Educational Review* 56. 4 (November 1986): 427–41.

10. John Dewey, *Democracy and Education* (New York: Macmillan, 1916), pp. 101–2.

11. Beverly Wildung Harrison, *Making the Connections: Essays in Feminist Social Ethics*, ed. Carol S. Robb (Boston: Beacon Press, 1985), p. 20, cited in Henry Giroux, *Schooling and the Struggle for Public Life: Critical Pedagogy in the Modern Age* (Minneapolis, University of Minnesota Press, 1988), p. 96.

12. Jonathan Kozol, *Savage Inequalities: Children in America's Schools* (New York: Crown, 1991), p. 3.

13. Norma Rees, comment during the meetings of the Massachusetts Board of Education/Board of Regents of Higher Education Task Force on Recruiting People of Color to the Teaching Profession, 1989.

14. Robert Reich, *The Work of Nations*, with a new Afterword by the author (New York: Vintage Books, 1992), p. 321.

15. Maxine Greene, "Excellence, Meanings and Multiplicity," *Teachers College Record*, 86.2 (Winter 1984): p. 296.

16. See especially Roger Kimball, *Tenured Radicals: How Politics Has Corrupted Our Higher Education* (New York: Harper & Row, 1991), and Dinesh D'Souza, "Illiberal Education," *The Atlantic Monthly*, March 1991, pp. 52–79.

17. Allan Bloom, *The Closing of the American Mind*, (New York: Vintage, 1988) and E. D. Hirsch, *Cultural Literacy: What Every American Needs to Know*, (New York: Vintage, 1988). Also, for an excellent critique, see Stanley Aronowitz and Henry Giroux, "Schooling, Culture, and Literacy in the Age of Broken Dreams: A Review of Bloom and Hirsch," *Harvard Educational Review* 58.2 (1988): 172–94.

18. Paul Berman, *Debating P.C.: The Controversy over Political Correctness on College Campuses* (New York: Laurel, 1992), p. 3. The quotation is Berman's summary of the charge, not his own considerably more judicious opinion.

19. See especially Roger Kimball, *Tenured Radicals: How Politics Has Corrupted Our Higher Education* (New York: Harper & Row, 1991), and D'Souza, "Illiberal Education," pp. 52–79.

20. Richard J. Herrnstein and Charles Murray, *The Bell Curve: Intelligence and Class Structure in American Life* (New York: Free Press, 1994). See also Arthur R. Jensen, *Genetics and Education* (New York: Harper & Row, 1972).

21. Russell Jacoby and Naomi Glauberman, *The Bell Curve Debate* (New York: Times Books, 1995), p. ix.

22. Robert Lerner, Althea K. Nagai, and Stanley Rothman, *Molding the Good Citizen: The Politics of High School History Texts* (Westport, Conn.: Praeger, 1995)

23. Jacoby and Glauberman, pp. ix–x.

24. Lerner et al., p. 1.

25. For the earlier version of this "morality play" approach to the history of education, see Lawrence A. Cremin, *The Transformation of the School: Progressivism in American Education, 1876–1957* (New York: A. Knopf, 1961), p. viii.

26. Lerner et al., p. 32.

27. While she was fired in the 1950s, Septima Clark's case of being fired for membership in the NAACP is not atypical, except for the importance of her later career as teacher to the Civil Rights movement. See Cynthia Stokes Brown, ed., *Ready from Within: Septima Clark and the Civil Rights Movement* (Trenton, N.J.: Africa World Press, 1990), pp. 35–39.

28. Ravitch, *The Trouble Crusade* (New York: Basic Books, 1983), see p. 54.

29. N. C. Turpen, "Cooperative Curricular Improvement: To Formulate a Plan for Securing Community Understanding, Cooperation, and Support in Making Basic Program Changes in the High Schools of Alabama (Ed.D. dissertation, Teachers College, Columbia University, 1941), p. 127.

30. In this assertion they contrast themselves positively with the "simplistic" (p. 2) histories of curriculum such as the work of Frances FitzGerald, *American Revised* (New York: Vintage, 1979) or Philip G. Altbach, Gail P. Kelly, Hugh G. Petrie, and Lois Weis, eds., *Textbooks in American Society: Politics, Policy, and Pedagogy* (Albany: State University of New York Press, 1991). In this author's judgment, both of these texts are considerably more careful and complex in their analysis than *Molding the Good Citizen*. More important, these authors ignore the magisterial work in curriculum history which has been done by Herbert M. Kliebard, *The Struggle for the American Curriculum* (New York: Routledge, 1987) and *Forging the American Curriculum* (New York: Routledge, 1992).

31. Lerner et al., p. 84.

32. Ibid.

33. Ibid, p. 56.

34. Ibid, p. 70.

35. Ibid, pp. 57 and 71.

36. Ibid, p. 71.

37. Ibid, pp. 55 and 85.

38. E. P. Thompson, *The Making of the English Working Class* (New York: Vintage Books, 1963, 1966) and Herbert G. Gutman, *Work, Culture and Society in Industrializing America* (New York: Vintage Books, 1966, 1977).

39. Thompson, p. 12.

40. Lerner et al., p. 157.

41. Ibid, p. 94.

42. Ibid, p. 152.

43. David Saville Muzzey, *A History of Our Country* (Boston: Ginn, 1943, 1952).

44. Lerner et al., p. 89.

45. Ibid, p. 93.

46. Ibid, p. 152.

47. Ibid, p. 155.

48. See William Holmes McGuffey, *New Sixth Eclectic Reader* (Cincinnati: Winthrop B. Smith, 1857) or Charles A. Goodrich, *A History of the United States of America: From the Discovery of the Continent by Christopher Columbus to the Present Time* (Hartford, Conn.: H. F. Sumner, 1822, 1833).

49. For a description of the role of the National Association of Manufacturers, the American Legion, and others in driving the progressive textbooks of Harold Rugg off the market in the late 1930s and 1940s, see Frances FitzGerald, *America Revised*, pp. 36–37.

50. Lerner et al., p. 152.

51. Diane Ravitch and Chester E. Finn Jr., *What Do Our 17-Year-Olds Know?* (New York: Harper & Row, 1987); Charles Murray and R. J. Herrnstein, "What's Really Behind the SAT-Score Decline?" *Public Interest* 15 (Winter 1992): 32–56.

52. Leon J. Kamin, "Lies, Damned Lies, and Statistics," in Jacoby and Glauberman, p. 103.

53. Adolph Reed Jr., "The Inherent Racism of The Bell Curve," *Rethinking Schools* 9.2 (Winter 1994): 14.

54. In addition to Jacoby and Glauberman's important work, the best analysis of *The Bell Curve* to date can be found in Joe Kincheloe, Shirley Steinberg, and Aaron Greeson III, editors, *Measured Lies: The Bell Curve Examined* (New York: St. Martin's Press, 1996).

55. Henry Giroux, *Border Crossings: Cultural Workers and the Politics of Education* (New York: Routledge, 1992), p. 230. This citation is from an essay co-

authored with David Trend. The Buchanan reference is from "In the War for America's Culture, the 'Right' Side is Losing, *Richmond News Leader*, June 24, 1989.

56. Ibid, p. 231.

57. John Dewey, *The Public and Its Problems* (New York: Henry Holt & Co, 1927) , p. 143.

58. Giroux, *Border Crossings*, p. 235.

59. Ibid, p. 248.

60. bell hooks, *Teaching to Transgress: Education as the Practice of Freedom* (New York: Routledge, 1994), p. 31.

61. Arthur M. Schlesinger, *The Disuniting of America* (Knoxville, Tenn.: Whittle Direct Books, 1991), p. 71. It has generally gone unremarked that Schlesinger's angry volume was first published by Whittle Communications and only later made available to the wider public through publication by Norton.

62. Neil Postman, *The End of Education: Redefining the Value of School* (New York: Knopf, 1995), pp. 50–58.

63. Ibid, p. 167.

64. Paulo Freire, *Pedagogy of Hope: Reliving Pedagogy of the Oppressed* (New York: Continuum, 1995), p. 152.

65. Ibid.

66. Adam Clayton Powell Jr., *Marching Blacks* (1945), cited in Vincent Harding, "We the People: The Long Journey Toward a More Perfect Union," Clayborne Carson et al., eds., *The Eyes on the Prize: Civil Rights Reader* (New York: Penguin, 1991), p. 31.

67. bell hooks, *Teaching to Transgress: Educating as the Practice of Freedom* (New York: Routledge, 1994), pp. 32–33.

68. Giroux, *Border Crossings,* p. 156.

69. James Baldwin, "A Talk to Teachers," 1963, reprinted in Rick Simonson and Scott Walker, editors, *The Graywolf Annual Five: Multi-Cultural Literacy: Opening the American Mind* (Saint Paul, Minn.: Graywolf Press, 1988), p. 4.

70. E. L. Doctorow, "A Gangsterdom of the Spirit," *The Nation*, 2 October 1989, p. 352–53.

4. Toward a New Child-Centered Curriculum

1. For a careful analysis of the split and the related problems, see Lawrence A. Cremin, *The Transformation of the School: Progressivism in American Education,*

1876–1957 (New York: Knopf, 1961), and Patrick Shannon, *The Struggle to Continue: Progressive Reading Instruction in the United States* (Portsmouth, N.H.: Heinemann Educational Books, 1990).

2. John Dewey, *The School and Society* (Chicago: The University of Chicago Press, 1900; revised 1915), pp. 6–7. Amy Gutman has challenged this statement in her *Democratic Education* (Princeton: Princeton University Press, 1987), and Theresa Perry and I have also followed Gutmann's lead in *Freedom's Plow: Teaching in the Multicultural Classroom* (New York: Routledge, 1993). There is a serious problem with the assumption which seems to lurk in Dewey's statement, that all children will need the same kind of education. Nevertheless, his basic goal, to unite the concern for the individual child and the need to build an educational system which brings this concern to every child remains as valid now as it was in 1900.

3. Gutmann, p. 14.

4. Samuel Bowles and Herbert Gintis, *Schooling in Capitalist America: Educational Reform and the Contradictions of Economic Life* (New York: Basic Books, 1976), p. 13; see also their thoughtful chapter on "Educational Alternatives," pp. 245–63.

5. See chapter 1 for a detailed analysis of the links between economic and educational changes in late-twentieth-century American society and also Robert Reich, *The Work of Nations* (New York: Vintage Books, 1991, 1992).

6. Jacqueline Jones, *The Dispossessed: America's Underclasses from the Civil War to the Present* (New York: Basic Books, 1992), pp. 269–70.

7. See, for example, Andrew Hacker, *Two Nations: Black and White, Separate, Hostile, Unequal* (New York: Scribner's, 1992), p. 188.

8. Marian Wright Edelman cited in an interview in *The New Yorker*, 15 January 1996, p. 26.

9. Jonathan Kozol, *Amazing Grace: The Lives of Children and the Conscience of a Nation* (New York: Crown, Inc., 1995), pp. 38–39.

10. Jones, pp. 269–88.

11. For an excellent analysis of the way economic statistics exclude women's concerns, see Marilyn Waring, *If Women Counted: A New Feminist Economics* (San Francisco: HarperSanFrancisco, 1988).

12. Barbara Ehrenreich, citation on the dust jacket of Kozol, *Amazing Grace.*

13. Jones, pp. 272–73.

14. Manning Marable, *The Crisis of Color and Democracy: Essays on Race, Class and Power* (Monroe, Maine: Common Courage Press, 1992), p. 259.

15. Horace Mann, "Tenth Annual Report" (1846), in Lawrence A. Cremin, *The Republic and the School: Horace Mann on the Education of Free Men* (New York: Teachers College Press, 1957), pp. 77–78.

16. Kozol, *Amazing Grace*, pp. 243–44.

17. *San Antonio School District v Rodriguez* 411 US 1 (1973), cited in David Fellman, ed., *The Supreme Court and Education* (New York: Teachers College Press, 1976), p. 295.

18. The specific quote is cited in Kozol, *Amazing Grace*, pp. 41–42, but virtually identical words can be heard on the talk shows portion of the radio band in any part of America.

19. Lisa Delpit, *Other People's Children: Cultural Conflict in the Classroom* (New York: New Press, 1995).

20. Charles E. Silberman, *Crisis in the Classroom: The Remaking of American Education* (New York: Random House, 1970), p. 11.

21. Christopher Jencks, *Inequality: A Reassessment of the Effect of Family and Schooling in America* (New York: Harper & Row, 1972), p. 253. For a useful response to Jencks, see Gutmann, pp. 152–59.

22. In Massachusetts, for example, the decade of the 1970s saw a state commission finding flagrant abuse in the building contracts for the new campus of the University of Massachusetts at Boston, while at the same time two members of the Boston School Committee were sent to jail on different graft convictions, and other school committee members came under serious suspicion.

23. Kozol, *Death at an Early Age,* (Boston: Houghton Mifflin, 1977).

24. David B. Tyack, Michael W. Kirst, and Elisabeth Hansot, "Educational Reform: Retrospect and Prospect," *Teachers College Record* 81.3 (Spring 1980): 254.

25. Shannon, p. 82.

26. George S. Counts, *Dare the School Build a New Social Order?* (Carbondale, Ill.: Southern Illinois University Press, 1978; original edition, 1932), pp. 4–5.

27. For an excellent analysis of the development of the deficit model of viewing children, see Ann Bastian, Norm Fruchter, Marilyn Gittell, Colin Greer, and Kenneth Haskins, *Choosing Equality: The Case for Democratic Schooling* (New York: New World Foundation, 1985), especially chapter 3.

28. *Making the Grade: Report of the Twentieth Century Fund Task Force on Federal Elementary and Secondary Education Policy* (New York: Twentieth Century Fund, 1983), pp. 11–13.

29. Paulo Freire, *Pedagogy of the Oppressed* (New York: Seabury Press, 1970), pp. 58–62.

30. Antonia Darder, "Buscando America: The Contribution of Critical Latino Educators to the Academic Development and Empowerment of Latino Students in the U.S.," in Christine E. Sleeter and Peter L. McLaren, eds., *Multicultural Education, Critical Pedagogy, and the Politics of Difference* (Albany: State University of New York Press, 1995), p. 320. See also Antonia Darder, *Culture and Power in the Classroom* (New York: Bergin & Garvey, 1991).

31. Two important voices in the research which has shown the negative impact of tracking—for students in the high as well as the low tracks—have been John I. Goodlad and Jeannie Oakes. See especially, John I. Goodlad, *A Place Called School: Prospects for the Future* (New York: McGraw-Hill, 1984), and Jeannie Oakes, *Keeping Track: How Schools Structure Inequality* (New Haven: Yale University Press, 1985). For a useful look at parental resistance to ending tracking see Amy Stuart Wells and Irene Serna, "The Politics of Culture: Understanding Local Political Resistance to Detracking in Racially Mixed Schools," *Harvard Educational Review* 66.1 (Spring 1996), pp. 93–118.

32. Anne Wheelock, *Crossing the Tracks: How "Untracking" Can Save America's Schools* (New York: New Press, 1992), p. vii.

33. Jeannie Oakes, "Foreword," in Wheelock, p. xiii.

34. Wheelock, p. 71.

35. Jerome Bruner, "The Relevance of Skill or the Skill of Relevance," in *The Relevance of Education*, 1973, cited in Wheelock, p. 188.

36. Wheelock, pp. 283–84.

37. bell hooks, *Feminist Theory: From Margin to Center* (Boston: South End Press, 1984), pp. 25, 35.

38. Joanne Hendrick and Terry Stange, "Do Actions Speak Louder Than Words? An Effect of the Functional Use of Language on Dominant Sex Role Behavior in Boys and Girls," ERIC/EDRS document ED 323039/ PS019059, p. 22.

39. Charlotte Bunch, "Feminism and Education: Not By Degrees," *Quest*, 5.1 (Summer 1979): 1–7, cited in hooks, p. 114.

40. Friedrich Froebel, *Pedagogics of the Kindergarten* (New York: D. Appleton and Company, 1914; translation of original German edition, Berlin: 1861), pp. 36–37.

41. Jeanne Brady, *Schooling Young Children: A Feminist Pedagogy for Liberatory Learning* (Albany: State University of New York Press, 1995), represents an important addition to the literature of early childhood education.

42. Walter Feinberg, "Fixing the Schools: The Ideological Turn," in Giroux and McLaren, p. 71.

43. Howard Gardner, *Teacher* magazine, November/December 1991, cited in Anne Wheelock, *Crossing the Tracks: How "Untracking" Can Save America's Schools* (New York: New Press, 1992), p. 179.

44. Counts, p. 15. For a more detailed analysis of these issues see chapter 1.

45. Lawrence A. Cremin, *The Transformation of the School: Progressivism in American Education, 1876–1957*, (New York: Knopf, 1961), p. 71. Cremin also cites, Adele Marie Shaw, "The True Character of New York Public Schools," *The World's Work*, 7 (1903-1904): 4204–21.

46. Michel Marriott, "As Students Come to Class Less Healthy, School Clinics Try to Offer More," *New York Times*, 30 January 1991.

47. Kozol, *Amazing Grace*, p. 107.

48. For a detailed and careful analysis of the issue raised here, see Joy G. Dryfoos, *Full-Service Schools: A Revolution in Health and Social Services for Children, Youth, and Families* (San Francisco: Jossey-Bass, 1994). For two excellent books on violence as a public health issue, see Deborah Prothrow-Stith with Michaele Weissman, *Deadly Consequences: How Violence Is Destroying Our Teenage Population and A Plan To Begin Solving The Problem* (New York: HarperCollins, 1991) and Nancy Carlsson-Paige and Diane E. Levin, *Who's Calling the Shots? How to Respond Effectively to Children's Fascination with War Play and War Toys* (Philadelphia: New Society Publishers, 1990).

49. The National Coalition of Advocates for Students, Board of Inquiry, *Barriers to Excellence: Our Children at Risk* (Boston: The National Coalition of Advocates for Students, 1985), p. 61.

50. Don Davies, cited in *Barriers to Excellence*, p. 101.

51. *Boston Teachers News Letter: Official Organ of the Boston Teachers Club*, February, 1917, pp. 10–11.

52. *Barriers to Excellence*, pp. 65–66.

53. Seymour B. Sarason, *Parental Involvement and the Political Principle: Why the Existing Governance Structure of Schools Should Be Abolished* (San Francisco: Jossey-Bass, 1995), p. 7. See also Susan Albers Mohrman and Priscilla Wohlstetter, *School-Based Management: Organizing for High Performance* (San Francisco: Jossey-Bass, 1994).

54. Mohrman and Wohlstetter, p. 13.

55. Ibid, p. 108.

56. Seymour B. Sarason, *The Culture of the School and the Problem of Change* (Boston: Allyn & Bacon, 1971), p. 159.

212   Notes

57. Ibid, pp. 159–60.

58. *Barriers to Excellence*, pp. 62–63.

59. *Barriers to Excellence*, p. 62.

60. Ronald Edmonds, "Effective Schools for the Urban Poor," *Educational Leadership*, October 1979, p. 22; see also Ronald Edmonds and J. R. Frederiksen, *Search for Effective Schools: The Identification and Analysis of City Schools that are Instructionally Effective for Poor Children* (Cambridge, Mass.: Harvard University, Center for Urban Studies, 1978).

61. *A Nation at Risk: The Imperative for Educational Reform* (Washington, D.C.: National Commission on Excellence in Education, 1983), pp. 5, 17.

62. Samuel Bowles and Herbert Gintis, "Can There Be a Liberal Philosophy of Education in a Democratic Society?" in Henry Giroux and Peter McLaren, eds., *Critical Pedagogy, the State, and Cultural Struggle* (Albany: State University of New York Press, 1989), p. 31.

63. George S. Counts, *Dare the School Build a New Social Order?* (Carbondale, Ill.: Southern Illinois University Press, 1978; original edition, 1932), pp. 33–34.

64. Counts, pp. 19–20.

65. John Dewey, *Democracy and Education* (New York: Macmillan, 1916), p. 87.

66. Many historians, notably Michael Katz, have examined the growing bureaucratization of schools, see Michael B. Katz, *Class, Bureaucracy, and Schools: The Illusion of Educational Change in America* (New York: Praeger, 1971); also for an excellent study of the growing powers of professional school administrators, see David Tyack and Elisabeth Hansot, *Managers of Virtue: Public School Leadership in America, 1820–1980* (New York: Basic Books, 1982); see also my "Who Were the Progressive Educators Anyway? A Case Study of the Progressive Education Movement in Boston, 1905–1925," *Educational Foundations*, 2.1 (Spring 1988): pp. 4–30.

67. Sheldon S. Wolin, "Editorial," *Democracy* 3.2 (Spring 1983): 5.

68. Seymour B. Sarason, *The Culture of the School*, p. 177.

69. The National Commission on Excellence in Education, *A Nation at Risk: The Imperative for Educational Reform* (Washington, D.C.: 1983), pp. 35–36.

70. Paulo Freire, *Pedagogy of the Oppressed* (New York: Seabury Press, 1970), pp. 57–58.

71. Dewey, *Democracy and Education*, p. 38.

72. John Dewey, "My Pedagogic Creed," *The School Journal* 54.3 (16 January 1897): 77–80, cited in Martin S. Dworkin, ed., *Dewey on Education* (New York: Teachers College Press, 1959), p. 31.

73. Maxine Greene, "In Search of Critical Pedagogy, *Harvard Educational Review* 56.4 (November 1986): 427–41.

5. Technology, Democracy, and School Policy

1. Seymour Papert, *The Children's Machine: Rethinking School in the Age of the Computer* (New York: Basic Books, 1993), ix.

2. Thomas Edison in *Dramatic Mirror*, 9 July 1913, cited in Paul Saettler, *A History of Instructional Technology* (New York: McGraw-Hill, 1968), p. 98.

3. Seymour Papert, "Trying to Predict the Future," *Popular Computing*, October 1984, p. 38. I am indebted to Larry Cuban, *Teachers and Machines: The Classroom Use of Technology since 1920* (New York: Teachers College Press, 1986) for helping to set the debate about the use of technology in schools in historical context.

4. Paulo Freire, *Pedagogy of the Oppressed* (New York: Seabury Press, 1970), pp. 57–58.

5. Douglas M. Sloan, "On Raising Critical Questions about the Computer in Education," *Teachers College Record*, 85.4 (Summer 1984): 542.

6. Rosemary E. Sutton, "Equity and Computers in the Schools: A Decade of Research," *Review of Educational Research* 61.4 (Winter 1991): 475–503.

7. Michael W. Apple, *Ideology and Curriculum* (Boston and London: Routledge & Kegan Paul, 1979).

8. *Teachers College Record* 85.4 (Summer 1984).

9. Neil Postman, with Charles Weingartner, *Teaching as a Subversive Activity* (New York: Knopf, 1979); *Technopoly: The Surrender of Culture to Technology* (New York: Knopf, 1992); *The End of Education* (New York: Knopf, 1995).

10. Kirkpatrick Sale, *Rebels against the Future: The Luddites and Their War on the Industrial Revolution: Lessons for the Computer Age* (Boston: Addison-Wesley, 1995), p. 273.

11. Michael W. Apple, *Teachers and Texts: A Political Economy of Class and Gender Relations in Education* (New York: Routledge, 1986), p. 169.

12. See, for example, Ann Bastian, Norm Fruchter, Marilyn Gittell, Colin Greer, and Kenneth Haskins, *Choosing Equality: The Case for Democratic Schooling* (Philadelphia: Temple University Press, 1986).

13. Apple, *Teachers and Texts*, p. 162.

14. Ella Flagg Young, *Isolation in the School* (Chicago: University of Chicago Press, 1901), pp. 106–7.

15. Margaret Haley, "Why Teachers Should Organize," National Education Association Addresses and Proceedings (St. Louis, 1904); reprinted in Nancy Hoffman, *Woman's "True" Profession: Voices from the History of Teaching* (Old Westbury, N.Y.: The Feminist Press, 1981), pp. 289–95; for an excellent historical overview of the imposition of new technologies on teachers, see Larry Cuban, *Teachers and Machines: The Classroom Use of Technology since 1920* (New York: Teachers College Press, 1986).

16. From a review in *School Library Journal* included on the cover of the paperback edition of Papert's *The Children's Machine* (1993).

17. Cuban, pp. 4–6.

18. Douglas M. Sloan, "On Raising Critical Questions about the Computer in Education," *Teachers College Record* 85.4 (Summer 1984): 541.

19. Tony Scott, Michael Cole, and Martin Engel, Laboratory of Comparative Human Cognition, "Computers and Education: A Cultural Constructivist Perspective," in Gerald Grant, ed., *Review of Research in Education 18* (Washington, D.C.: American Educational Research Association, 1992), p. 209.

20. Laboratory of Comparative Human Cognition, University of California, San Diego, "Kids and Computers: A Positive Vision of the Future," *Harvard Educational Review* 59.1 (February 1989): 73–74.

21. Neil Postman, *The End of Education: Redefining the Value of School* (New York: Knopf, 1995), pp. 45–46.

22. Papert, *The Children's Machine*, p. 64.

23. Paul N. Edwards, "The Army and the Microworld: Computers and the Politics of Gender Identity," *Signs: Journal of Women in Culture and Society*, 16.1 (Autumn 1990): 109.

24. Seymour Papert, *Mindstorms: Children, Computers, and Powerful Ideas* (New York: Basic Books, 1980), p. 21. In addition to *Mindstorms*, see also Seymour Papert, "Teaching Children Thinking," and "Teaching Children to be Mathematicians" in Robert Taylor, ed., *The Computer in the School: Tutor, Tool, Tutee* (New York: Teachers College Press, 1980). For an introduction to the most relevant work of Piaget to this discussion, see Jean Piaget, "Piaget's Theory," in *Handbook of Child Psychology*, 4th ed., ed. Paul H. Mussen (New York: John Wiley, 1983), 1:103–28.

25. Papert, *The Children's Machine*, p. 62.

26. Joanne Koltnow, "Planning for Educational Change," *Apple Education Review* (1991–1992 School Year, Issue 1): 2-6.

27. Paulo Freire, *Pedagogy of the Oppressed* (New York: Seabury Press, 1970), p. 57, 63–64.

28. Paulo Freire and Seymour Papert met twice in the early 1990s. It is to be hoped that more of their dialogue is yet to be made public. Brief references to their conversations are noted in Papert's *The Children's Machine*.

29. Scott et al., in Grant, pp. 192, 197–98.

30. Judah L. Schwartz, "Intellectual Mirrors: A Step in the Direction of Making Schools Knowledge-Making Places," *Harvard Educational Review* 59.1 (February 1989): 51.

31. Ibid, p. 57.

32. Sylvia Weir, "The Computer in Schools: Machine as Humanizer," *Harvard Educational Review* 59.1 (February 1989): 63.

33. Ibid.

34. Ibid, p. 62.

35. Linda Laverty, "The Switch Hitters—Creative and Competitive Activities for the Physically Impaired," *The Computing Teacher*, December/January, 1991–1992, pp. 41-43.

36. Terrel H. Bell and Donna L. Elmquist, "Technical Interaction in the Classroom," *Vocational Education Journal* 67.3 (March 1992): 22.

37. Joel Spring, *The Sorting Machine Revisited: National Educational Policy Since 1945* (New York: Longman, 1989).

38. Marie M. Clay, public lecture, Lesley College, Cambridge, Mass., 31 March 1992; see also Marie M. Clay, *Becoming Literate: The Construction of Inner Control* (Auckland, New Zealand: Heinemann, 1991).

39. Melvin Kranzberg, "Science-Technology-Society: It's as Simple as XYZ!," *Theory into Practice* 30.4 (Autumn 1991): 236; see also Melvin Kranzberg, "Technology and History: Kranzberg's Laws," *Technology and Culture* 27, pp. 544–60.

40. John Dewey, *Individualism Old and New* (New York: G.P. Putnam's Sons, Capricorn Books, 1962; originally published, 1929), cited in Harriet K. Cuffaro, "Microcomputers in Education: Why Is Earlier Better?" *Teachers College Record*, 85.4 (Summer 1984): 566.

41. Sutton, pp. 478–79.

42. J. Hayes, "Equality and Technology," *Learning and Leading with Technology*, October 1995, pp. 51–53, cited in Bradley Scott, "Access to Educational Technology: What's Going On?" *Intercultural Development Research Association Newsletter*, November/December 1995, p. 7.

43. Ibid, p. 481.

44. Ibid, p. 482; see also H. J. Blecker and C. W. Sterling, "Equity in School Computer Use: National Data and Neglected Considerations," *Journal of Educational Computing Research* 3 (1987): 289–311.

45. K. A. Whooley, "Gender Differences in Computer Use" (Unpublished master's thesis, University of California, San Diego 1986), p. 15, cited in Scott et al., p. 228.

46. Kori Inkpen, Rena Upitis, Maria Klawe, Joan Lawry, Ann Anderson, Mutindi Ndunda, Kamran Sedighian, Steve Leroux, and David Hsu, "'We Have Never-Forgetful Flowers in Our Garden:' Girls' Responses to Electronic Games," (Unpublished paper, University of British Columbia and Queens University, 1993).

47. Karrie Jacobs, "RoboBabes: Why Girls Don't Play Video Games," *The International Design Magazine*, May/June 1994, p. 43.

48. Scott et al., pp. 229–30.

49. Whooley, p. 125, 122, cited in Scott, et al., pp. 228–29.

50. Scott, et al, p. 229; see L. C. Moll and S. Diaz, "Change as the Goal of Educational Research," *Anthropology and Educational Quarterly* 18 (1987): 300–11; and B. Bellman and A. Arias, "Computer-mediated Classrooms for Culturally and Linguistically Diverse Learners," *Computers and School* 7.1–2 (1990): pp. 227–41.

51. Papert, *The Children's Machine*, p. 213.

52. Ibid, p. 225.

53. Scott et al., p. 229.

54. Michelle Fine, *Framing Dropouts: Notes on the Politics of an Urban Public High School* (Albany: State University of New York Press, 1991), p. 61.

55. See, Thomas Hehir and Thomas Latus, eds., *Special Education at the Century's End: Evolution of Theory and Practice since 1970*, Reprint Series No. 23 (Cambridge, Mass.: Harvard Educational Review, 1992).

56. Linda Laverty, "The Switch Hitters—Creative and Competitive Activities for the Physically Impaired," *The Computing Teacher*, December/January 1991–1992, pp. 41–43. It is important to note that it is not only special education students who gain new options in art education through the use of computers. Thus James A. Hoffmann reports on "Computer-Aided Collaborative Music Instruction," *Harvard Educational Review* 61.3 (August 1991): 270–78.

57. Weir, p. 65.

58. Alan Cromer, "Of Chalk and Chips," chapter 7 in *Connected Knowledge* (New York: Oxford University Press, forthcoming).

59. James Baldwin, "A Talk to Teachers," 1963, reprinted in Rick Simonson and Scott Walker, eds., *The Graywolf Annual Five: Multi-Cultural Literacy: Opening the American Mind* (Saint Paul, Minn.: Graywolf Press, 1988), p. 9.

60. Baldwin, p. 6.

61. Maxine Greene, "In Search of a Critical Pedagogy," *Harvard Educational Review* 56.4 (November 1986): 441.

62. B. Winston, *Misunderstanding Media* (Cambridge, Mass.: Harvard University Press, 1986), p. 137, cited in Scott et al., in Grant, p. 193.

63. Postman, *Technopoly*, p. 3.

64. "Vocational Education: A New Opportunity for Educational and Community Change," in Center for Law and Education, *Newsnotes* December 1991, p. 1.

65. See chapter 1 for a more detailed analysis of the perils and potential of vocational education in supporting a democratized schooling.

66. Douglas Noble, Computer Literacy and Ideology," *Teachers College Record* 85.4 (Summer 1984): 605.

67. See, for example, Henry M. Levin and Russell W. Rumberger, "The Educational Implications of High Technology," *Technology Review* (August/September, 1983).

68. For a detailed analysis of the impact of the changing American economy on schools, see chapter 1 of this text, and also Robert B. Reich, *The Work of Nations: Preparing Ourselves for 21st-Century Capitalism* (New York: Vintage Books, 1991).

69. Laboratory of Comparative Human Cognition, "Kids and Computers: A Positive Vision of the Future," *Harvard Educational Review* 59.1 (February 1989): p. 73.

70. Cuban, p. 160.

71. See for example, Scott et al., in Grant, pp. 192–95.

72. Postman, *The End of Education*, p. x.

73. I make the distinction here because I am uncomfortable with Gerald Graff's proposals to "teach the conflict." Clearly it is important for schools to teach conflicts and to engage students in an understanding of differing perspectives on any significant conflict. But teaching the conflict can be terrible passive. It can maintain the intellectual distance of the safe observer. It can fail to meet George Counts demand that we not only engage the minds but the passions and the ardent commitments of our students. See George S. Counts, *Dare the School Build a New Social Order?* (Carbondale, Ill.: Southern Illinois University Press, 1978; original edition, 1932).

74. Kirkpatrick Sale, *Rebels against the Future: The Luddites and Their War on the Industrial Revolution: Lessons for the Computer Age* (Boston: Addison-Wesley, 1995), pp. 261–78.

75. Papert, *The Children's Machine*, p. 225.

76. *Pedagogy of the Oppressed*, pp. 84–85.

77. Lawrence A. Cremin, *Popular Education and Its Discontents* (New York: Harper & Row, 1990), p. 125.

6. Preparing Teachers for Democratic Schools

1. *What Matters Most: Teaching for America's Future*, (New York: National Commission on Teaching and America's Future, 1996).

2. *A Nation Prepared: Teachers for the 21st Century: The Report of the Task Force on Teaching as a Profession*, (New York: Carnegie Forum on Education and the Economy, 1986); *Tomorrow's Teachers: A Report of the Holmes Group* (East Lansing Mich.: Holmes Group, 1986).

3. Among the best known of the "first stage reports' issues in 1983 and 1984 were National Commission on Excellence in Education, *A Nation at Risk* (Washington, D.C.: GPO 1983); and the Twentieth Century Fund, *Making the Grade: Report of the Twentieth Century Fund Task Force on Federal Elementary and Secondary Education Policy* (New York: Twentieth Century Fund, 1983). Also included in the public discussions of education reform in the early 1980s were John I. Goodlad, *A Place Called School: Prospectus for the Future* (New York: McGraw-Hill, 1984); and Theodore R. Sizer, *Horace's Compromise: The Dilemma of the American High School* (Boston: Houghton Mifflin, 1984). Still when one talks of the reform reports of 1983 and 1984, *A Nation at Risk* is the one which usually comes to mind first.

4. For what is probably the most thorough review of the 1980s debates about reform efforts in teacher education, see Margo Okazawa-Rey, James Anderson, and Rob Traver, *Teachers, Teaching, and Teacher Education* (Cambridge, Mass.: Harvard Educational Review, 1987); and Thomas S. Popkewitz, *Critical Studies in Teacher Education: Its Folklore, Theory and Practice* (London: Falmer Press, 1987).

5. Carnegie, p. 3.

6. For example, most studies of the Progressive Era point to an amazing lack of impact on school classroom practice—as opposed to administrative structures—of all of the Progressive Era publications. See Lawrence Cremin, *The Transformation of The School: Progressivism in American Education, 1876–1957* (New York: Random House, 1961).

7. Courtney Leatherman, "Reforms in Education of Schoolteachers Face Tough New Challenges," *The Chronicle of Higher Education*, 20 April 1988.

8. In two very thorough studies, Ellen Condliffe Lagemann has traced the role of Carnegie money in the transformation of many institutions in this society throughout the twentieth century. See Ellen Condliffe Lagemann, *Private Power for the Public Good: A History of the Carnegie Foundation for the Advancement of Teaching* (Middletown, Conn.: Wesleyan University Press, 1983) and Ellen Condliffe Lagemann, *The Politics of Knowledge: A History of the Carnegie Corporation of New York* (Middletown, Conn.: Wesleyan University Press, 1987).

9. The Holmes Group, *Tomorrow's Schools: Principles for the Design of Professional Development Schools* (East Lansing, Mich.: 1990); idem, *Tomorrow's Schools of Education* (East Lansing, Mich.: 1995). For a thoughtful—and critical—analysis of the reports, especially the 1995 one, see David F. Labaree, "A Disabling Vision: Rhetoric and Reality in *Tomorrow's Schools of Education*," *Teachers College Record* 97.2 (Winter 1995): 166–205.

10. Maxine Greene, "In Search of a Critical Pedagogy, *Harvard Educational Review* 56.4 (November 1986): 427.

11. Ibid, p. 440.

12. bell hooks, *Teaching to Transgress: Education as the Practice of Freedom* (New York: Routledge, 1994), p. 207.

13. See also Roger Soder, "Teaching the Teachers of the People," in Roger Soder, editor, *Democracy, Education, and the Schools* (San Francisco: Jossey-Bass, 1996), pp. 244–74.

14. One place which is attending to the issue of putting a progressive vision of teacher education into practice is the Center for Educational Renewal at the University of Washington led by John Goodlad and his colleagues. The consortium of "Goodlad schools of education" or centers of excellence in teacher education is making an important contribution to the development of new models. However, I continue to be frustrated with their lack of attention to the needs of urban schools, students and teachers of color, and perhaps most of all the Civil Rights heritage which is described here in the work of Greene, hooks, and others.

15. Greene, p. 438.

16. Henry Giroux and Peter McLaren, "Teacher Education as a Counter-public Sphere: Notes Toward a Redefinition," in Popkewitz, ed., p. 269.

17. See Lawrence A. Cremin, *The Transformation of the School*.

18. Ann Bastian, Norm Fruchter, Marilyn Gittell, Colin Greer, and Kenneth Haskins, *Choosing Equality: The Case for Democratic Schooling* (New York: New World Foundation, 1985).

19. See for example, Henry A. Giroux, *Teachers as Intellectuals: Toward a Critical Pedagogy of Learning* (Granby, Mass.: Bergin & Garvey, 1988). Of course, half a century earlier, similar questions about the role of teachers were raised by George S. Counts, *Dare the School Build a New Social Order?* (New York: John Day, 1932).

20. Henry Giroux and Peter McLaren, "Teacher Education and the Politics of Engagement: The Case for Democratic Schooling," *Harvard Educational Review* 56.3 (August 1986): 216.

21. For a useful review of the current debates about the political purposes of the liberal arts, see Stanley Aronowitz and Henry A. Giroux, "Schooling Culture, and Literacy in the Age of Broken Dreams: A Review of Bloom and Hirsch," *Harvard Educational Review* 58.2 (May 1988): 172–94.

22. Maxine Greene, "Liberal Arts and Professional Studies," unpublished lecture, Lesley College, Cambridge, Mass., January 1991.

23. Susan Laird, "Reforming 'Women's True Profession': A Case for 'Feminist Pedagogy' in Teacher Education?" *Harvard Educational Review* 58.4 (November 1988): 449–63; see also Jane Roland Martin, "Reforming Teacher Education, Rethinking Liberal Education," *Teachers College Record* 88 (1987): 406–09.

24. Theresa Perry, "Is Text Also Context or Does the Significant Representation of Students and Faculty of Color in a Teacher Preparation Program Necessarily Shape the Conversation," paper presented at the American Educational Research Association, Chicago, 3 April 1991.

25. These issues are discussed in considerable depth in Ernest L. Boyer, *College: The Undergraduate Experience in America* (New York: Harper & Row, 1987); for an especially useful review of the current critical discussion of the undergraduate experience in today's colleges and universities, see Ursula Elisabeth Wagener, "Quality and Equality: The Necessity for Imagination," *Harvard Educational Review* 59.2 (May 1989): 240–50.

26. Giroux and McLaren, "Teacher Education as a Counter-public Sphere," 269–70.

27. Maxine Greene, "Liberal Arts and Professional Studies."

28. Ibid. For examples of the argument against the arts and sciences major, see Daryl Siedentop, "The Great Teacher Education Legend," *Physical Education Professional Preparation*, pp. 48–57, and Patricia Ashton and Linda Crocker, "Systematic Study of Planned Variations: The Essential Focus of Teacher Education Reform," *Journal of Teacher Education*, May–June 1987, pp. 2–8.

29. Henry Giroux and Donaldo Macedo, "Editorial Comment," *Journal of Urban and Cultural Studies* 1.1 (1990): p. 4.

30. Giroux and McLaren, "Teacher Education as a Counter-public Sphere," p. 273.

31. John Silber, in *Straight Shooting: What's Wrong with America and How to Fix It* (New York: Harper & Row, 1989), makes the argument for abolishing methods courses in favor of an arts and sciences only preparation with special drama. Like most of the other arguments in the book, this one seems designed more to strengthen the position of an intellectual elite—of which Silber considers himself the best example—rather than a serious attempt to wrestle with the issues of teaching and learning which are faced by teachers on a daily basis in today's schools.

32. I have benefited from many discussions of this issue with Theresa Perry, Marian Darlington Hope, and James Jennings. I am grateful to each of them for sharing ideas which are certainly reflected in this section of this chapter. For a thoughtful analysis of the issues discussed in this section, see Mary E. Dilworth, ed., *Diversity in Teacher Education: New Expectations* (San Francisco: Jossey-Bass, 1992).

33. Karen Kepler Zumwalt criticized an earlier version of this chapter for saying that the "Holmes report is silent on the issue of recruiting people of color." The two more recent Holmes reports make a significant contribution in this area, but the original report only mentions the issue once on the last page. This is hardly serious attention to the issue. See Karen Kepler Zumwalt, "A Response," *Teachers College Record,* 94.1 (Fall 1992), pp. 51–52.

34. "Recruitment and Support of Minorities in Teacher Education Programs," The University of the State of New York, State Education Department, Albany, New York, September 1989, p. 1.

35. For an especially thoughtful analysis of the barriers which face people of color who are interested in teaching careers and for a range of possible strategies for dealing with these barriers see "The Recruitment and Retention of People of Color in the Teaching Profession in Massachusetts," A Report Prepared by the Statewide Committee on the Recruitment of Minority Teachers for the Board of Regents and the Board of Education of Massachusetts (March 1990), and also June A. Gordon, "Why Students of Color Are Not Entering Teaching: Reflections from Minority Teachers," *Journal of Teacher Education* 45:5 (November–December 1994), 346–53.

36. Willis D. Hawley, "The Importance of Minority Teachers to the Racial and Ethnic Integration of American Society," *Equity and Choice* 5.2 (March 1989): 33.

37. Ibid, p. 31.

38. Lisa Delpit, *Other People's Children: Cultural Conflict in the Classroom* (New York: New Press, 1995), p. xiv.

39. Ibid, p. 11.

40. *Making Teaching a Major Profession: Report of the Joint Task Force on Teacher Preparation.* The "JTTP Report" implemented many of the recommendations which were part of the Holmes and Carnegie recommendations, but with some unique innovations in areas such as recruiting people of color.

41. For a review and analysis of the Wheelock program, see James W. Fraser, Theresa Perry, Shirley Malone-Fenner, and Ella Burnett, "Preparing Liberal Arts Graduates for Multicultural Classrooms: An Alternative Approach," panel presentation at the American Educational Research Association, Chicago, April 1991.

42. *A Nation Prepared*, p. 79.

43. For useful information on the problems of competency testing, see George F. Madaus, "Test Scores: What Do They *Really* Mean in Education Policy," New Jersey Education Association Convention, Atlantic City, New Jersey, 11 November 1983; George F. Madaus, ed., *The Courts, Validity, and Minimum Competency Testing* (Boston: Kluwer-Nijhoff, 1983) and Leonard C. Beckum, "Diversifying Assessment: A Key Factor in the Reform Equation," in Mary E. Dilworth, ed., *Diversity in Teacher Education: New Expectations* (San Francisco: Jossey-Bass, 1992), pp. 215–28.

44. See Robert I. Sperber to Superintendent Laval Wilson, "Recruiting Boston Public School Students to Become Future Boston Teachers," Memorandum, 20 October 1988.

45. See "The Recruitment and Retention of Black, Latino, and Asian Descent Teachers in Massachusetts," A Report Prepared by the Statewide Committee on the Recruitment of Minority Teachers and sponsored by the Board of Regents and the Board of Education of Massachusetts, 1989.

46. See for example, Linda Darling-Hammond, Karen Pittman, and Cecilia Ottinger, "Career Choices for Minorities: Who Will Teach?." National Education Association and Council of Chief State School Officers—Task Force on Minorities in Teaching (October 1987).

47. "The Recruitment and Retention of People of Color in the Teaching Profession in Massachusetts," p. 15.

48. For a good look at the experience of a new teacher of color in the public schools, see Valerie Ooka Pang, "Ethnic Prejudice: Still Alive and Hurtful," *Harvard Educational Review* 58.3 (August 1988): 375–79.

49. *A Nation Prepared*, p. 59.

50. Giroux and McLaren, in Popkewitz, p. 287.

51. Ibid., p. 279.

52. Ibid, pp. 269–70.

53. Michael W. Apple, *Teachers and Texts: A Political Economy of Class & Gender Relations in Education* (New York: Routledge & Kegan Paul, 1986), p. 161.

54. Giroux and McLaren, in Popkewitz, p. 271; see also Apple, *Teachers and Texts*, and Michael W. Apple and Linda K. Christian-Smith, *The Politics of the Textbook* (New York: Routledge, Chapman and Hall, 1991).

55. Ella Flagg Young, *Isolation in the School* (Chicago: University of Chicago Press, 1901), pp. 106–07. For a more detailed analysis of the development of teachers councils in the Progressive Era, see my "Agents of Democracy: Urban Elementary-School Teachers and the Conditions of Teaching," in Donald R. Warren, ed., *American Teachers: Histories of a Profession at Work* (New York: Macmillan, 1989).

56. John Dewey, "Professional Organization of Teachers," *Journal of Education*, 30 October 1919, p. 428.

57. Giroux and McLaren, in Popkewitz, p. 273.

58. For one set of examples of a teacher education program which breaks out of the traditional model, which rejects "the notion of children—and teachers—as empty vessels," see Margaret Yonemura, "Reflections on Teacher Empowerment and Teacher Education," *Harvard Educational Review* 56.4 (November 1986), 473–80.

59. Theresa Perry, "Teacher Preparation and Its Impact on Black and Latino Communities," Conference on Blacks and Education in Boston: Issues, Problems and Resolutions, College of Public & Community Service, University of Massachusetts at Boston, 9 December 1988.

60. Apple, *Teachers and Texts*, pp. 187–88.

61. Delpit, p. 167.

62. Ibid, p. 168.

63. For a more detailed discussion of these issues, see my "An Unnoticed Bicentennial: Some Thoughts on School Committee Structure," *Equity and Choice*, September 1989; and Ann Bastian, Norm Fruchter, Marilyn Gittell, Colin Greer, and Kenneth Haskins, *Choosing Equality: The Case for Democratic Schooling* (New York: New World Foundation, 1985).

64. Young, pp. 89, 104.

65. *A Nation Prepared*, p. 55.

66. See, for example, Kenneth M. Ludmerer, *Learning to Heal: The Development of American Medical Education* (New York: Basic Books, 1985).

67. Burton J. Bledstein, *The Culture of Professionalism: The Middle Class and the Development of Higher Education in America* (New York: Norton, 1976), p. 90.

68. Christopher Lash, *The Revolt of the Elites and the Betrayal of Democracy* (New York: Norton, 1995), pp. 5, 45.

69. See Paulo Freire, *Pedagogy of the Oppressed* (New York: Seabury Press, 1970).

70. The undergraduate elementary student teaching program at the University of Wisconsin, Madison, meets many of the same goals as those I have proposed for graduate level programs. See Kenneth M. Zeichner and Daniel P. Liston, "Teaching Student Teachers to Reflect," *Harvard Educational Review* 57.1 (February 1987): 1–22.

71. The 1990 and 1995 Holmes reports seems to call for similar school based graduate programs. At the same time, it is essential to maintain the tension between theory and practice, between teaching and critical reflection on teaching and on the social context in which teaching takes place. In this regard it is important to heed David Labaree's criticism of especially the 1995 Holmes Report which is included in his reminder that a professional education must not cut itself off from practice, "But at the same time, it should not so immerse itself in the world of practice that it loses sight of its responsibility to pursue a theoretical understanding of this world from an appropriate intellectual distance." Labaree, p. 198. Both the engagement and the distance are essential if teachers are to be critical intellectuals.

72. See Donald A. Schon, *Educating the Reflective Practitioner* (San Francisco: Jossey-Bass, 1987). As part of the state education reform law of 1993, Massachusetts has begun to require continued professional development and recertification for teachers. Other states have done the same. This is an important step in the right direction.

73. See Ellen Condliffe Lagemann, "The Politics of Knowledge: The Carnegie Corporation and the Formulation of Public Policy," *History of Education Quarterly* 27.2 (Summer 1987): pp. 205–20.

74. For a good analysis of the problems with a permanent core of master teachers, see Sara Freedman, "Master Teacher/Merit Pay—Weeding Out Women from 'Women's True Profession: A Critique of the Commissions on Education,' " *Radical Teacher* 25 (1983).

75. Giroux and McLaren in Popkewitz, p. 288.

76. See for example Margaret Yonemura, "Reflections on Teacher Empowerment and Teacher Education, *Harvard Educational Review*, 56.4 (November 1986): 473–80.

77. *W. E. B. Du Bois: A Reader*, ed. Meyer Weinberg (New York: Harper Torchbooks, 1970), pp. 153–54.

78. Maxine Greene, "In Search of a Critical Pedagogy," in Margo Okazawa-Rey, James Anderson, and Rob Traver, eds., *Teachers, Teaching, and Teacher Education*, (Cambridge, Mass.: Harvard Educational Review, 1987), p. 247.

BIBLIOGRAPHY

Introduction

Counts, George S. *Dare the School Build a New Social Order?* Carbondale, Ill.: Southern Illinois University Press, 1978. (Original edition, 1932.)

Freire, Paulo. *Pedagogy of Hope: Reliving Pedagogy of the Oppressed.* New York: Continuum, 1995.

Kohl, Herbert. *"I Won't Learn from You" and Other Thoughts on Creative Maladjustment.* New York: The New Press, 1994.

Macedo, Donaldo. *Literacies of Power: What Americans Are Not Allowed to Know.* Boulder, Colorado: Westview Press, 1994.

Marable, Manning. *The Crisis of Color and Democracy: Essays on Race, Class and Power.* Monroe, Maine: Common Courage Press, 1992.

Chapter 1: Education Reform and Economic Renewal

Alterman, Eric. *Sound and Fury: The Washington Punditocracy and the Collapse of American Politics.* New York: HarperCollins, 1992.

Anderson, James D. *The Education of Blacks in the South, 1860–1935.* Chapel Hill: University of North Carolina Press, 1988.

Apple, Michael W. "Do the Standards Go Far Enough? Power, Policy, and Practice in Mathematics Education." *Journal for Research in Mathematics Education* 23.5 (1992): 412–31.

Apple, Michael W., and James A. Beane. *Democratic Schools.* Alexandria, Va.: Association for Supervision and Curriculum Development, 1995.

Aronowitz, Stanley. *The Politics of Identity: Class, Culture, Social Movements.* New York: Routledge, 1992.

Aronowitz, Stanley, and William DiFazio. *The Jobless Future: Sci-Tech and the Dogma of Work.* Minneapolis: University of Minnesota Press, 1994.

Bacon, David. "Upsizing Labor." *The Nation*, 18 September 1995.

Boston Public Schools. *Promotion Policy Grades 1–12.* Boston: The Boston School Committee, 1983.

Bowles, Samuel, and Herbert Gintis. *Schooling in Capitalist America: Educational Reform and the Contradictions of Economic Life*. New York: Basic Books, 1976.

———. *Democracy and Capitalism: Property, Community, and the Contradictions of Modern Social Thought*. New York: Basic Books, 1986.

Carnegie Forum on Education and the Economy. *A Nation Prepared: Teachers for the 21st Century: The Report of the Task Force on Teaching as a Profession*. New York: Carnegie Forum on Education and the Economy, 1986.

Coontz, Stephanie. *The Way We Never Were: American Families and the Nostalgia Trap*. New York: Basic Books, 1992.

Cremin, Lawrence A. *The Republic and the School: Horace Mann on the Education of Free Men*. New York: Teachers College Press, 1957.

Daily Labor Report [Online] Available. Nexis Library, News File: DLABRT.

Dewey, John. *Democracy and Education*. New York: Macmillan, 1916.

———. Philosophy of Education," *American Journal of Education* 100.4 (August 1992): 409.

Dow, Peter B. *Schoolhouse Politics: Lessons from the Sputnik Era*. Cambridge, Mass.: Harvard University Press, 1991.

Edmonds, Ronald. "Effective Schools for the Urban Poor." *Educational Leadership* (October 1979): 15–24.

Fellman, David, ed. *The Supreme Court and Education*. (New York: Teacher's College Press, 1976.

Greene, Maxine. *The Dialectic of Freedom*. New York: Teachers College Press, 1988.

Halberstam, David. *The Fifties*. New York: Fawcett Columbine Books, 1933.

Harrison, Bennett, and Barry Bluestone. *The Deindustrialization of America*. New York: Basic Books, 1982.

———. *The Great U-Turn*. New York: Basic Books, 1988.

Johnston, William B. *Workforce 2000: Work and Workers for the 21st Century*. Indianapolis: Hudson Institute, 1987.

Kilborn, Peter T. "Militant Is Elected Head of A.F.L.-C.I.O., Signaling Sharp Turn for Labor Movement." *New York Times*, 26 October 1995, D25.

Kopkind, Andrew. "Bobby's in the Basement: Doctor Reich's Economic Rx." *The Nation*, 17–24 August 1992.

Kozol, Jonathan. *Savage Inequalities: Children in America's Schools*. New York: Crown, 1991.

Malcolm X. *The Autobiography of Malcolm X*. New York: Grove Press, 1964.

Marshall, Ray, and Marc Tucker. *Thinking for a Living: Education and the Wealth of Nations*. New York: Basic Books, 1992.

Meier, Deborah W. "Get the Story Straight: Myths, Lies and Public Schools." *The Nation*, 21 September 1992.

———. *The Power of Their Ideas*. Boston: Beacon Press, 1995.

Meier, Deborah, and Paul Schwartz, "Central Park East Secondary School: The Hard Part Is Making It Happen." In *Democratic Schools*, ed. Michael W. Apple and James

A. Beane. Alexandria, Va.: Association for Supervision and Curriculum Development, 1995.

Melman, Seymour. *Our Depleted Society*. New York: Holt, Rinehart and Winston, 1965.

"Mr. Justice Marshall Dissenting," in *San Antonio School District v Rodriguez* 411 US 1 (1973), in The S*upreme Court and Education*, ed. David Fellman. New York: Teacher's College Press, 1976.

National Coalition of Advocates for Students. *Barriers to Excellence: Our Children at Risk*. Boston: National Coalition of Advocates for Students, 1985.

The National Commission on Excellence in Education. *A Nation at Risk: The Imperative for Educational Reform*. Washington, D.C.: U.S. Government Printing Office, 1983.

National Education Goals Panel. "The National Education Goals Report." Washington, D.C.: The National Education Goals Panel, 1993, 1994.

Phillips, Kevin. B*oiling Point: Democrats, Republicans, and the Decline of Middle-Class Prosperity*. New York: Random House, 1993.

Reich, Robert B. *The Work of Nations: Preparing Ourselves for 21st-Century Capitalism*. New York: Vintage Books, 1991, 1992.

Republican National Committee. *Contract with America*. New York: Times Books, 1994.

Rosenstock, Larry and Adria Steinberg, "Beyond the Shop: Reinventing Vocational Education." In *Democratic Schools*, ed. Michael W. Apple and James A. Beane. Alexandria, Va.: Association for Supervision and Curriculum Development, 1995.

Serrano v Priest, 5 Cal, 3d 584, 96 Cal Rptr. 601, 487 p. 2d 1241 (1971). In *The Supreme Court and Education*, ed. David Fellman. New York: Teachers College Press, 1976.

Spring, Joel. *The Sorting Machine Revised: National Educational Policy since 1945*. New York: Longman, 1989.

Steinberg, Adria "Making School Work More Like Real Work" (tentative title). New York: Routledge, forthcoming.

Stratman, David. *We Can Change the World: The Real Meaning of Everyday Life*. Boston: New Democracy Books, 1991.

Thurow, Lester C. *The Future of Capitalism*. New York: William Morrow, 1996.

Traub, James. "It's Elementary." *The New Yorker,* 17 July 1995.

Weis, Lois. *Working Class Without Work: High School Students in a De-Industrializing Economy*. New York: Routledge, 1990.

Chapter 2. Defining Democracy, Defining Democratic Education

Alterman, Eric. *Sound & Fury: The Washington Punditocracy and the Collapse of American Politics*. New York: HarperCollins, 1992.

Anderson, James D. *The Education of Blacks in the South, 1860–1935*. Chapel Hill: University of North Carolina Press, 1988.

Apple, Michael, and James A. Beane. *Democratic Schools*. Alexandria, Va.: Association for Supervision and Curriculum Development, 1995.

Butterfield, L. H., Marc Friedlaender, and Mary-Jo Klein, eds. *The Book of Abigail and John: Selected Letters of the Adams Family, 1762-1784*. Cambridge, Mass.: Harvard University Press, 1975.

Clark, Steve. *Malcolm X Talks to Young People: Speeches in the U.S., Britain & Africa*. New York: Pathfinder Press, 1991.

Cremin, Lawrence A. *The Republic and the School: Horace Mann on the Education of Free Men*. New York: Teachers College Press, 1957.

————. *The Transformation of the School: Progressivism in American Education, 1876–1957*. New York: Vintage Books, 1961.

de Tocqueville, Alexis. *Democracy in America*, ed. Richard D. Heffner New York: New American Library, 1956.

Dewey, John. *The School and Society*. Chicago: University of Chicago Press, 1899, second edition, 1915.

————. *The Public and Its Problems*. New York: Henry Holt, 1927.

DuBois, W. E. B. *Black Reconstruction in America: An Essay toward a History of the Part Which Black Folk Played in the Attempt to Reconstruct Democracy in America, 1860–1880*. Cleveland: World, Meridian Books, 1962. (Originally published 1935.)

————. "The Meaning of Education." In *Against Racism: Unpublished Essays, Papers, Addresses, 1887–1961*, ed. Herbert Aptheker. Amherst: The University of Massachusetts Press, 1985.

————. *Color and Democracy: Colonies and Peace*. In Manning Marable, *The Crisis of Color and Democracy: Essays on Race, Class and Power*. Monroe, Maine: Common Courage Press, 1992.

Finkelstein, Barbara. "Education and the Retreat from Democracy in the United States, 1979–198?" *Teachers College Record* 86 (1984): 280–81.

Freire, Paulo. *Pedagogy of the Oppressed*. New York: The Seabury Press, 1970.

Gooding-Williams, Robert, ed. *Reading Rodney King: Reading Urban Uprisings*. New York: Routledge, 1993.

Gramsci, Antonio. *Selections from Prison Notebooks*. Quintin Hoare and Geoffrey Nowell-Smith, eds. and trans. New York: International Publishers, 1971.

Hughes, Langston. "In Explanation of Our Times," *Selected Poems of Langston Hughes*. New York: Vintage Books, 1959.

————. "Freedom's Plow," in *Selected Poems of Langston Hughes*. New York: Vintage Books, 1959.

Kozol, Jonathan. *Savage Inequalities: Children in America's Schools*. New York: Crown, 1991.

————. "Corporate Raid on Education: Whittle and the Privateers." *The Nation*, 21 September 1992.

Lee, Gordon C. *Crusade against Ignorance: Thomas Jefferson on Education*. New York: Bureau of Publications, Teachers College, Columbia University, 1961.

Marable, Manning. *Race, Reform and Rebellion: The Second Reconstruction in Black America, 1945–1990*. Jackson: University Press of Mississippi, 1991.

———. *The Crisis of Color and Democracy: Essays on Race, Class and Power*. Monroe, Maine: Common Courage Press, 1992.

Parker, Walter C., ed. *Educating the Democratic Mind*. Albany: State University of New York Press, 1996.

Renyi, Judith. *Going Public: Schooling for a Diverse Democracy*. New York: New Press, 1993.

Report of the National Advisory Commission on Civil Disorders [The Kerner Commission]. New York: E. P. Dutton, 1968.

Schlesinger, Arthur M. Jr. *The Disuniting of America*. Knoxville, Tenn.: Whittle Direct Books, 1991; republished New York: Norton, 1992.

Soder, Roger, ed. *Democracy, Education, and the Schools*. San Francisco: Jossey-Bass Publishers, 1996.

Thomson, J. A. K., trans. *The Ethics of Aristotle* [*Nicomachean Ethics*]. New York: Penguin, 1953.

Chapter 3. The School and Multicultural Democracy

Alba, Richard D. *Ethnic Identity: The Transformation of White America*. New Haven: Yale University Press, 1990.

Altbach, Philip G., Gail P. Kelly, Hugh G. Petrie, and Lois Weis, eds. *Textbooks in American Society: Politics, Policy, and Pedagogy*. Albany: State University of New York Press, 1991.

Apple, Michael W. *Official Knowledge: Democratic Education in a Conservative Age*. New York: Routledge, 1993.

Apple, Michael W., and Linda K. Christian-Smith. *The Politics of the Textbook*. New York: Routledge, 1991.

Aronowitz, Stanley, and Henry Giroux. "Schooling, Culture, and Literacy in the Age of Broken Dreams: A Review of Bloom and Hirsch." *Harvard Educational Review* 58.2 (1988): 172–94.

Baldwin, James. "A Talk to Teachers," 1963. *The Graywolf Annual Five: Multi-Cultural Literacy: Opening the American Mind*, ed. Rick Simonson and Scott Walker. Saint Paul, Minn.: Graywolf Press, 1988.

Berman, Paul. *Debating P.C.: The Controversy over Political Correctness on College Campuses*. New York: Laurel, 1992.

Bloom, Allan. *The Closing of the American Mind*. New York: Vintage Books, 1988.

Brown, Cynthia Stokes, ed. *Ready from Within: Septima Clark and the Civil Rights Movement*. Trenton, N.J.: Africa World Press, 1990.

Castellanos, Diego. *The Best of Two Worlds: Bilingual-Bicultural Education in the U.S.* Trenton, N.J.: New Jersey State Department of Education, 1983.

Crawford, James. *Bilingual Education: History, Politics, Theory, and Practice*. Trenton, N.J.: Crane, 1989.

Cremin, Lawrence A. *The Transformation of the School: Progressivism in American Education, 1876–1957*. New York: Knopf, 1961.

Dewey, John. *Democracy and Education*. New York: Macmillan, 1916.

Doctorow, E. L. "A Gangsterdom of the Spirit." *The Nation*, 2 October 1989.

D'Souza, Dinesh. "Illiberal Education." *The Atlantic Monthly*, March 1991, 52–79.

FitzGerald, Frances. *America Revised*. New York: Vintage Books, 1979.

Freire, Paulo. *Pedagogy of Hope: Reliving Pedagogy of the Oppressed*. New York: Continuum, 1995.

Giroux, Henry. *Schooling and the Struggle for Public Life: Critical Pedagogy in the Modern Age*. Minneapolis: University of Minnesota Press, 1988.

Giroux, Henry. *Border Crossings: Cultural Workers and the Politics of Education*. New York: Routledge, 1992.

Goodrich, Charles A. *A History of the United States of America: From the Discovery of the Continent by Christopher Columbus to the Present Time*. Hartford, Conn.: H. F. Sumner, 1822, 1833.

Greene, Maxine. "Excellence, Meanings and Multiplicity." *Teachers College Record* 86.2 (Winter 1984): 296.

———. "In Search of a Critical Pedagogy." *Harvard Educational Review* 56:4 (November 1986): 427–41.

Gutman, Herbert G. *Work, Culture and Society in Industrializing America*. New York: Vintage Books, 1966, 1977.

Harding, Vincent. "We the People: The Long Journey toward a More Perfect Union." In *The Eyes on the Prize Civil Rights Reader*. ed. Clayborne Carson et al. New York: Penguin, 1991.

Harrison, Beverly Wildung. *Making the Connections: Essays in Feminist Social Ethics*, ed. Carol S. Robb. Boston: Beacon Press, 1985.

Heath, Shirley Brice, and Milbrey W. McLaughlin, eds. *Identity and Inner-City Youth: Beyond Ethnicity and Gender*. New York: Teachers College Press, 1993.

Hehir, Thomas and Thomas Latus, eds. *Special Education at the Century's End: Evolution of Theory and Practice Since 1970*. Reprint Series No. 23. Cambridge, Mass.: Harvard Educational Review, 1992.

Herrnstein, Richard J., and Charles Murray. *The Bell Curve: Intelligence and Class Structure in American Life*. New York: Free Press, 1994.

Hirsch, E. D. *Cultural Literacy: What Every American Needs to Know*. New York: Vintage Books, 1988.

hooks, bell. *Teaching to Transgress: Education as the Practice of Freedom*. New York: Routledge, 1994.

Jacoby, Russell, and Naomi Glauberman. *The Bell Curve Debate*. New York: Times Books, 1995.

Jensen, Arthur R. *Genetics and Education*. New York: Harper & Row, 1972.

Kamin, Leon J. "Lies, Damned Lies, and Statistics." In *The Bell Curve Debate,* ed. Russell Jacoby and Naomi Glauberman. New York: Times Books, 1995.

Kimball, Roger. *Tenured Radicals: How Politics Has Corrupted Our Higher Education.* New York: Harper & Row, 1991.

Kincheloe, Joe, Shirley Steinberg, and Aaron Greeson III, eds. *Measured Lies: The Bell Curve Examined.* New York: St. Martin's Press, 1996.

Kliebard, Herbert M. *The Struggle for the American Curriculum.* New York: Routledge, 1987.

Kliebard, Herbert M. *Forging the American Curriculum.* New York: Routledge, 1992.

Kozol, Jonathan. *Savage Inequalities: Children in America's Schools.* New York: Crown, 1991.

Lerner, Robert, Althea K. Nagai, and Stanley Rothman. *Molding the Good Citizen: The Politics of High School History Texts.* Westport, Conn.: Praeger, 1995.

Levine, David, Robert Lowe, Bob Peterson, and Rita Tenorio. *Rethinking Schools: An Agenda for Change.* New York: New Press, 1995.

McGuffey, William Holmes. *New Sixth Eclectic Reader.* Cincinnati: Winthrop B. Smith, 1857.

Murray, Charles, and Richard J. Herrnstein. "What's Really Behind the SAT-Score Decline?" *Public Interest* 15 (Winter 1992): 32–56.

Muzzey, David Saville. *A History of Our Country.* Boston: Ginn, 1943, 1952.

A Nation Prepared: Teachers for the 21st Century: The Report of the Task Force on Teaching as a Profession. New York: Carnegie Forum on Education and The Economy, 1986.

Perry, Theresa, and James W. Fraser. *Freedom's Plow: Teaching in the Multicultural Classroom.* New York: Routledge, 1993.

Postman, Neil. *The End of Education: Redefining the Value of School.* New York: Knopf, 1995.

Ravitch, Diane, and Chester E. Finn Jr. *What Do Our 17-Year-Olds Know?* New York: Harper & Row, 1987.

Reich, Robert. *The Work of Nations.* With a new Afterword by the Author. New York: Vintage Books, 1992.

Schlesinger, Arthur M. Jr. *The Disuniting of America.* Knoxville, Tenn.: Whittle Direct Books, 1991; republished New York: Norton, 1992.

Sleeter, Christine E., and Peter L. McLaren, eds. *Multicultural Education, Critical Pedagogy, and the Politics of Difference.* Albany: State University of New York Press, 1995.

Thompson, E. P. *The Making of the English Working Class.* New York: Vintage Books, 1963, 1966.

U.S. Commission on Civil Rights. *The Excluded Student: Educational Practices Affecting Mexican Americans in the Southwest, Mexican American Education Study, Report III.* Washington, D.C.: GPO, 1972.

Chapter 4. Toward a New Kind of Child-Centered Curriculum

Bastian, Ann, Norm Fruchter, Marilyn Gittell, Colin Greer, and Kenneth Haskins. *Choosing Equality: The Case for Democratic Schooling.* New York: New World Foundation, 1985.

Bowles, Samuel, and Herbert Gintis. *Schooling in Capitalist America: Educational Reform and the Contradictions of Economic Life.* New York: Basic Books, 1976.

———. "Can There Be a Liberal Philosophy of Education in a Democratic Society?" In *Critical Pedagogy, the State, and Cultural Struggle.* ed. Henry Giroux and Peter McLaren. Albany: State University of New York Press, 1989.

Brady, Jeanne. *Schooling Young Children: A Feminist Pedagogy for Liberatory Learning.* Albany: State University of New York Press, 1995.

Bruner, Jerome. *The Relevance of Education.* New York: Norton, 1971.

Bunch, Charlotte. "Feminism and Education: Not By Degrees." *Quest* 5.1 (Summer 1979).

Burdell, Pat. "Teen Mothers in High School: Tracking Their Curriculum," In *Review of Research in Education 21, 1995–1996,* ed. Michael W. Apple. Washington, D.C.: American Educational Research Association, 1995.

Carlsson-Paige, Nancy, and Diane E. Levin. *Who's Calling the Shots? How to Respond Effectively to Children's Fascination with War Play and War Toys.* Philadelphia: New Society Publishers, 1990.

Counts, George S. *Dare the School Build a New Social Order?* Carbondale, Ill.: Southern Illinois University Press, 1978; original edition, 1932.

Cremin, Lawrence A. *The Republic and the School: Horace Mann on the Education of Free Men.* New York: Teachers College Press, 1957.

———. *The Transformation of the School: Progressivism in American Education, 1876–1957.* New York: Knopf, 1961.

Darder, Antonia. *Culture and Power in the Classroom: A Critical Foundation for Bicultural Education.* New York: Bergin & Garvey, 1991.

Delpit, Lisa. *Other People's Children: Cultural Conflict in the Classroom.* New York: New Press, 1995.

Dewey, John "My Pedagogic Creed." *The School Journal* 54.3 (January 1897).

———. *The School and Society.* Chicago: University of Chicago Press, 1900, revised 1915.

———. *Democracy and Education.* New York: Macmillan, 1916.

Dryfoos, Joy G. *Full-Service Schools: A Revolution in Health and Social Services for Children, Youth, and Families.* San Francisco: Jossey-Bass, 1994.

Dworkin, Martin S., ed. *Dewey on Education.* New York: Teachers College Press, 1959.

Edmonds, Ronald. "Effective Schools for the Urban Poor." *Educational Leadership* (October 1979): 22.

Edmonds, Ronald, and J. R. Frederiksen. *Search for Effective Schools: The Identification and Analysis of City Schools that are Instructionally Effective for*

Poor Children. Cambridge, Mass.: Harvard University, Center for Urban Studies, 1978.

Feinberg, Walter. "Fixing the Schools: The Ideological Turn." In *Critical Pedagogy, the State, and Cultural Struggle*, ed. Henry Giroux and Peter McLaren. Albany: State University of New York Press, 1989.

Fraser, James W. "Who Were the Progressive Educators Anyway? A Case Study of the Progressive Education Movement in Boston, 1905–1925." *Educational Foundations* 2.1 (Spring 1988): 4–30.

Freire, Paulo. *Pedagogy of the Oppressed*. New York: Seabury Press, 1970.

Froebel, Friedrich. *Pedagogics of the Kindergarten*. New York: D. Appleton and Company, 1914; translation of original German edition, Berlin: 1861.

Gardner, Howard, and Thomas Hatch. "Multiple Intelligences Go to School: Educational Implications of the Theory of Multiple Intelligences." *Educational Researcher* 18.8 (November 1989).

Goodlad, John I. *A Place Called School: Prospects for the Future*. New York: McGraw-Hill, 1984.

Greene, Maxine. "In Search of Critical Pedagogy." *Harvard Educational Review* 56:4 (November 1986): 427–41.

Grubb, W. Norton, and Marvin Lazerson. *Broken Promises: How Americans Fail Their Children*. Chicago: University of Chicago Press, 1982, 1988.

Gutman, Amy. *Democracy and Education*. Princeton, N.J.: Princeton University Press, 1987.

Hacker, Andrew. *Two Nations: Black and White, Separate, Hostile, Unequal*. New York: Scribner's, 1992.

Hendrick, Joanne and Terry Stange. "Do Actions Speak Louder Than Words? An Effect of the Functional Use of Language on Dominant Sex Role Behavior in Boys and Girls." ERIC/EDRS document ED 323039/ PS019059, p. 22.

hooks, bell. *Feminist Theory: From Margin to Center*. Boston: South End Press, 1984.

———. *Talking Back: Thinking Feminist, Thinking Black*. Boston: South End Press, 1989.

———. *Teaching to Transgress: Education as the Practice of Freedom*. New York: Routledge, 1994.

Jencks, Christopher. *Inequality: A Reassessment of the Effect of Family and Schooling in America*. New York: Harper & Row, 1972.

Jones, Jacqueline. *The Dispossessed: America's Underclasses from the Civil War to the Present*. New York: Basic Books, 1992.

Katz, Michael B. *Class, Bureaucracy, and Schools: The Illusion of Educational Change in America*. New York: Praeger, 1971.

Kozol, Jonathan. *Amazing Grace: The Lives of Children and the Conscience of a Nation*. New York: Crown, 1995.

Making the Grade: Report of the Twentieth Century Fund Task Force on Federal Elementary and Secondary Education Policy. New York: Twentieth Century Fund, 1983.

Marable, Manning. *The Crisis of Color and Democracy: Essays on Race, Class and Power*. Monroe, Maine: Common Courage Press, 1992.

Marriott, Michel. "As Students Come to Class Less Healthy, School Clinics Try to Offer More." *New York Times*, 30 January 1991.

Martin, Jane Roland. *The School Home: Rethinking Schools for Changing Families*. Cambridge, Mass.: Harvard University Press, 1992.

Mohrman, Susan Albers, and Priscilla Wohlstetter. *School Based Management: Organizing for High Performance*. San Francisco: Jossey-Bass, 1994.

The National Coalition of Advocates for Students, Board of Inquiry. *Barriers to Excellence: Our Children at Risk*. Boston: National Coalition of Advocates for Students, 1985.

The National Commission on Excellence in Education. *A Nation at Risk: The Imperative for Educational Reform*. Washington, 1983.

Oakes, Jeannie. *Keeping Track: How Schools Structure Inequality*. New Haven: Yale University Press, 1985.

Perry, Theresa, and James W. Fraser. *Freedom's Plow: Teaching in the Multicultural Classroom*. New York: Routledge, 1993.

Prothrow-Stith, Deborah, with Michaele Weissman. *Deadly Consequences: How Violence Is Destroying Our Teenage Population and a Plan to Begin Solving the Problem*. New York: HarperCollins, 1991.

Reich, Robert. *The Work of Nations*. New York: Vintage Books, 1991, 1992.

San Antonio School District v. Rodriguez 411 US 1 (1973). In Fellman, *The Supreme Court and Education*. New York: Teachers College Press, 1976.

Sarason, Seymour B. *The Culture of the School and the Problem of Change*. Boston: Allyn & Bacon, 1971.

———. *Parental Involvement and the Political Principle: Why the Existing Governance Structure of Schools Should Be Abolished*. San Francisco: Jossey-Bass, 1995.

Shannon, Patrick. *The Struggle to Continue: Progressive Reading Instruction in the United States*. Portsmouth, N.H.: Heinemann Educational Books, 1990.

Shaw, Adele Marie. "The True Character of New York Public Schools." *The World's Work* 7 (1903–1904): 4204–21.

Silberman, Charles E. *Crisis in the Classroom: The Remaking of American Education*. New York: Random House, 1970.

Tyack, David B., Michael W. Kirst, and Elisabeth Hansot. "Educational Reform: Retrospect and Prospect." *Teachers College Record* 81.3 (Spring 1980): 254.

Tyack, David, and Elisabeth Hansot. *Managers of Virtue: Public School Leadership in America, 1820–1980*. New York: Basic Books, 1982.

Waring, Marilyn. *If Women Counted: A New Feminist Economics*. San Francisco: Harper San Francisco, 1988.

Wells, Amy Stuart, and Irene Serna. "The Politics of Culture: Understanding Local Political Resistance to Detracking in Racially Mixed Schools." *Harvard Educational Review* 66.1 (Spring 1996): 93–118.

Wheelock, Anne. *Crossing the Tracks: How "Untracking" Can Save America's Schools*. New York: New Press, 1992.

Wolin, Sheldon S. "Editorial." *democracy* 3.2 (Spring 1983): 5.

Chapter 5. Technology, Democracy, and School Policy

Apple, Michael W. *Ideology and Curriculum*. Boston and London: Routledge & Kegan Paul, 1979.

———. *Teachers and Texts: A Political Economy of Class and Gender Relations in Education*. New York: Routledge, 1986.

Baldwin, James. "A Talk to Teachers." 1963. Reprinted in *The Graywolf Annual Five: Multi-Cultural Literacy: Opening the American Mind*. ed. Rick Simonson and Scott Walker. Saint Paul, Minn.: Graywolf Press, 1988.

Bastian, Ann, Norm Fruchter, Marilyn Gittell, Colin Greer, and Kenneth Haskins, eds. *Choosing Equality: The Case for Democratic Schooling*. Philadelphia: Temple University Press, 1986.

Bell, Terrel H., and Donna L. Elmquist. "Technical Interaction in the Classroom." *Vocational Education Journal* 67.3 (March 1992): 22.

Blecker, H. J., and C. W. Sterling. "Equity in School Computer Use: National Data and Neglected Considerations." *Journal of Educational Computing Research* 3 (1987): 289–311.

Center for Law and Education. "Vocational Education: A New Opportunity for Educational and Community Change." December 1991.

Clay, Marie M. *Becoming Literate: The Construction of Inner Control*. Auckland, New Zealand: Heinemann, 1991.

Counts, George S. *Dare the School Build a New Social Order?* Carbondale, Ill.: Southern Illinois University Press, 1978; original edition 1932.

Cremin, Lawrence A. *Popular Education and Its Discontents*. New York: Harper & Row, 1990.

Cuban, Larry. *How Teachers Taught: Constancy and Change in American Classrooms, 1890–1980*. New York: Longman, 1984.

———. *Teachers and Machines: The Classroom Use of Technology since 1920*. New York: Teachers College Press, 1986.

———. "Computers Meet Classroom; Classroom Wins." *Commentary Education Week* (November 1992): 36.

Cummins, Jim, and Dennis Sayers. *Brave New Schools: Challenging Cultural Illiteracy Through Global Learning Networks*. New York: St. Martin's Press, 1995.

Cummins, Robert A. and Margot P. Prior. "Autism and Assisted Communication: A Response to Biklen." *Harvard Education Review* 62.2 (Summer 1992): 228–41.

Dewey, John. *Individualism Old and New*. New York: G. P. Putnam's Sons, Capricorn Books, 1962; originally published, 1929.

Edison, Thomas. *Dramatic Mirror* July 1913. Cited in Paul Saettler, *A History of Instructional Technology*. New York: McGraw-Hill, 1968.

Edwards, Paul N. "The Army and the Microworld: Computers and the Politics of Gender Identity." *Signs: Journal of Women in Culture and Society* 16.1 (Autumn 1990): 109.

Fine, Michelle. *Framing Dropouts: Notes on the Politics of an Urban Public High School*. Albany: State University of New York Press, 1991.

Freire, Paulo. *Pedagogy of the Oppressed*. New York: Seabury Press, 1970.

Greene, Maxine. "In Search of a Critical Pedagogy." *Harvard Educational Review* 56:4 (November 1986).

Haley, Margaret. "Why Teachers Should Organize." St. Louis, Mo.: National Education Association Addresses and Proceedings, 1904.

Hoffmann, James A. "Computer-Aided Collaborative Music Instruction." *Harvard Educational Review* 61.3 (August 1991): 270–78.

Hoffman, Nancy. *Woman's "True" Profession: Voices from the History of Teaching*. Old Westbury, N.Y.: Feminist Press, 1981.

Koltnow, Joanne. "Planning for Educational Change." *Apple Education Review* (1991–1992 School Year, Issue 1): 2–6.

Kranzberg, Melvin. "Science-Technology-Society: It's as Simple as XYZ!" *Theory into Practice* 30.4 (Autumn 1991): 236.

———. "Technology and History: Kranzberg's Laws." *Technology and Culture* 27: 544–60.

Laboratory of Comparative Human Cognition, University of California, San Diego. "Kids and Computers: A Positive Vision of the Future." *Harvard Educational Review* 59.1 (February 1989): 73–74.

Laverty, Linda. "The Switch Hitters—Creative and Competitive Activities for the Physically Impaired." *The Computing Teacher*, December/January 1991–1992, 41–43.

Levin, Henry M., and Russell W. Rumberger. "The Educational Implications of High Technology." *Technology Review*, August/September 1983.

Moll, L. C., and S. Diaz. "Change as the Goal of Educational Research." *Anthropology and Educational Quarterly* 18 (1987): 300–11.

Noble, Douglas. "Computer Literacy and Ideology." *Teachers College Record* 85.4 (Summer 1984): 605.

Papert, Seymour. *Mindstorms: Children, Computers, and Powerful Ideas*. New York: Basic Books, 1980.

———. "Teaching Children Thinking," and "Teaching Children to be Mathematicians." In *The Computer in the School: Tutor, Tool, Tutee*, ed. Robert Taylor. New York: Teachers College Press, 1980.

———. "Trying to Predict the Future." *Popular Computing*, October 1984.

———. *The Children's Machine: Rethinking School in the Age of the Computer*. New York: Basic Books, 1993.

Piaget, Jean. "Piaget's Theory." In *Handbook of Child Psychology*, 4th ed., ed. Paul H. Mussen. New York: John Wiley, 1983.

Postman, Neil. *Technopoly*. New York: Knopf, 1993.

———. *The End of Education: Redefining the Value of School*. New York: Knopf, 1995.

Postman, Neil, and Charles Weingartner. *Teaching as a Subversive Activity*. New York: Knopf, 1979.

Reich, Robert B. *The Work of Nations: Preparing Ourselves for 21st-Century Capitalism*. New York: Vintage Books, 1991.

Sale, Kirkpatrick. *Rebels against the Future: The Luddites and Their War on the Industrial Revolution: Lessons for the Computer Age*. Boston: Addison-Wesley, 1995.

Scott, Tony, Michael Cole, and Martin Engel of the Laboratory of Comparative Human Cognition. "Computers and Education: A Cultural Constructivist Perspective." In *Review of Research in Education 18*, ed. Gerald Grant. Washington, D.C.: American Educational Research Association, 1992.

Schwartz, Judah L. "Intellectual Mirrors: A Step in the Direction of Making Schools Knowledge-Making Places." *Harvard Educational Review* 59.1 (February 1989).

Sloan, Douglas M. "On Raising Critical Questions about the Computer in Education." *Teachers College Record* 85.4 (Summer 1984).

Spring, Joel. *The Sorting Machine Revisited: National Educational Policy since 1945* New York: Longman, 1989.

Sutton, Rosemary E. "Equity and Computers in the Schools: A Decade of Research." *Review of Educational Research* 61.4 (Winter 1991): 475–503.

Weir, Sylvia. "The Computer in Schools: Machine as Humanizer." *Harvard Educational Review* 59.1 (February 1989): 63.

Whooley, K. A. "Gender Differences in Computer Use." Unpublished Ph.D. diss., University of California, San Diego, 1986.

Winston, B. *Misunderstanding Media*. Cambridge, Mass.: Harvard University Press, 1986.

Young, Ella Flagg. *Isolation in the School*. Chicago: University of Chicago Press, 1901.

6. Preparing Teachers for Democratic Schools

Apple, Michael W. *Teachers and Texts: A Political Economy of Class and Gender Relations in Education*. New York: Routledge & Kegan Paul, 1986.

Apple, Michael W., and Linda K. Christian-Smith. *The Politics of the Textbook*. New York: Routledge, Chapman and Hall, 1991.

Aronowitz, Stanley, and Henry A. Giroux. "Schooling Culture, and Literacy in the Age of Broken Dreams: A Review of Bloom and Hirsch." *Harvard Educational Review* 58.2 (May 1988): 172–94.

Ashton, Patricia, and Linda Crocker. "Systematic Study of Planned Variations: The Essential Focus of Teacher Education Reform." *Journal of Teacher Education* (May–June 1987): 2–8.

Bastian, Ann, Norm Fruchter, Marilyn Gittell, Colin Greer, and Kenneth Haskins. *Choosing Equality: The Case for Democratic Schooling.* New York: New World Foundation, 1985.

Beckum, Leonard C. "Diversifying Assessment: A Key Factor in the Reform Equation." In *Diversity in Teacher Education: New Expectations*, ed. Mary E. Dilworth. San Francisco: Jossey-Bass, 1992.

Bledstein, Burton J. *The Culture of Professionalism: The Middle Class and the Development of Higher Education in America.* New York: Norton, 1976.

Boyer, Ernest L. *College: The Undergraduate Experience in America.* New York: Harper & Row, 1987.

The Carnegie Forum on Education and the Economy. *A Nation Prepared: Teachers for the 21st Century: The Report of the Task Force on Teaching as a Profession.* New York: Carnegie Forum on Education and the Economy, 1986.

Counts, George S. *Dare the School Build a New Social Order?* New York: John Day, 1932.

Cremin, Lawrence. *The Transformation of The School: Progressivism in American Education, 1876–1957.* New York: Random House, 1961.

Darling-Hammond, Linda Karen Pittman, and Cecilia Ottinger. "Career Choices for Minorities: Who Will Teach?" National Education Association and Council of Chief State School Officers, Task Force on Minorities in Teaching (October 1987).

Delpit, Lisa. *Other People's Children: Cultural Conflict in the Classroom* New York: New Press, 1995.

Dewey, John. "Professional Organization of Teachers." *Journal of Education*, 30 October 1919.

Dilworth, Mary E., ed. *Diversity in Teacher Education: New Expectations.* San Francisco: Jossey-Bass, 1992.

Fraser, James W. "An Unnoticed Bicentennial: Some Thoughts on School Committee Structure." *Equity and Choice* 1.1 (September 1989).

———. "Agents of Democracy: Urban Elementary-School Teachers and the Conditions of Teaching." In *American Teachers: Histories of a Profession at Work*, ed. Donald R. Warren, New York: Macmillan, 1989.

Freedman, Sara. "Master Teacher/Merit Pay—Weeding Out Women from 'Women's True Profession': A Critique of the Commissions on Education." *Radical Teacher* 25 (1983).

Giroux, Henry A. *Teachers as Intellectuals: Toward a Critical Pedagogy of Learning.* Granby, Mass.: Bergin & Garvey, 1988.

Giroux, Henry, and Donaldo Macedo. "Editorial Comment." *Journal of Urban and Cultural Studies* 1.1 (1990): 4.

Giroux, Henry, and Peter McLaren "Teacher Education as a Counter-public Sphere: Notes Toward a Redefinition." In *Critical Studies in Teacher Education: Its*

Folklore, Theory and Practice, ed. Thomas S. Popkewitz. London: Falmer Press, 1987.

————. "Teacher Education and the Politics of Engagement: The Case for Democratic Schooling." *Harvard Educational Review* 56.3.

Goodlad, John I. *A Place Called School: Prospectus for the Future*. New York: McGraw-Hill, 1984.

————. *Teachers for Our Nation's Schools*. San Francisco: Jossey-Bass, 1990.

Gordon, June A. "Why Students of Color Are Not Entering Teaching: Reflections from Minority Teachers." *Journal of Teacher Education* 45.5 (November–December 1994).

Greene, Maxine. "In Search of a Critical Pedagogy." *Harvard Educational Review* 56.4 (November 1986): 427.

Harrison, Beverly Wildung. Making the Connections: Essays in *Feminist Social Ethics*, ed. Carol S. Robb. Boston: Beacon Press, 1985.

Hawley, Willis D. "The Importance of Minority Teachers to the Racial and Ethnic Integration of American Society." *Equity and Choice* 5.2 (March 1989): 33.

Holmes Group. *Tomorrow's Teachers: A Report of The Holmes Group*. East Lansing, Mich.: The Holmes Group, 1986.

————. *Tomorrow's Schools: Principles for the Design of Professional Development Schools*. East Lansing, Mich.: The Holmes Group, 1990.

————. *Tomorrow's Schools of Education*. East Lansing, Mich.: The Holmes Group, 1995.

hooks, bell. *Teaching to Transgress: Education as the Practice of Freedom*. New York: Routledge, 1994.

Labaree, David F. "A Disabling Vision: Rhetoric and Reality in *Tomorrow's Schools of Education*." *Teachers College Record* 97.2 (Winter 1995): 166–205.

Lagemann, Ellen Condliffe. *Private Power for the Public Good: A History of the Carnegie Foundation for the Advancement of Teaching*. Middletown, Conn.: Wesleyan University Press, 1983.

————. "The Politics of Knowledge: The Carnegie Corporation and the Formulation of Public Policy." *History of Education Quarterly* 27:2 (Summer 1987): 205–20.

————. *The Politics of Knowledge: A History of the Carnegie Corporation of New York*. Middletown, Conn.: Wesleyan University Press, 1987.

Laird, Susan. "Reforming 'Women's True Profession': A Case for 'Feminist Pedagogy' in Teacher Education?" *Harvard Educational Review* 58.4 (November 1988): 449–63.

Lash, Christopher. *The Revolt of the Elites and the Betrayal of Democracy*. New York: Norton, 1995.

Leatherman, Courtney. "Reforms in Education of Schoolteachers Face Tough New Challenges." *The Chronicle of Higher Education*, 20 April 1988.

Ludmerer, Kenneth M. *Learning to Heal: The Development of American Medical Education*. New York: Basic Books, 1985.

Madaus, George F., ed. *The Courts, Validity, and Minimum Competency Testing.* Boston: Kluwer-Nijhoff, 1983.

Making Teaching a Major Profession: Recommendations of the Joint Task Force on Teacher Preparation. Boston: Commonwealth of Massachusetts Board of Regents of Higher Education and Board of Education, 1987.

Martin, Jane Roland. "Reforming Teacher Education, Rethinking Liberal Education." *Teachers College Record* 88 (1987): 406–9.

Massachusetts Statewide Committee on the Recruitment of Minority Teachers. "The Recruitment and Retention of People of Color in the Teaching Profession in Massachusetts." Boston: Massachusetts Board of Regents of Higher Education and Board of Education, 1990.

McLaren, Peter and Henry Giroux. "Teacher Education as a Counter-Public Sphere: Notes Towards a Redefinition." In *Critical Studies in Teacher Education: Its Folklore, Theory and Practice*, ed. Thomas S. Popkewitz. London: Falmer Press, 1987.

National Commission on Excellence in Education. *A Nation at Risk.* Washington, D.C.: GPO, 1983.

National Commission on Teaching and America's Future. *What Matters Most: Teaching for America's Future.* New York: 1996.

Novak, John M. ed. *Democratic Teacher Education: Programs, Processes, Problems, and Prospects.* Albany: State University of New York Press, 1994.

Okazawa-Rey, Margo, James Anderson, and Rob Traver. *Teachers, Teaching, and Teacher Education.* Cambridge, Mass.: Harvard Educational Review, 1987.

Pang, Valerie Ooka. "Ethnic Prejudice: Still Alive and Hurtful." *Harvard Educational Review* 58.3 (August 1988): 375–79.

Perry, Theresa. "Teacher Preparation and Its Impact on Black and Latino Communities." Conference on Blacks and Education in Boston: Issues, Problems and Resolutions, College of Public & Community Service, University of Massachusetts at Boston, 9 December 1988.

———. "Is Text Also Context or Does the Significant Representation of Students and Faculty of Color in a Teacher Preparation Program Necessarily Shape the Conversation." Paper presented at the American Educational Research Association, Chicago, Ill. 3 April 1991.

Popkewitz, Thomas S. *Critical Studies in Teacher Education: Its Folklore, Theory and Practice.* London: Falmer Press, 1987.

"Recruitment and Support of Minorities in Teacher Education Programs." The University of the State of New York, State Education Department, Albany, New York, September 1989.

Schon, Donald A. *Educating the Reflective Practitioner.* San Francisco: Jossey-Bass, 1987.

Silber, John. *Straight Shooting: What's Wrong with America and How to Fix It.* New York: Harper & Row, 1989.

Sizer, Theodore R. *Horace's Compromise: The Dilemma of the American High School.* Boston: Houghton Mifflin, 1984.

Soder, Roger. "Teaching the Teachers of the People." In *Democracy, Education, and the Schools*, ed. Roger Soder. San Francisco: Jossey-Bass, 1996.

The Twentieth Century Fund. *Making the Grade: Report of the Twentieth Century Fund Task Force on Federal Elementary and Secondary Education Policy*. New York: Twentieth Century Fund, 1983.

Wagener, Ursula Elisabeth. "Quality and Equality: The Necessity for Imagination." *Harvard Educational Review* 59.2 (May 1989): 240–50.

Weinberg, Meyer, ed. *W. E. B. Du Bois: A Reader*. New York: Harper Torchbooks, 1970.

Yonemura, Margaret. "Reflections on Teacher Empowerment and Teacher Education." *Harvard Educational Review* 56.4 (November 1986): 473–80.

Young, Ella Flagg. *Isolation in the School*. Chicago: University of Chicago Press, 1901.

Zeichner, Kenneth M., and Daniel P. Liston. "Teaching Student Teachers to Reflect." *Harvard Educational Review* 57.1 (February 1987): 1–22.

Zumwalt, Karen Kepler. "A Response." *Teachers College Record* 94.1 (Fall 1992): 51–52.

INDEX

243

246   Index